Beyond Consolation

Reading
WOMEN
Writing

**a series edited by
Shari Benstock and Celeste Schenck**

Reading Women Writing is dedicated to furthering international feminist debate. The series publishes books on all aspects of feminist theory and textual practice. *Reading Women Writing* especially welcomes books that address cultures, histories, and experience beyond first-world academic boundaries. A complete list of titles in the series appears at the end of the book.

Beyond Consolation

DEATH, SEXUALITY, AND THE
CHANGING SHAPES OF ELEGY

Melissa F. Zeiger

Cornell University Press

ITHACA AND LONDON

First published 1997 by Cornell University Press

Printed in the United States of America

Library of Congress Cataloging-in-Publication Data
Zeiger, Melissa F. (Melissa Fran), 1957–
    Beyond consolation : death, sexuality, and the changing shapes of
elegy / Melissa F. Zeiger.
        p.   cm.—(Reading women writing)
    Includes bibliographical references and index.
    ISBN 0-8014-3110-7 (cloth : alk. paper)
    ISBN 0-8014-8441-3 (pbk. : alk. paper)
    1. Elegiac poetry—History and criticism.   2. Death in literature.
3. Sex in literature.   4. Orpheus (Greek mythology) in literature.
I. Title.   II. Series.
PN1389.Z45   1997
809.1'93548—dc21   97-7929

Cornell University Press strives to utilize environmentally responsible suppliers and materials to the fullest extent possible in the publishing of its books. Such materials include vegetable-based, low-VOC inks and acid-free papers that are also either recycled, totally chlorine-free, or partly composed of nonwood fibers.

Cloth printing   10 9 8 7 6 5 4 3 2 1
Paperback printing   10 9 8 7 6 5 4 3 2 1

To my father, Arthur Zeiger,
with love, admiration, and gratitude

Contents

Acknowledgments

I am grateful to the American Council of Learned Societies for supplying crucial encouragement and research time at an early stage of this project. It is a pleasure to acknowledge the generosity of Jonathan Crewe, Marianne Hirsch, Brenda Silver, and Susanne Zantop, who read and made extensive comments on innumerable drafts of every chapter of the manuscript, and who still claim "to enjoy every word." Others who contributed important comments, as well as inspiration, at various stages are Lynda Boose, William Cook, Louise Fradenburg, Terrence Holt, Stacy Hubbard, Keala Jewell, Dorothy Mermin, Beth Newman, Peter Saccio, the late Walt Slatoff, Jon Stallworthy, Peter Swaab, Virginia Swain, Arthur Waldhorn, and Arthur Zeiger. I also thank others who offered me warmth and intellectual support during the composition of the book: Tony Dangerfield, Laurence Davies, Judy Frank, Carla Freccero, Tassie Gwilliam, Nancy Harrowitz, Alexis Jetter, Joke Kardux, Veronica Kelly, Laurie Langbauer, Lisa Miles, Matthew Neuburg, Annelise Orleck, Matthew Rowlinson, Paul Sawyer, Ivy Schweitzer, Tom Sleigh, Jonathan Speaker, Frank Stringfellow, Sasha Torres, and Eduard van der Bilt. My mother, Sophia Pelkey, called down good spirits to aid me. I have been unusually lucky in my research assistants over the years, and thank Martha Viehmann, Rob Miotke, Jonathan Eburne, Doug Bachman, and Michelle Angers for invaluable scholarly support. I also want to acknowledge a large debt of gratitude to Bernhard Kendler, executive editor at Cornell University Press, for his encouragement. My two Press readers, Celeste Schenck and Debra Fried, responded to an earlier version with such extraordinary insight—and exigency—that they helped call three new chapters, and in a sense the book itself, into being. My very special thanks go to Jessica and Jonathan Crewe, who gave soul-saving pleasure and love during hard times.

A version of the Swinburne chapter has already appeared, in somewhat different form, as " 'A Muse Funereal': The Critique of Elegy in Swinburne's 'Ave atque Vale,' " in *Victorian Poetry* 24 (summer 1986): 173–88.

Excerpts from "Lycidas" from *John Milton: Complete Poems and Prose*, ed. by Merritt Y. Hughes. Copyright © 1957 by The Odyssey Press. Reprinted by permission of Macmillan General Books.

From *Shelley's "Adonais": A Critical Edition*, edited by Anthony D. Knerr. Copyright ©1984 by Columbia University Press. Reprinted with permission of the publisher.

From *The Poems of Matthew Arnold* by Matthew Arnold, ed. by Kenneth Allot. Copyright © 1979. Reprinted by permission of Addison Wesley Longman Ltd.

Reprinted by permission of the publishers and the Loeb Classical Library from Ovid, *Metamorphosis: Book X*, translated by Frank Justus Miller, Cambridge, Mass.: Harvard University Press, 1946.

Excerpts from "Hugh Selwyn Mauberly" from *Persona* by Ezra Pound. Copyright © 1926 by Ezra Pound. Reprinted by permission of New Directions Publishing Corp. and Faber and Faber Ltd.

From "Epitaphs of War" from *Rudyard Kipling's Verse: Definitive Edition* by Rudyard Kipling. Copyright © 1940. Reprinted by permission of Doubleday, Doran and Co.

Excerpts from *The War Poems of Siegfried Sassoon* by Siegfried Sassoon. Published by William Heinemann. Reprinted by permission of Reed Books, Ltd.

From *Poems* by Edward Thomas. Copyright © 1917. Reprinted by permission of Henry Holt and Company, Inc.

Excerpts from Ivor Gurney, *Collected Poems of Ivor Gurney*. Copyright © 1982 by Oxford University Press. Reprinted by permission of Oxford University Press.

Excerpts from Wilfred Owen, *Collected Poems of Wilfred Owen*. Copyright © 1963 by Chatto & Windus, Ltd. Reprinted by permission of Chatto & Windus and New Directions Publishing Corp.

From *Winter Numbers* by Marilyn Hacker. Copyright © 1994 by Marilyn Hacker. Reprinted by permission of the author, W. W. Norton & Company, Inc., and Frances Collin, literary agent.

Excerpts from *The Complete Works of Algernon Swinburne*, Vols. 2 & 3, by Algernon Swinburne. Published by William Heinemann. Reprinted by permission of Reed Books, Ltd.

Excerpts from "After a Journey," "The Convergence of the Twain," "The Shadow of the Stone," "Your Last Drive," and "The Haunter" from *Thomas Hardy: The Complete Poems* by Thomas Hardy. Reprinted by permission of Macmillan General Books.

Charles Baudelaire: excerpts from "My Old Great-Hearted Nurse Who Stirred Your Jealousy," copyright © 1991 by William H. Crosby. Reprinted from *The Flowers of Evil and*

Georgie Yeats; copyright renewed © 1968 by Bertha Georgie Yeats, Michael Butler Yeats, and Anne Yeats. Also reprinted with the permission of A. P. Watt Ltd., London.

Excerpts from "Daddy," "Lady Lazarus," and "Electra on Azalea Path" from *Collected Poems* by Sylvia Plath. Copyright © 1981. Reprinted with permission of HarperCollins Publishers.

From *The Inner Room* by James Merrill. Copyright © 1988 by James Merrill. Reprinted by permission of Alfred A. Knopf, Inc.

Excerpts from *Love Alone* by Paul Monette. Copyright © 1988 by Paul Monette. Reprinted by permission of St. Martin's Press Incorporated.

Reprinted by permission of Farrar, Straus & Giroux, Inc., and Faber and Faber, Ltd.: Excerpts from "Lament," "Courtesies of the Interregnum," "The Man with Night Sweats," "The Reassurance," "The Missing," and "Her Pet" from *The Man with Night Sweats* by Thom Gunn. Copyright © 1994 by Thom Gunn.

Reprinted by permission of Farrar, Straus & Giroux, Inc., and the author: Excerpts from "v." from *V. and Other Poems* by Tony Harrison. Copyright © 1990 by Tony Harrison.

"American Wedding," "Heavy Breathing," "In the Life," and "When My Brother Fell" from *Ceremonies* by Essex Hemphill. Copyright © 1992 by Essex Hemphill. Used by permission of Dutton Signet, a division of Penguin Books USA Inc.

Excerpts from "Atlantis" and "Homo Will Not Inherit" from *Atlantis* by Mark Doty. Copyright © 1995. Reprinted with permission of HarperCollins Publishers.

Selections from "The Garbo Index" and "Erotic Collectibles" from *Rhapsodies of a Repeat Offender* by Wayne Koestenbaum, copyright © 1994 by Wayne Koestenbaum. Reprinted by permission of Persea Books, Inc.

From *Turtle, Swan* by Mark Doty. Reprinted by permission of David R. Godine, Publisher, Inc. Copyright © 1987 by Mark Doty.

From *Bethlehem in Broad Daylight* by Mark Doty. Reprinted by permission of David R. Godine, Publisher, Inc. Copyright © 1991 by Mark Doty.

Excerpts from *These Waves of Dying Friends* and "Terrors of Resurrection" reprinted with the permission of the Estate of Michael Lynch. "Terrors of Resurrection" also reprinted with the permission of the University of Illinois Press.

Selections from "The Answer Is in the Garden" from *Ode to Anna Moffo and Other Poems* by Wayne Koestenbaum, copyright © 1990 by Wayne Koestenbaum. Reprinted by permission of Persea Books, Inc.

Excerpt from "One by One" was reprinted with the permission of the Estate of Melvin Dixon.

From "Dreaming the Breasts" from *The Book of Folly*. Copyright © 1972 by Anne Sexton. Reprinted by permission of Houghton Mifflin Co. All rights reserved.

From "Child" from *Bulletins from a War* by Helen Webster. Reprinted with permission of Word Works, Washington, D.C.

From *The Great Mother and Other Poems* and *A Haunting* by Michelle Murray. Reprinted with permission of Sheed & Ward, 115 E. Armour Blvd., Kansas City, Mo. 64111. To order, call (800) 333-7373.

From "To My Mother" by Claire Henze, collected in *Cancer Stories: Creativity and Self-Repair* by Esther Dreifuss-Kattan. Reprinted with permission of Analytic Press, Mahwah, N.J.

"125th Street and Abomey" from *The Black Unicorn* by Audre Lorde. Copyright © 1978 by Audre Lorde. "Today Is Not the Day," "Speechless," "Restoration: A Memorial—9/18/91," "East Berlin," "Hugo I," "Construction," "The Night-Blooming Jasmine," "Girlfriend," and "Lunar Eclipse" from *The Marvelous Arithmetics of Distance: Poems 1987–1992* by Audre Lorde. Copyright © 1993 by Audre Lorde. Reprinted by permission of W. W. Norton & Company, Inc., and Charlotte Sheedy, Literary Agency.

M. F. Z.

Beyond Consolation

Introduction

During the past twenty years, elegies have been more prolifically written, intensively studied, and resourcefully theorized than poems in practically any other traditional genre. At the same time, writing in other genres has become more elegiac as writers have increasingly addressed themes of loss and mourning. Although it has proved intellectually rewarding, this broad cultural turn to elegy is painful insofar as it attests to the psychic and social threat of contemporary life-threatening diseases like AIDS and breast cancer. It is a turn that also betrays the pervasiveness of cultural melancholia at the end of a century that has repeatedly witnessed unimaginable loss of life, from World War I through the Holocaust and Hiroshima to Cambodia and Bosnia. If the resources of elegy have often been called upon, and sometimes found wanting, it is partly because elegiac occasions have been so numerous and so dire.

It is not only contemporary direct threats of mortality, however, that have stimulated interest in elegy. Elegy's high place among traditional poetic forms—it remains an object of lofty poetic ambition to some poets even in the late twentieth century—has recently prompted intensive critical reexamination of its literary history and political implications. In criticism as in twentieth-century poetry, many cultural norms of sexuality, gendered identity, cultural inheritance, and permissible response to death have been at once challenged and actively renegotiated by feminists among others. Because of its privileged poetic status, elegy has been a primary site of critical renegotiation.

I review some of the recent critical discussion in the chapters to come.

Insofar as gender polemics remain unavoidable in dealing with the topic of elegy, I have not sought to avoid them, nor do I profess indifference to their outcome. Even the most studious literary-historical approach to the genre cannot be neutral, a fact to which all recent major books on elegy attest. I have not myself tried to produce a feminist literary history of elegy. Nor have I tried to map the genre or the critical field comprehensively. What I have undertaken is a study, mainly focused on twentieth-century poems, of the literary and cultural politics of the genre. I have centered this study on the story of Orpheus in elegy—or, more tellingly, on the story of Orpheus and Eurydice.

Since classical times, elegiac poetry has been shaped or informed by the narrative of Orpheus and Eurydice. The story has served as a template—a structural paradigm, even an ominous, self-fulfilling prophecy—for elegiac production. The rich complexity of the traditional narrative, with its differing versions, diverse topics, and multiple plots, has facilitated a wide range of poetic variations. At the same time, the story's allegorical potentiality—its expression of the powers and limitations of the poet with respect to human mortality—has been exploited by elegiac poets in every period. The status of the elegist as culture hero and communal spokesperson has often been tacitly at issue in retellings of Orpheus's story.

In gender-political terms, Orphean motifs include men's fears, on the one hand, of victimization by angry, thwarting, or vengeful women and, on the other hand, of being imprisoned without release in a sphere of "female" grieving and mortality. Additionally, the complex, often fraught interplay between male homoerotic desire and heterosexual cultural norms embodied in marriage is prefigured in the Orpheus story, as is the conflict between the erotically charged impulses of the living to remain connected to the dead or aggressively disconnect themselves from them. In short, the story's wealth of implications has proved attractive to poets while the diversity of its topics has resisted any fully integral or definitive rendering.

Nevertheless, elegy has retained a certain narrative focus on the key plot sequence of Eurydice's death, Orpheus's descent to the underworld, and the fatal turn that restores Eurydice to death while Orpheus lives on as the exemplary poet-mourner. This sequence, which encodes a set of recurrent elegiac problems and motifs, has repeatedly attracted elegiac poets, making it a singularly germinal episode for elegiac rewriting. It is also an episode that has shaped critical thinking about elegy and even about language in general: witness Roland Barthes's lifelong fascination with the sequence as reported by Edmund White: "one of his favorite images was of Orpheus (the signifier) condemning Eurydice (the signified) to eternal death by looking back at her."[1] Tellingly, Eurydice's return to the underworld is no sad accident here; it is an active, ruthless condemnation performed in the guise of an anxious backward glance.

The routine cultural misogyny of Barthes's reading is consistent with the celebratory fixation of many male poets on the figure of Orpheus: on the multiple threats to his vocation and on his triumphant apotheosis as a user of poetic language. However culturally sanctioned this "higher strain" in elegy may be, it alone does not justify elegy, nor does it confer value on it. An identificatory fixation on Orpheus and his poetic success is all too compatible with a repressive, death-denying, and self-canonizing masculinist compulsion in elegy *and* in its reception, which now calls for critical reevaluation. In the chapters to come, I hope to display the wealth of poetic alternatives to Orphean identification and apotheosis.

Elegy in Criticism and Theory

Recent critical preoccupation with elegy as a form has coincided with a widespread theoretical exploration of loss, mourning, and, lately, trauma. Psychoanalytic as well as deconstructive theorizations of lack, absence, or loss as the origin of all linguistic performance or cultural construction have given elegy a generally exemplary status, since the genre is already predicated on loss. The specific theorization of elegy has proved to be one of the most productive undertakings of post-structuralist poetics. Any further progress in the discussion of elegy requires some preliminary consideration of this critical heritage.

Until very recently, two powerful models have dominated the discussion of elegy: an anxiety-of-influence model derived from Harold Bloom, and a work-of-mourning model based on Freud's "Mourning and Melancholia."[2] While the first model conceives elegy as a rivalrous attack on a dead but still overwhelming precursor figure, the second conceives the genre as a translation into literature of the grieving process following a death, leading to resignation or consolation. Peter

Sacks's well-known book *The English Elegy* examines elegiac patterning mainly in the light of Freud's "Mourning and Melancholia," yet it aligns that essay with other Freudian texts that treat loss. Sacks rehearses three narratives of adjustment to loss, each centering upon renunciation. In the first, following "Mourning and Melancholia," mourning for a death, if it is not to become fixated in melancholia, requires the detachment of libido from the lost object and its transfer to a new one. In the second, oedipal resolution requires a substitutive transfer of loyalty in the family structure from mother to father, and it involves a castrative "symbolic self-chastening" that placates the father and prevents his vengeance in the form of real castration or death. In the third narrative, the elegiac process is compared to the *fort-da* game played by Freud's grandson: a game of throwing away and retrieving a wooden spool in order, Freud argues, to rehearse the disappearances of the child's mother. Sacks, and almost all psychoanalytic readers of elegy, cast these and other analogous self-taught consolations as heroic male narratives of renunciation. Whatever the merits of this treatment— and they are great, for in its theoretical sophistication and explanatory scope Sacks's book elevated the criticism of elegy to a new level—it has too often been legislated and uncritically normalized. As Louise O. Fradenburg notes, "When 'health' is defined as submission to the rule of law, a subjection for which we are to be compensated by figures that transcend mortality and individuality, then we need a political reading of the elegy, of theories of the elegy, and of elegiac theory."[3]

The need for political consciousness in this arena becomes even more apparent when criteria of success and failure are invoked: of "successful" mourning in the first place, but then of cultural "success" as its reward and counterpart. Sacks's own cultural mythology draws on Ovid's telling of several stories of poetic origin about Apollo and Daphne and a female object for which a substitution is made:

> Only when Apollo turns to the projected founding of a sign, the laurel wreath, does he appear to accept his loss, by having invented some consoling substitute for Daphne. . . . Apollo is having to refer to the nymph, or to the whole tree, by focusing on a detached part of that tree, the fragmentary sign alone which he can attach to his lyre, his quiver, or his hair, and which he already projects as a sign in the future absence of either nymph or tree. . . . What Apollo or the poet pursues turns into a sign not

only of his lost love but also of his very pursuit—a consoling sign that carries in itself the reminder of the loss on which it has been founded.[4]

While one might query the term "lost love" as applied to Apollo's feeling for Daphne—in this as in so many Ovidian stories of origin, rape is in prospect—the question Whose loss? apparently does not arise: it is Apollo's only. Daphne's metamorphosis, followed by the fragmentation of her physical being which yields up, for the male poet, "a consoling sign" in the guise of the laurel wreath or the pan pipes, simply does not count as a loss for her. Sacks's "successful" mourners are typically the winners, performing tasks that define elegy at its best:

> Unlike many other grievers in the *Metamorphoses*, such as Cycnus, Pyramus and Thisbe, Egeria, Niobe, and even Orpheus—all of whom fail to invent or accept an adequate figure for what they have lost and all of whom are consequently altered or destroyed—Apollo and Pan are successful mourners. (The fact that they are, after all, gods may tell us something of Ovid's pessimism regarding the difficulty of their task.)[5]

Success is rendered somewhat ironic, however, by its masochistic subservience ("invent or *accept* [my emphasis] an adequate substitute"), while the unremarked consumption of the woman in this triumphal scenario might well arouse some misgivings.[6] So too might Sacks's canonization of the Apollo and Daphne story as the story of elegiac success: while it is an important myth of origin, it is generally less important in elegy than Orpheus and Eurydice.

The "political reading" Fradenburg calls for has, in fact, been powerfully elaborated in her own work as well as in work by other feminist scholars such as Celeste Schenck and Juliana Schiesari. These critics have directed attention to elegy as a site of male bonding, power production, and authorial self-identification, and to the privileging of male melancholia and concomitant appropriation of mourning by a melancholic male poet and culture hero. All these critics focus on the ways in which men's losses are made to seem the ones that count: women as characters and authors are systematically written out of the picture. If, as Schenck argues, elegy is a male initiation ritual and achieving a successful elegy stands for being a successful male subject, then women have been positively barred from the traditional genre, and the elegies of women poets must be read as a countertradition with a revisionist agenda.[7] Fradenburg shows, conversely, how inconsolability and elegiac silence are at the heart of a politics of "elegiac misogyny" which attempts to distance loss and femininity. She also points out the political implications of the association of women with death: "For if, and when, woman is constructed as the site of loss—made responsible, in any way, for mortality—her capacity to participate in that form of tribal or cultural knowledge which we call history, will inevitably be in doubt or denied altogether."[8]

Finally, Schiesari discusses how male suffering has been culturally "accredited" as melancholia, and female suffering correspondingly discredited as hysteria or depression, throughout the enormously consequential history of melancholia since classical antiquity.[9] One consequence of this difference in accreditation is that women's suffering must be subsumed and effaced in the melancholic man's suffering if it is to receive credit at the highest level. In effect, the articulation of all human suffering, including the woman's, becomes the martyred vocation of the male melancholic culture hero, particularly after the Renaissance, while the suffering of women is doomed to remain speechless, incoherent, or excessive. Insofar as the male melancholic gives words to women's grief, he thereby incorporates "the feminine" into his own highly privileged cultural persona.[10] The male melancholic thus at once denies symbolic expression to women's grief and loss and appropriates it as a symbol. Against this cultural predisposition, however, Schiesari shows how Italian woman poets of the Renaissance, while situating themselves within masculine norms of poetic achievement and propriety, nevertheless try to transform loss, grief, and mourning—the valuable cultural property of the male melancholic—into a communal bond between women.[11] In my view, these points are extremely well taken, and the production of these critiques has coincided with a sustained scholarly effort to gain a hearing for women as poets and elegists; their historical existence has now effectively been made visible.

As a feminist, one might conclude that elegiac fixation on the figure of Orpheus expresses both the fear that women (the maenads) have the power to kill and survive men, and a pathos-infused narcissistic identification with the destroyed male culture hero. The poet appears as a shattered hero of life and culture, scorned, hated, and ultimately killed by women. In the background of these destroying women, urging them on, as it were, are figures of powerful, arbitrarily regulating, and punitive male authority: Pluto or Bacchus or Apollo, depending on the event and the version. But the anger that might be expected to fix on these powerful male deities is deflected onto the female figures. Men are often cast as gentle; women, murderous. Orpheus in fact appears from time to time as a teacher of nonviolence.[12] Better, then, that Eurydice should remain in Hades; in the upper air she is made of the same material as the maenads who dismembered her husband.[13]

The English Elegy

Milton's "Lycidas," resonantly influential for most later English elegy, creates a suggestive connection between female proliferation and the beleaguered figure of Orpheus not only as ur-poet but also as stand-in, always available, for the male poet considering the fate of his own project. The death of Orpheus at the hands of the angry maenads is merely the culminating item in a list of poets' vocational sufferings: the list is full of threatening or abandoning women.

In representing the threatened or martyred poet, "Lycidas" sets up a series of relationships with female figures culminating in the death of Orpheus:

> Where were ye, nymphs, when the remorseless deep
> Clos'd o'er the head of your loved Lycidas?
> For neither were ye playing on the steep,
> Where your old Bards, the famous Druids lie,
> Nor on the shaggy top of Mona high,
> Nor yet where Deva spreads her wizard stream:
> Ay me! I fondly dream—
> Had ye been there—for what could that have done?
> What could the Muse herself that Orpheus bore,
> The Muse herself, for her enchanting son
> Whom Universal nature did lament,
> When by the rout that made the hideous roar,
> His gory visage down the stream was sent,
> Down the swift Hebrus to the Lesbian shore?[14]

Each set of female figures in the passage—nymphs, Muse, murderous maenads—is succeeded by one still more vital and threatening, and even when they are not directly responsible for the deaths of the men they encounter, all outlive those men. The Druids, those other magical poet-priests who, like Lycidas, might be imagined as the successors to Orpheus, are dead, and under the heartless power—and feet—of the vital and indifferent nymphs. Those nymphs have now abandoned Lycidas as well, and although Milton goes on to deny their power, in a flourish of melancholy *correctio*, he establishes and strengthens their ascendancy, twelve lines after this passage, in the apocalyptic image of the life-ending Atropos. She is a Fury-Fate (Milton's own conflation):[15]

> Comes the blind Fury with th'abhorred shears,
> And slits the thin spun life.
>
> (75–76)

The nymphs' close association with the Muse, moreover, makes their possible hostility and their proven unreliability as allies particularly significant. Calliope, or one of her sisters, is indeed "the thankless Muse" (66) who will presently be reproached for exacting heavy prices without certain profit. Later in "Lycidas," female figures lure the aspiring poet into the "shade" and "tangles" of sexual play;[16] finally, when the poem turns from grief and rage toward the consoling apotheosis, they disappear from the poem. They create, in other words, a network of various dangers whose center is the male poet-subject; they therefore confirm the importance of his project at the same time that they threaten its accomplishment, both because they create a world of opposition that magnifies the poet's struggle and because they place culture (the poet, the elegized figure, poetry, and any social context in which the particular poet imagines poetry functioning) in such danger that their defeat acquires moral urgency.

This tale of female threat and masculine poetic *Bildung* is somewhat belied, however, by another story told *by* "Lycidas"—by its triumphant success as a poem—as well as *in* it. This story, which is one of continuous enablement by women and the incorporation of them, also comprises elements of the Orpheus myth: the victory of Orpheus's art over death in the recovery of his dead spouse, Eurydice; the implicitly sacrificial second loss of Eurydice; Eurydice's part in creating the greatness of Orpheus's poetry; and even the role of the maenads in sending Orpheus's head down the river to Lesbos, where his oracular poetic voice will be apotheosized despite the dismemberment of his body. However wanting Orpheus may be found as a pagan prototype in the Christianized context of "Lycidas," both these Orphean stories, the one told in the poem and the one told by it, set monumentally important precedents for later English and American elegists.

In "Lycidas," the use of the Orpheus myth is overt. Yet the story—and its problematic gender politics—haunts elegy as a potent shadow-text even when not overtly invoked. It haunts "Adonais," for example, where Shelley creates a feminized, ambivalent portrait of the "gentle" Keats as an amalgam of Orpheus and Eurydice. Shelley intimates that Keats died after reading a cruel review of his "Endymion"; the anonymous snakelike reviewer hated Keats, we are to understand, for his implicitly Orphean "magic tone" and lyre, and so caused him to die, as Eurydice died, of snakebite. The references in the following passage to lyre and magic form part of a conventional poetic shorthand for Orpheus:[17]

> Our Adonais has drunk poison—oh!
> What deaf and viperous murderer could crown
> Life's early cup with such a draught of woe?
> The nameless worm would now itself disown:
> It felt, yet could escape the magic tone
> Whose prelude held all envy, hate, and wrong,
> But what was howling in one breast alone,
> Silent with expectation of the song
> Whose master's hand is cold, whose silver lyre unstrung.[18]

Shelley imagines Keats as both Orpheus and Eurydice: like the Thracian poet, he is destroyed by a "howling," envious, maddened enemy; but he is also soft, isolated, and vulnerable like Eurydice:[19]

> Oh, gentle child, beautiful as thou wert,
> Why didst thou leave the trodden paths of men
> Too soon, and with weak hands though mighty heart
> Dare the unpastured dragon in his den?
> Defenceless as thou wert.
>   (235–39)

In this presentation Shelley can distance and negotiate his uncertainties about his own poetic vocation and genres; are they as manly as the public, political ones of Byron and Milton? The "conventional poetic shorthand for Orpheus" mentioned above can also be understood as a condensation of identifications and anxieties precipitated by the multivalent story of Orpheus.

In "Thyrsis," Matthew Arnold evokes the world of Orpheus to place the elegized poet, his friend Arthur Hugh Clough, in a nostalgically imagined and significantly feminized past, one in which poetry had more power to move its audience:

> Alack, for Corydon no rival now!—
>   But when Sicilian shepherds lost a mate,
>   Some good survivor with his flute would go,
>   Piping a ditty sad for Bion's fate,
>   And cross the unpermitted ferry's flow,
>   And relax Pluto's brow,
>   And make leap up with joy the beauteous head
>   Of Proserpine, among whose crownèd hair
>   Are flowers first open'd on Sicilian air,
>   And flute his friend, like Orpheus, from the dead.[20]

This is a rewriting of the Orpheus and Eurydice story. Clough is Thyrsis, Corydon's erstwhile rival. He is also, through a complicated series of hypothetical associations, the classical elegist whom an Orpheus figure—here presumably Bion's own elegist, Moschus—would bring back from the dead. Yet he undoes the compliment of making Clough this honored figure by reminding his audience that classical glory has departed: no heroic elegists exist any longer to rescue or be rescued. Moreover, Clough is Eurydice too: or, more exactly, he occupies the position that Eurydice fills in the traditional version of the story which, in a radical—and almost invisibly homoerotic—movement of departure, Arnold has altered by substituting a male "friend" for Eurydice. Eurydice disappears completely, and Clough stands in as the passive spouse to Arnold's wishful fluting. Thyrsis is feminized, however, partly to exorcise femaleness; and the woman's exorcism is repeated throughout the poem, where women are noted only as absences: the tavern-keeper Sibylla whose (resonant) name has vanished from the tavern's sign, the girl who had once tended boats on the river, and Proserpine, who, already a figure of loss in her abduction from the upper world, is no longer accessible at all. If the poem laments a failure of Orphean power and masculine poetic identity, the discovery of that "lack" facilitates an appropriation of the "feminine" and a simultaneous erasure of women. The gender politics of this self-consciously "weak" Orphean scenario are not necessarily more hospitable to women than are those of the "strong" ones.

Gender dynamics of this kind remain visible throughout the readings that follow, yet they are not the whole story. Orpheus, the poet whose ambiguously successful war against mortality depends upon a poetic power to which death itself seemingly gives him further access, is the ur-elegist for many postclassical poets, including the antitraditional or nonnormative ones I discuss in my concluding chapters.

Masculinity and the Threat of Women in Elegy

As we have seen, female figures abound in the major, canonical English elegies, occupying constantly shifting roles as enabling or threatening adjuncts to the poetic process. Although the proliferation and multiple functioning of female figures in the traditional English elegy may serve to consolidate male literary authority, the sheer excess of these figures tends to betray an insecurity at the heart of that authority. Harry Berger, Jr., for example, has argued that when Spenser announces himself as Orpheus at the beginning of his "Epithalamion," he introduces, amid the poem's opening celebration, the darkness that governs the poem's ending. Berger foregrounds "the close functional interdependence between poetic power and [masculine] erotic failure."[21]

The Orpheus myth also addresses the fear that to grieve at all, but especially to write elegy, is to be unmasculine. Because Orpheus is represented sometimes approvingly as a powerful poet and a brave quester, but sometimes scornfully as a weak-willed lover and "only" a poet, his story crystallizes poets' anxieties about their gendered identity. The topic of the poet's "manliness" or "strength of will" is, tellingly, a major matter for debate in literature about Orpheus. Orpheus's fatal breach of Pluto's law can be read as irrational weakness. Aurelia Ghezzi summarizes as follows:

> That a man who had enough courage to defy death in its kingdom would be so mindless or weak-willed that he could not resist looking back makes very little psychological sense; and while in the classical sources no special emphasis is placed on this crucial instant, in the modern versions that are the object of this study the decisive moment is given focal attention.... According to Apollodorus' *Library*: "Orpheus did not believe Plutus, turned around and saw his wife, and she (as a result) returned to Hades...." Here Orpheus' looking back was a form of hubris. In Virgil's Georgics Orpheus turns back "immemor": "Incautum dementia cepit amantem" and, while vanishing again forever Eurydice asks him "Quis tantus furor?" ... Orpheus is not thinking, forgetful of his obligations. Eurydice blames his action on "furor," a sort of irrational lack of control that often accompanies love in Virgil. In Ovid's *Metamorphoses*: "ne deficeret metuens avidusque videndi flexit amans oculos et protinus illa relapsa est." ... His desire for her was his motive here, but it destroys her for the second time. In these cases Orpheus' looking back is considered unintentional, due to emotional, not rational motivations. The transgression, although decisive, is attributed to human frailty, to a form of irrationality, Orpheus is a victim of too-human nature.[22]

Orpheus lacks, moreover, the martial attributes that would make him a hero like Achilles, Herakles, Jason, Perseus, Oedipus, Odysseus, or Agamemnon. All of these are, "whatever else they may be, great killers."[23]

The Orpheus myth also prompts ongoing questions about the manliness or propriety of grieving at all, let alone in the flamboyantly dramatic modes of Orpheus, or of elegy. This uncertainty has long informed elegy and other public modes of grieving. Mourning has been women's work since at least classical antiquity.[24] Perhaps for that reason, it has definitively not been men's work. Discussing consolation manuals in the early part of the sixteenth century, but making the point for modern culture and elegy as well, G. W. Pigman III, for instance, writes about the (stoic) cultural injunction that men suppress grief, which is seen by the writers of the manuals as subversive of the rule of reason and domestic and social order: "The bereaved are likely to feel—and be made to feel—that their grief reveals their irrationality, weakness, inadequate self-control, and impiety. The major purpose of consolation is to induce the bereaved to suppress grief."[25] The denial of loss, grief, and fear, to the degree that it is constitutive of masculinity and of social order, requires outlets and displacements; women and homosexual men are useful, in different but related ways, as sites of displacement. But the displacement creates new difficulties and contaminating connections, so the movement is an ambivalent and anxious one, constantly being reworked.[26]

Additionally, the legendary status of Orpheus as the "inventor" of male homosexuality imports into many elegiac poems a tense interplay between heterosexual and homosexual motifs, as well as between misogyny and homophobia.[27] No doubt male homosexuality in the Orpheus story is conceived heterosexually—it certainly is so in some later retellings—as a disappointed or frustrated retreat from the love of the "opposite" sex rather than as desire for one's own. Because he has lost Eurydice twice, Orpheus will love no other women:

> He set the example for the peoples of Thrace
> Of giving his love to tender boys,
> And enjoying the springtime
> And first flower of their youth.[28]

Nevertheless, the presence of a male homoerotic "sequel"—one that seems retroactively to forestall loss and grieving in an eternal springtime of happy homoerotic consumption—brings heterosexual love and marriage into disconcerting proximity, as well into apparent opposition, with homoerotic desire. The opposition threatens at least on occasion to preempt the proximity. Tennyson, for example, was sufficiently embarrassed late in his life by jokes about the feeling he had expressed for Hallam, the subject of his poem *In Memoriam*, to issue distancing proclamations: "If anybody thinks I ever called him 'dearest' in his life they are much mistaken, for I never even called him 'dear.' "[29] The Orpheus story acts variously, in other words, not only as a template for elegiac production but also as a nexus of often contradictory, anxiety-creating impulses central to poetic production.

Continuity and Discontinuity

To focus on the story of Orpheus and Eurydice in elegy is to risk abstracting a set of motifs without reference to the historical contexts of their deployment. For the Renaissance, after all, Orpheus is dominantly a humanist poet-hero of the civilizing impulse, creating heavenly harmony through his music and upholding marriage, while the Romantics value him for his tragic love and willingness to brave the powers of darkness. These perspectives can also cross: Shelley as a Romantic could see Orpheus as a savior figure, enlightening a despiritualized world with his "magic tone."[30] The modernist crisis in poetry is particularly strongly marked in elegy through the failure of religious belief and consolation, hence of redemptive elegiac narrative and poetic closure. As we shall see, the fortunes of Orpheus vary considerably depending on historical circumstances.

One such circumstance to mention here, partly because it produces a moment of drastic discontinuity in elegiac production and partly because, for obvious reasons, it is actively recalled in both AIDS and breast cancer writing, is the catastrophe of World War I. Coming just after Thomas Hardy's elegiac *Poems of 1912–13*, the war apparently precipitated an even greater crisis for elegy than the post-Victorian one of religious faith. The strain that the war experience placed on traditional (especially pastoral) elegiac conventions and decorums is registered in a number of pithy locutions ranging from Wilfred Owen's "What passing bells for those who die as cattle?" through Virginia Woolf's "[A shell exploded. Twenty or thirty young men were blown up in France, among them Andrew Ramsay, whose death, mercifully, was instantaneous]," through Ezra Pound's

> Died some, pro patria
> non "dulce" non
> "et decor."[31]

Neither traditional elegiac forms nor the figure of Orpheus could weather this crisis. On the contrary, elegiac pastoralism has been increasingly implicated in the political deception that led to World War I. It was Rudyard Kipling, after all, not a soldier-pacifist, who wrote: "If any question why we died, / Tell them, because our fathers lied."[32]

Elegy, to the extent that it continued to be written during World War I, tended to become virulently anti-pastoral; at the same time, the physical separation of fighting men from women left at home, and the domesticated intimacy of trench life, resulted in a frequently negative reconstruction of gender relations in World War I poetry. Women are repeatedly held to blame for men's misfortunes, and are projected as hostile, threatening, or inadequate.[33] This misogynistic representation is consistent with the Miltonic one of the destructive maenad horde, yet the confidence Milton had placed in the defensive power of masculine poetic vocation apparently fails.

Siegfried Sassoon writes bitterly in his "Glory of Women":

> You crown our distant ardours while we fight,
> And mourn our laurelled memories when we're killed.[34]

Women, placing laurels, will now share or usurp male access to the conventions and poetic triumphs of elegy. Neither the gender-interactive scenarios nor the Orphean figurations of previous elegiac writing are much in evidence in the elegiac writing of World War I and its aftermath, whether the poets are combatants or, like Eliot, Pound, and Yeats, noncombatants. Instead, anti-elegy prevails, frequently charged with misogynistic animus. Only a few poems written in the trenches make a most tentative return to Orphean motifs.

A masculine idyll, now destroyed and only a memory, forms the background for much World War I poetry—a "we drove afield" nostalgia for an all-male world of pleasure and autonomy.[35] The loss of this idyll has damaged not only happiness but grief: those who have lost can no longer mourn:

> It seems I have no tears left. They should have fallen—
> Their ghosts, if tears have ghosts, did fall—that day
> When twenty hounds streamed by me, not yet combed out
> But still all equals in their rage of gladness.[36]

Repeatedly, the poet of the war will make this complaint: that he can neither love nor mourn. This incapacity is virtually prohibitive for any Orphean narrative or identification. "To His Love," by the minor World War I poet Ivor Gurney, who spent most of his postwar life confined to an asylum, illustrates the impasse. The poem alludes to, but finds useless, the old conventions of the elegiac genre.

> He's gone, and all our plans
> Are useless indeed.
> We'll walk no more on Cotswold
> Where the sheep feed
> Quietly and take no heed.[37]

Like the mourning swain and Lycidas, this narrator and his friend seem to have shared a beginning, "nursed," perhaps, "upon the self-same hill." Yet the poem's eroticized memory of the young male body's vitality and male penetrative power is devalued by what replaces it:

> You would not know him now . . .
> But still he died
> Nobly, so cover him over
> With violets of pride
> Purple from Severn side.
>
> Cover him, cover him soon!
> And with thick-set
> Masses of memoried flowers—
> Hide that red wet
> Thing that I must somehow forget.
>
> (11–20)

No poetic burial, elegiac apotheosis, or postcastrative recuperation will transform the "red wet thing."

Given the wartime traumatic overload and the failure of cultural therapies, many poets gesture toward reunion with the dead, or number themselves among the already dead. These reunions tend to take place in a classically inflected underworld setting which looks both like Hades and like the mines dug by soldiers in order to explode the other side's entrenchments. The Orphean return from the dead receives grimly parodic treatment from Siegfried Sassoon in "The Rear-Guard":

> At last, with sweat of horror in his hair,
> He climbed through darkness to the twilight air,
> Unloading hell behind him step by step.[38]

Wilfred Owen's "Strange Meeting" plays out a similar descent:

> It seemed that out of battle I escaped
> Down some profound dull tunnel, long since scooped
> Through granites which titanic wars had groined.
>
> Yet also there encumbered sleepers groaned,
> Too fast in thought or death to be bestirred.
> Then, as I probed them, one sprang up, and stared
> With piteous recognition in fixed eyes,
> Lifting distressful hands, as if to bless.
> And by his smile, I knew that sullen hall,—
> By his dead smile I knew we stood in Hell.[39]

The sleepers of the poem, wishing to remain undisturbed, resemble shades of a classical underworld, or in Dante's Hell, locked in oblivion, yet also exhausted, traumatized, virtually catatonic victims of stress. Moments of true encounter or shared recognition *in extremis* are prized above poetic apotheosis, while the difference between the exhausted or neurasthenic living and the dead is so close to being imperceptible that it has to be physically "probed." Under these conditions, the Orphean shadow-text all but disappears, or remains only faintly discernible.[40]

These instances of historical difference and discontinuity are paralleled by political and cultural ones. The sheer fact of discontinuity, even when Orphean motifs persist, is not just apparent but violently marked in, for example, Tony Harrison's recent elegiac poem titled "v.," which I will discuss more extensively in due course.[41] The referential field of this hyper-masculinist, arguably homophobic, yet brilliant poem includes the Holocaust, English class conflict and soccer hooliganism, and the alienating consequences of upward mobility through the modern English educational system. All these topics may make the poem seem at once disconnected from and jarringly antipathetic to the contexts and decorums of earlier pastoral elegy. Yet even so disconcerting an example as "v." shows, in fact, how current elegiac writing is intelligibly connected to seemingly remote precedents, and how much its own intelligibility depends on those precedents rather than its immediate topics of reference. Among other things, the poem's explicit repudiation of a "Greek" ethos—meaning both a Hellenistic literary tradition and the erotic scenarios associated with it—implies aggressive consciousness on Harrison's part of the literary-historical continuum from which he seeks to remove himself.

Shifting from Harrison's "v." to AIDS elegies may produce a further experience of discontinuity or disorientation, yet it also occasions debate and repositioning within a poetic continuum. Harrison's "no more Greek" is answered by AIDS elegies. As Gregory Woods points out, "A long string of funeral elegies connects the literature of classical Greece with our own. Milton's 'Lycidas,' Shelley's 'Adonais,' Arnold's 'Thyrsis,' and Tennyson's *In Memoriam*—all marking the deaths of male friends—stand at the very center of the so-called 'mainstream' of English verse, refusing to be marginalized."[42] Although potentially just as reductive and partial in the end as the exclusively straight characterization of mainstream elegy, this gay counterreading rebukes the cultural vandalism of the skinhead's "no more Greek"; it also invokes the power of a poetic continuum to traverse fields of historical and cultural difference.

The Field of Inquiry

So far, my examples have mainly been drawn from the masculine pastoral elegiac tradition in English poetry and from criticism that addresses that poetry. In the chapters to come, however, I examine elegiac poems *written* by women (some of those poems in the especially painful, politicized context of breast cancer) and by AIDS-threatened gay men. However much the terms of their writing may be conditioned by "mainstream" elegiac norms and conventions, these authors are no longer simply figures in elegy or figments of masculine poetic imagining: it makes a categorical as well as an individual difference who is writing. I have attempted to negotiate a transition from the mainstream elegiac tradition to these contemporary poems instead of simply producing an oppositional or dissociative account. When discussing "mainstream" writers, however, I have focused on ones whose relation to the elegiac tradition already seems somewhat anomalous or problematizing (notably Swinburne and Hardy). While all the poets I consider were intensely engaged with elegiac legacies and imperatives, these writers were skeptical or ambivalent in ways that anticipate contemporary elegiac refiguration. Their poems, moreover, serve as relays between the mainstream elegiac tradition and contemporary elegy. By choosing to discuss Swinburne, the somewhat "perverse" Decadent, rather than the officially meliorist Tennyson of *In Memoriam*, for example, I want to emphasize the contradictions that Swinburne's poetry embraces and that Tennyson's conformist Victorian ideology of marriage subsumes or suppresses.[43] As for Hardy, his anomalousness stems from his elegiac focus on a woman rather than a dead male peer, and on a specifically conceived historical woman rather than a mythological personage. This focus on a real woman functions at once as a private mechanism of Hardy's poetics of loss and as a reading—evaluative, reflective, revisionary—of the elegies of the past. As the exemplary productions of a "poet's poet," too, Hardy's poems become a definitively important source for later elegists; for example, Douglas Dunn in his *Elegies*.

Among modern poets, Robert Lowell might seem a more natural choice than Berryman to represent both elegiac writing in America after World War II and a certain shift of poetic initiative and major ambition from England to the United States in the same period. A noted elegist, more central to his generational group than Berryman and arguably a better poet as well, Lowell recommends himself. Yet Berryman's elegies, especially in *The Dream Songs*, that decades-long accretion, have an obsessive, return-to-the-scene-of-the-crime quality that the more assured elegies of Lowell do not. Berryman worries the issues of authorship, gender position, and relationship to the dead with an intensity and repetitiveness that the more comfortable cultural inheritor escapes; in his position of cultural insecurity, Berryman is less definitively the inheriting male elegist than his more confident peer, and perhaps more revealing.

In seeing elegies written by women as transitional from Hardy to Berryman, I am guided more by thematic concerns than literary-historical ones, yet readers may feel that a significant literary-historical gap opens up at this point. If nothing else, the major elegies of Yeats and Auden might seem to call for attention, as might the shift from English to American writing. If, like Sacks, one prizes above all the "classical" elegy and the uninterrupted poetic succession into which such poets as Yeats, Auden, and Lowell insert themselves as inheritors, a gap may indeed seem to open up in my argument between Hardy and Berryman. Yet it is from precisely this standpoint—of canonical poetic succession—that the revisionary elegiac writing of women, including H.D. and Edna St. Vincent Millay in the interwar period, often remains unseen or gets passed over as inconsequential.

In fact, the increasingly significant access of women to privileged poetic roles and forms of discourse from the interwar period onward can be seen not only in the diverse careers of poets like H.D., Edna St. Vincent Millay, Louise Bogan, Elizabeth Bishop, Sylvia Plath, Anne Sexton, and Adrienne Rich. It can also be seen in the conscious and increasingly "normal" recognition of women's perspectives and issues in poetic discourse, and finally, in the responses of male poets to their female contemporaries.[44] Canonically acknowledged woman poets cease to be rare exceptions, like Rossetti or Dickinson, in English and American writing.

The effect of these cumulative changes can be read, among other things, in Berryman's *Dream Songs*. Berryman reveals the increasingly beleaguered self-consciousness of the male poet, now without assured cultural privilege, being driven into frustrated or parodic relation to mainstream poetic forms and ambitions. However problematic or displacing it may be, Berryman's homage to Anne Bradstreet as an American founding *mother* is telling, as is his subtextual dialogue in *The Dream Songs* with Sylvia Plath as an exemplary yet threatening woman contemporary.[45] As a somewhat marginalized and highly anxious male elegist, Berryman brings into view both a poetic history and a gender agon that are generally kept out of sight in treatments of the "classical" elegy in the twentieth century. Chronologically speaking, the poets in my chapter on women's elegies include Berryman's contemporaries and successors, yet they also include important predecessors in a twentieth-century poetic history that is not exclusively one of male succession, nor, as we shall see, one in which Orpheus always has the last word.

AIDS and Breast Cancer Elegies

While a gay-identified poet such as James Merrill may aspire to major poetic status, and thus invite comparison with English predecessors such as Swinburne and Hardy, the genre of AIDS elegies also imports a communal politics and an overriding sense of *shared* catastrophe into the sphere of poetic production. As regards shared (political) catastrophe, the poems of World War I offer a precedent for AIDS elegies; a poet such as Wilfred Owen may stand out individually, but the common experience continues to define a poetic category. While less programmatically communal than AIDS poems, breast cancer elegies also negotiate between individual poetic achievement and the interests of women—or women with breast cancer—as a class.

To a significant degree, AIDS elegies bear out Simon Watney's now famous dictum that AIDS is "a crisis of representation,"[46] just as they bear out Paula Treichler's corollary characterization of AIDS as "an epidemic of signification."[47] Watney and Treichler do anything but underplay the actual human devastation involved: that devastation, and the rage at injustice it demands, are at the center of their AIDS writing and speech. Yet their own terms point to the difficulty of producing an adequate discursive response to something as ideologically dense and resiliently irrational as AIDS discourse has been. Because hatred of people with illnesses, and of gay men and women, is naturalized at so many levels, discursive refiguration has had to take place in moral, emotional, sexual, metaphysical, aesthetic, and political terms as well as medical ones. Part of the powerful and continuing discourse of AIDS has been a large outpouring of politically informed and often brilliant poetry. As a mode of cultural discourse, AIDS elegy has been no less activist in many of its manifestations than what Cindy Patton calls AIDS "agitprop,"[48] yet it has also (and not only in its "Greek" preoccupations) maintained a strongly interactive dialogue with earlier conventions of poetic elegy, thereby functioning as a means for the gay community to "think and feel our way through this dangerous period in all of our lives."[49]

In important respects, of course, the cultural work done in AIDS elegies, written predominantly by and for gay men and from explicitly gay subjectivities, almost necessarily *does* differ from that done in many earlier elegies.[50] The social positioning of gay men interrupts "normative" scenarios of cultural reproduction and inheritance, while the drastic social circumstances of AIDS elegies, like those of certain other inescapably politicized poems—elegizing victims of the Holocaust, deaths by political assassination, or martyrs among the politically oppressed—have distanced these poems from earlier norms. The effects of this distancing have not been simple, any more than have relations between gay men and women generally—or between gay men and lesbians specifically: painful resentments have developed, for example, over the distribution of public funds for AIDS and breast cancer research.[51] Yet although AIDS poems focus mainly on relations—sexual, social, political—between men, contingent changes in the gender dynamics of elegy amount to a small revolution in the genre. Possibilities of mutual recognition and affinity open up between AIDS elegies and women's breast cancer elegies, where norms of cultural construction and inheritance are also questioned. Although I would certainly not want to assert any "natural" alignment between AIDS elegies and women's elegies on that account, some exploration of the affinities seems legitimate.

In both AIDS and breast cancer elegies, as in Holocaust elegies, certain consciously investigated topics—social silencing and fear of contamination, vengefulness toward the person who suffers and dies, and the sacrifice of an abjected body to purify and regenerate the larger culture—are recognizable from my investigation of Orphean structures in earlier elegies. AIDS and breast cancer elegies participate with other overtly political elegies, however, in a larger debate about the propriety of different kinds of cultural mourning and remembrance. Central to this debate has been the question of whether the exposure of horrors is either morally necessary or politically effective. Debates also center on the decorum of representing or not representing physical disfigurement. Joseph Cady, for instance, argues for what he calls an "immersive" mode of AIDS writing, one in which "the reader is thrust into a direct imaginative confrontation with the special horrors of AIDS," both psychic and physical.[52] Yet as the work of Elaine Scarry among others would suggest, the revelation of horrors can be bent to either progressive or reactionary purposes: to investigate the representation of pain is to understand the very complicated and mobile "way other persons become visible to us, or cease to be visible to us."[53] It is the hostile or sensationalistic description of the physical suffering of people with AIDS, meant to dissociate them from daily experience and therefore from the human, that many activists wish to counter with images of healthy people busy with their lives.

Although AIDS and breast cancer elegies address illness and its effects, they also make connections to a wider range of political analysis and praxis. Questioning often begins with an analysis of the speaker's own stake in, or relation to, the status quo. A heightened understanding of mechanisms of escapism, on the one hand, and of scapegoating, on the other, leads to repositioning in solidarity or refuge with the ill, as in David Bergman's "In the Waiting Room," where the healthy are imagined as having walled themselves off in a polluted city.[54] Audre Lorde calls for political self-recognition *and* self-revelation among the survivors of breast cancer: "what would happen if an army of one-breasted women descended upon Congress and demanded that the use of carcinogenic, fat-stored hormones in beef-feed be outlawed?"[55] In Michael Lynch's *These Waves of Dying Friends*, the connections made throughout the sequence between government inactivity about AIDS and other failures of democracy ("a familiar / country who fail to cross with me the divides") culminate in a scene set at a march on the Capitol:

> Mourning that treasures
> and elegies that hold convert this day
> to other arts: the pageantry of protest, televised.[56]

Social critique and self-critique tend to be pursued concurrently. In "The Mirror and the Tank: 'AIDS,' Subjectivity, and the Rhetoric of Activism," Lee Edelman, for example, rebukes what he sees as a co-ercive, puritanical and self-isolating tendency of some *in* the gay community to "refashion the gay subject in terms of an 'AIDS activist' identity that deploys, on occasion, as the mirror image against which it would call itself into being, a contemptuous depiction of non-'activist' gay men as narcissists addicted to pleasure, resistant to struggle, and therefore themselves responsible for the continuing devastations of 'AIDS.' "[57] Activism is necessary, but not to be pursued at the cost of "the complex and contradictory vision—at once social, political, and erotic—that vitalizes our community."[58]

Making a similar point, Douglas Crimp insists upon the creative and the erotic as central to a visionary politics: "Having learned to support and grieve for our lovers and friends; having joined the fight against fear, hatred, repression, and inaction; having adjusted our sex lives so as to protect ourselves and one another—we are now reclaiming our subjectivities, our communities, our culture . . . and our promiscuous love of sex."[59] Similarly, when the speaker of Marilyn Hacker's "Year's End" hears by phone that yet another woman she knows has died of cancer—and is driven to ask by the rising statistics, "Tell me, senators, what you call abnormal?"—she returns to making love:

> we went back to each other's hands and
> mouths as to a requiem where the chorus
> sings death with irrelevant and amazing
> bodily music.[60]

According to these writers, pairing resistance with pleasure, not abstinence, offers the least sanction to received and repressive structures.

I have been speaking of AIDS and breast cancer poems almost interchangeably here because they tend to share a set of political preoccupations. They also tend implicitly to refuse the traditionally gendered narrative and closure of Orphean elegy. Traditional Orphean narrative comprises an ostensibly mourning—but in reality a dissociative—movement away from a feminized world of the dead and of female figures toward a reconciliation with a masculinized social, political, and ultimately "natural" order. That order, based in heterosexual masculinity, would be disrupted by further grief for the dead; its reassertion is often heralded in elegy by a staged marriage ceremony.[61] I would suggest that the repetition of this narrative in the elegiac tradition coincides to some degree with an *unconscious* politics of cultural masculinity, to the compulsions of which Harrison's "v." still attests. Insofar as women's elegies, AIDS elegies, and breast cancer elegies bring this gender politics to consciousness—an achievement certainly facilitated by concurrent theoretical work—the story of Orpheus and Eurydice may simply appear to lose its power for elegy. Yet, as I will argue in the chapters to come, that story retains its simultaneously promising and threatening paradigmatic character, while the dialogue with older elegiac discourses is sustained throughout both AIDS and breast cancer poems.

In my final chapter, I again link breast cancer elegies, and, more broadly, breast cancer poems by women, to AIDS elegies, seeking, among other things, to identify affinities and shared purposes between them. At the same time, I distinguish between the articulateness of AIDS elegies as a mode of poetic and political discourse and the curious reticence of breast cancer poems. To link the two genres in this way is to incur some risk of distinguishing invidiously in one direction or the other between AIDS and breast cancer poems—and, correlatively, between the respective political and ethical merits of articulation and reticence, between sufferers from AIDS and from breast cancer, and between gay men and women. To this risk must be added the risk of producing an overpolarized distinction between men's AIDS elegies as a genre of flamboyant expressiveness and women's elegies as a genre of decorous reticence—a distinction pre-encoded, so to speak, in the cultural languages of homophobia and misogyny. Both the distinction *and* its undoing are preempted insofar as both genres can be viewed under patriarchy as inferior "feminine" ones. Yet despite these risks, it seems possible (even necessary) to pursue the benefits that might accrue from recognizing affinity, disarming suspicion, and engaging in a strategic dialogue, however threateningly overdetermined, that can barely be said to have started.

1
Unwriting Orpheus:
Swinburne's "Ave atque Vale"
and the "New" Elegy

Algernon Charles Swinburne wrote his elegy for Charles Baudelaire, "Ave atque Vale," in April 1867. The poem established a set of elegiac issues and modalities foreign to the English tradition of pastoral elegy highlighted by canonical poems like "Lycidas," "Adonais," and "Thyrsis."[1] In addition to being centered on a French poet-mentor and, perhaps, being self-consciously Decadent, Swinburne's poem is pointedly unconsoled, even anti-consolatory. It at once exposes and resists the English neoclassical elegy's triumphant relegation of death and the mortal to a feminized, distanced, and disembodied realm of nonbeing. In its different relation to issues of consolation and elegiac closure, "Ave atque Vale" undertakes a revision of elegiac ideology, reexamining the originary status of Orpheus, especially in his role as an exemplary figure of male power, and the relation between winners and losers and between gain and loss. It is for these reasons above all that Swinburne's poem constitutes a significant point of departure for my own examination of elegiac writing. For the same reasons, the poem— canonical (if marginally) and thus not wholly disruptive—institutes an elegiac counterdiscourse that significantly anticipates the counterdiscourses of women's elegies, AIDS elegies, and breast cancer elegies. More centrally even than "Lycidas," "Ave atque Vale" foregrounds the symbolic workings of gender in elegy. Swinburne's poem reveals his passionate interest in the way elegy has traditionally encoded masculinity, hence the world of masculine imagining, and he imagines different, although certainly not what I would call feminist, relations to being male.

As I indicated in the introduction, because the Orpheus story focuses with uncomfortable intensity the elegist's anxieties about poetry and masculinity, about loss and gain, it recurs obsessively in elegy; so too in "Ave atque Vale." A classical hero of unparalleled daring and the supreme poet of heterosexual love, Orpheus is also, in both classical and Christian revisions of the story, a failure and an outsider, both as a poet and as a man. In some versions Orpheus is the inventor of male homosexuality, a fact which, for Swinburne, can hardly have failed to make him a figure of attraction and anxiety, possibly emphasizing his own outsider relation to masculine norms.[2] Yet in Swinburne's poem this compromised masculinity enables Orpheus to cross with female figures, the most important of whom is Sappho, in ways that allow him an innovative reentry into elegiac tradition.

In "Ave atque Vale," Swinburne embeds a punning reference to Orpheus in a comparison between Baudelaire and Sappho:

> For always thee the fervid languid glories
>   Allured of heavier suns in mightier skies;
>   Thine ears knew all the wandering watery sighs
> Where the sea sobs round Lesbian promontories,
>   The barren kiss of piteous wave to wave
>   That knows not where is that Leucadian grave
> Which hides too deep the supreme head of song.
>   Ah, salt and sterile as her kisses were,
>   The wild sea winds her and the green gulfs bear
> Hither and thither, and vex and work her wrong,
>   Blind gods that cannot spare.[3]

The "head of song" is not only the greatest of all poets, as Swinburne steadfastly insisted Sappho was, and the originator of lyric poetry, but also a singing head: Orpheus after the maenads have killed him.[4] Sappho and Orpheus are traditionally associated because Orpheus's head and lyre washed up on Lesbos; in several versions of the myth, it was this event that consecrated Lesbos to lyric poetry ever after, making it the home not only of Sappho but also of Terpander and Alcaeus.[5] According to legend, Sappho makes a suicidal leap from the cliffs of Leucas—a martyrdom to love, like Orpheus's ultimately fatal devotion to the dead Eurydice. Sappho's broken body and the fragments that re-

main of her verse recall Orpheus's dismemberment. Even Sappho's descent into the ocean echoes that of Orpheus to the underworld. But the
strong identification of the two in "Ave atque Vale" is Swinburne's
innovation.

As I have already argued, Swinburne's reference to Orpheus participates in a tradition; it serves as the elegist's marker of investment in
the elegiac canon. In this context it signals as well a difficult set of
connected issues for the male elegist: his need to take death as his
subject, but also his longing for poetic power and his vexed relationship
to ideals of masculinity. In "Ave atque Vale," a poem of passion as
well as of ambivalence and questioning about poetry and the elegiac
project, Orpheus is vividly present. Yet Swinburne comes at him
obliquely, evoking him through (or hiding him behind) a favorite and,
significantly, female heroic figure. In her legendary bisexual role as
lover of women and of Phaon, Sappho can stand in for both Orpheus—
the lover of women, the shattered but resurgent poet, the receiver of
god-given poetic gifts—and Eurydice, the faithful lover of her male
poet, the irrevocably dead woman, the source of poetic inspiration.[6]

Sappho supplies a more complicated figure for identification and distancing than the poem's other women—characters from Baudelaire's
poetry, Venus, Clytemnestra, Niobe. It is important that all the poem's
female figures confirm its movement toward irredeemable loss, and all,
like Eurydice, are themselves lost or losing. In this richly intertextual
poem every character imported from Baudelaire's poetry is female, including one generally assumed to be male—and partly disguised as
such: the old servant of Swinburne's epigraph (a quotation from
Baudelaire). This invocation of female figures is no conventional summoning of the Muses: Swinburne's female figures generally function in
ways more complex than do the maternal-erotic, engendering Muses.
This point is already addressed by Thaïs Morgan in her examination of
Swinburne's ventriloquy of female voices in poems about poetic inspiration: he speaks so often through female voices because "poetics and
the politics of gender are interdependent for Swinburne."[7]

Always implicit in this complex, "interdependent" poetics and politics of gender is a calculus of loss and gain, the ratio between which is
often a gendered one, although it has not always been discussed as
such. In an influential book, Jahan Ramazani, for example, sees as a
major concern of the genre "the economic problem of poetic mourning

... [an] elegiac trade-off between aesthetic gain and mortal loss"; he instances Tennyson's "trying to 'find in loss a gain to match.' "[8] The economic issue of profit and loss (whose profit, whose loss?) is sufficiently well established in elegiac tradition for Hardy later to ask, in one of his elegies for his wife:

> Dear ghost, in the past did you ever find
> The thought, "What profit," move me much?[9]

This question and the way of putting it suggest, however, what is troubling as well as appealing to elegists about the economic model. It requires a suppression of either the compassionate or the ambitious impulse: compassion becomes equated with loss while callous ambition becomes equated with gain. From this equation another may follow: denial of loss is seen as constitutively masculine, while adherence to loss is seen as feminine. Finally (and most importantly for Swinburne) the economic model threatens to render poetry wholly instrumental, binding it to the production of ulterior gain rather than allowing it to remain suspended as a powerful, literary, alternate world in its own right.

It is for the "real" masculine world of male rivalry and action, of striving toward unmistakable gain, that Swinburne in "Ave atque Vale" apparently substitutes a prolifically feminized, textual, other (or under-) world, ruled over, tellingly, by "Proserpine's veiled head" (83).[10] In this deathly realm of female dominance, worldly distinctions fade or become illegible, and loss and gain may suffuse each other inseparably. The focus of Swinburne's elegy is "the place where white dreams dwell" (175), a textual "place" itself problematically situated, filled with the illegibilities, uncertainties, and anxieties belonging to poetic production, and spectrally feminine in character.

Issues of gendered value play out in Swinburne's intensely paradoxical attitudes toward loss and gain in the public arena of literature. His temperamental—perhaps aristocratic—repugnance for the idea of profit, and for a goal beyond experience itself, governs the range of his topics and interests, as does his aversion to the idea of poetry for political or moral change; to the instrumentalization of sexuality, as in marriage, in the service of social goals; to life only as redeemed in an afterlife. Yet the pressures of a normative, thus socially engaged, Romanticism continue to be discernible in Swinburne's revolutionary enthusiasm, in his adoration of Blake and Shelley, and, perhaps above all, in his relation to the paternal, tutelary figure of Victor Hugo, curiously and ambivalently identified, as we shall see, with Orpheus in Swinburne's poems.

From childhood on, Swinburne had been drawn in the direction of political poetry by the work of admired Romantics. Among the living, he regarded Victor Hugo most highly. The nationalist Mazzini and, later, Hugo himself had urged the younger poet not to restrict himself to poetry of individual passion, but to use his voice for higher purposes.[11] Indeed, Swinburne's volume of 1871, *Songs before Sunrise*, is an answer to Mazzini's urging: the sun will rise, Swinburne hopes, on the successful republican struggles of Europe, particularly those of Italy and France. Throughout his life, in other words, Swinburne was deeply drawn to the idea of political poetry, and at least until his last years, emancipatory views on almost all topics of his day informed his poetry, even when the poetry was at its most hermetic.[12] However reactionary his politics became, he tried to hold onto an early, idealized image of his own radicalism. In a late preface to the first *Poems and Ballads* series, for example, he defended his stance against Irish home rule: "Monarchists and anarchists may be advocates of national dissolution and reactionary division: republicans cannot be."[13] Swinburne's attachment to public, revolutionary goals, no less than his panics and regressions in the face of revolutionary practice—his retreats to the family scene, to the admiral father and the genteelly literary mother[14]—may indeed contribute to the famous paradoxicality of his work. Attachment and retreat contribute as well to the palpable ambivalence of the strongly asserted, self- consciously heroic emancipatory impulse in Swinburne's writing.[15]

Going back at least as far as Plato's *Symposium*, which Swinburne knew well, the Orpheus story could be read as one distinguishing pejoratively between the hero and the poet.[16] Speaking of love as an incentive to military valor, Phaedrus remembers the Orpheus story, and his eloquence falters:

> Thus heaven itself has a peculiar regard for ardor and resolution in the cause of Love. And yet the gods sent Orpheus away from Hades empty-handed, and showed him the mere shadow of the woman he had come

to seek. Eurydice herself they would not let him take, because he seemed, like the mere minstrel that he was, to be a lukewarm lover, lacking the courage to die as Alcestis died for love, and choosing rather to scheme his way, living, into Hades. And it was for this that the gods doomed him, and doomed him justly, to meet his death at the hands of women.[17]

In conceiving of an "Orphean" Hugo, Swinburne seemingly attempts to reintegrate the poetic with the heroic, yet the very attempt to effect this reintegration apparently results in radical failure and hence in a quest for alternative models.

Throughout the letters, Swinburne refers to Hugo as "Maître," "Cher Maître," "Maître des Maîtres," recalling proudly that Hugo's first letter to him was addressed "Mon fils"; and he was devastated by Hugo's death.[18] The poem "To Victor Hugo," published in the first *Poems and Ballads* volume, praises Hugo and reviles those who sent him into exile; it mourns the failure of Hugo's political hopes; and it dwells on Swinburne's own ambivalent identification with France, not only as a place of greater aestheticism and sensuality than Britain, but also of revolutionary ideals in decline.[19] In this poem, Hugo represents for Swinburne a combination of Orpheus and Prometheus, a rebellious figure who undoes the stereotypical Orphean opposition between the self-absorbed poet and the altruistic man of action who defies unjust laws (of gods or state) and whose poetry can move man and animal, not simply to strong emotion, but to new vision and purpose:[20]

> For thee man's spirit stood
> Disrobed of flesh and blood,
> And bare the heart of the most secret hours;
> And to thine hand more tame
> Than birds in winter came
> High hopes and unknown flying forms of powers,
> And from thy table fed, and sang
> Till with the tune men's ears took fire and rang.
>
> Even all men's eyes and ears
> With fiery sound and tears
> Waxed hot, and cheeks caught flame and eyelids light,
> At those high songs of thine
> That stung the sense like wine,
> Or fell more soft than dew or snow by night,

> Or wailed as in some flooded cave
> Sobs the strong broken spirit of a wave.[21]

Like Prometheus, Hugo has an affinity with fire, emblematic of his rebellious courage, and he dares the anger of those who can punish him in
order to advance human progress and liberty. Like Orpheus, however,
Hugo crosses to where the human being is only spirit, but does so in the
world of the living: "For thee man's spirit stood / Disrobed of flesh and
blood." Swinburne has created a fairly traditional Orphean context, but
one that eventually registers as strangely out of place in this poem: he
chooses the Orpheus who is a powerful, magical poet, but thereby paradoxically questions Hugo's power. Hugo is in exile, out of range of his
country and compatriots, and the influence of his fiery song has diminished. The imagery surrounding his song is suspicious; perhaps, since it
"stung the sense like wine," the visions it produced were illusory—and
the spirit of the wave, though "strong," is "broken." France may have
forgotten Hugo in its degeneracy, yet Hugo's own potencies are rendered questionable by the defection of his people:

> fled like dreams
> The feet of freedom and the thought of thee;
> And all between the skies and graves
> The mirth of mockers and the shame of slaves.[22]

Unlike Orpheus, Hugo has seen the efficacy of his song die before him.
   Songs before Sunrise, Swinburne's second volume of poetry, includes
the sonnet "Eurydice: To Victor Hugo," which can be read as a revi-
sionary gloss on "To Victor Hugo." This sonnet allegorizes France as
Eurydice, drugged and sleeping under false rule, awaiting rescue by
Orpheus (Hugo):

> Orpheus, the night is full of tears and cries,
>   And hardly for the storm and ruin shed
>   Can even thine eyes be certain of her head
> Who never passed out of thy spirit's eyes,
> But stood and shone before them in such wise
>   As when with love her lips and hands were fed,
>   And with mute mouth out of the dusty dead
> Strove to make answer when thou bad'st her rise.

Yet viper-stricken must her lifeblood feel
  The fang that stung her sleeping, the foul germ
  Even when she wakes of hell's most poisonous worm,
Though now it writhe beneath her wounded heel.
  Turn yet, she will not fade nor fly from thee;
  Wait, and see hell yield up Eurydice.[23]

Swinburne has reshaped the story in bold strokes, and yet the syntactic difficulty of the lines impedes the programmatic radicalism of the retelling. Both narrative and values are reversed: Eurydice takes vengeance on the serpent, and Orpheus must be enjoined, rather than forbidden, to turn.[24] The sestet's opening "yet" is ambiguous: although it appears at first to mean "but," it must actually mean "still," since the following sentence is not opposed to what has come before. The new version of the story, then, seems to run this way: Eurydice has been, and continues to be, slowed by the snake's venom: "yet viper-stricken must her lifeblood feel"; in Swinburne's version, as opposed to Virgil's and Ovid's, she has been stung in her sleep rather than in fleeing a rapist. Moreover, it is Orpheus rather than she who must be summoned. If Hugo is Orpheus, then this makes sense: he is in exile, imagining his beloved France only in his "spirit's eyes." But it also introduces a strange attribute of reluctance into the picture of Orpheus, elsewhere the over-eager lover. At the same time, Eurydice gains new agency: it is she who "strove to make answer," who will grind the snake beneath her foot (recalling that action of the biblical Eve), who will remove herself to the upper world. Interestingly, in this eulogy to a heroic figure of action, the action is displaced from the male to the female figure, although not without anxiety, since the Eurydice who will save herself from Hell is clearly related to the Eve who, tempting her passive mate, cast humanity out of Paradise.[25]

Swinburne speaks of Baudelaire with significantly calmer collegiality than he does of Hugo: Baudelaire is "a man whom I deeply admired and believed in." After Baudelaire's death, Swinburne would sometimes refer to him with proprietary affection as "my poor Baudelaire."[26] In "Ave atque Vale" Baudelaire is a "brother" ("mon semblable, mon frère"?) not a father or master.[27] Like Hugo, however, though in a different way, Baudelaire becomes another exemplarily failed Orpheus. His failure is that he cannot come back from the underworld, with or without Eurydice: he is hostage forever to "the solemn earth, a fatal mother," and his only triumph is that "there lies not any troublous thing before" (191, 195). Given the apparent failure of Hugo as the integral figure of the poet-hero, and given, furthermore, the apparent failure of paternal transmission from Hugo as father/master, a more complex circulation of identities and differences—including fraternal ones triangulated by the figure of Sappho as poetic, phallic "mother"— become apparent in "Ave atque Vale"; in the Baudelaire elegy, the story of Orpheus is present only as a buried text, or subtext.

The choice of Sappho as a displacing cover figure for Orpheus makes the references to her at once a conflation of the two legendary poets and a refusal of Orpheus: if Sappho is the supreme head of song, Orpheus is not, and has been misunderstood (or displaced) as such.[28] By routing his Orphic longings for poetic power and knowledge of the dead through the figure of Sappho, Swinburne can distance the specific anxieties the Orpheus myth both raises and partly articulates—especially those pertaining to gender. Sappho initiates the poet, as her devotee, into a textual world figured in the poem simultaneously as a classical underworld and the place of writing—the place of what Derrida calls "graphic relations between the living and the dead."[29]

Sappho, sometimes conflated with Baudelaire in "Ave atque Vale," becomes one version of the "elder singer." In doing so, however, she unavoidably precipitates a conflict between the elegiac program of "Ave atque Vale" and that of another "elder singer."[30] This elder singer is Milton, whose image of Orpheus in "Lycidas" is sharply evoked in "Ave atque Vale."

The reference to Orpheus/Sappho as "head of song" cannot but recall Milton's images of the decapitation of Orpheus and its aftermath:[31]

> When by the rout that made the hideous roar
> His gory visage down the stream was sent,
> Down the swift Hebrus to the Lesbian shore.
> (61–63)

In "Lycidas," Orpheus is associated not only with the elegy's subject, Edward King, but with Christ as a resurrected deity. Christ's return is, of course, metaphysically superior to that of Orpheus in Milton's poem, pointing to the poem's closure in spiritual rather than bodily salvation.

Yet Swinburne rejects Milton's revision of the pagan toward the Christian; for modern poets, "Lycidas," with its consolation and strong closure, is an epitome of the old elegy, and "Ave atque Vale" confronts both "Lycidas" and the tradition it represents directly. Swinburne's elegy responds to three famous English elegies: "Lycidas," "Adonais," and "Thyrsis."[32] "Ave atque Vale" is an acknowledgment of poetic debt and an assertion of revisionary rights as well as the commemoration of an individual.[33]

The most powerful condensation of this revisionary impulse occurs in Swinburne's revision of the imagery of the head. It is as though, for Swinburne, "Lycidas" were primarily a poem about the decapitation of Orpheus. In *The English Elegy*, Peter Sacks points out the proximity of the line "which hides too deep the supreme head of song" ("Ave atque Vale") to "That sunk so low that sacred head of thine" ("Lycidas")—"in content, meter, and syntax."[34] The sun becomes associated with the head, and ultimately with faith and challenges to faith, throughout "Lycidas":

> Together both, ere the high lawns appeared
> Under the opening eyelids of the morn,
> We drove afield.
>
> (26–27)

Apollo, the sun god, chides the speaker for insufficient faith, touching his ear (77). The absence of the sun, recalling its earlier eclipse during the crucifixion, destroys the head:

> It was that fatal and perfidious bark,
> Built in th' eclipse, and rigged with curses dark,
> That sunk so low that sacred head of thine.
>
> (100–103)

The sun's return after a night "beneath the watery floor," where Lycidas is, presages the spiritual resurrection of the dead man:

> So sinks the day-star in the ocean bed,
> And yet anon repairs his drooping head.
>
> (168–69)

Finally, the setting sun puts the world to rest as the swain sings—but not without the promise of its return in the morning (190–94). Although the pagan world has been too powerfully evoked to be wholly erased, the "pagan" interpretation of the sun in "Lycidas" gives way to the Christian.[35]

And in Milton's poem the female gives way to the male, with the disappearance of all threatening female figures. Swinburne, however, creates a different pattern. Rewriting Orpheus through Sappho as he does, and maintaining the focus on female figures, Swinburne implicitly conflates elegiac closure with the masculinist and Christian, refusal of consolation with the female and pagan. If the set of head images becomes more emphatically solar in Milton, pointing to spiritual rebirth and freedom from the vulnerability of the body, in Swinburne an equally central set of head images grows progressively darker, more bodily.

The first of these images, a reminiscence of Baudelaire's "La Géante," suggests repose, although it also resonates with an awed sadness that foreshadows the later section of Swinburne's elegy:

> Hast thou found place at the great knees and feet
> Of some pale Titan-woman like a lover,
> Such as thy vision here solicited,
> Under the shadow of her fair vast head.
>
> (58–61)

This relatively benign image is overwhelmed by the next, of a female head as chilling emissary from the world of death:

> Some dim derision of mysterious laughter
> From the blind tongueless warders of the dead,
> Some gainless glimpse of Proserpine's veiled head,
> Some little sound of unregarded tears
> Wept by effaced unprofitable eyes,
> And from pale mouths some cadence of dead sighs—
> These only, these the hearkening spirit hears,
> Sees only such things rise.
>
> (81–88)

Faces are central to the frustration and eeriness of this passage: Proserpine's head leads the rest in invisibility and inaudibility; the effacement of their "unprofitable" eyes and the pallor of their mouths suggests decay and horror behind her veil as well. Entry into the afterlife meets only with the frustration of encountering more veils, more unspeaking mouths: "Proserpine's veiled head," "the blind tongueless warders of the dead." Echoing the "blind mouths" of "Lycidas," this line constitutes a nightmare version—"gainless," "unprofitable"—of Orpheus's (initially) successful journey: in the old story, the shades of the dead wept too, but at the beauty of Orpheus's music; his glimpse of Proserpine was not gainless, but rendered up Eurydice.

The final stanzas of "Ave atque Vale" accrete gestures and depictions of mourning, violence, and death. The speaker will "lay, Orestes-like, across the tomb / A curl of severed hair" (120–21). These lines recall, by contrast, Lycidas's "oozy locks" washed clean in heavenly nectar. Yet although the mourner may be Orestes-like in his grief, he can undertake no revenge to soothe his spirit, for Baudelaire's death does not impose heroic obligation:

> But by no hand nor any treason stricken,
>   Not like the low-lying head of Him, the King,
>   The flame that made of Troy a ruinous thing,
> Thou liest, and on this dust no tears could quicken.
>   (122–25)

Baudelaire's is merely a human death, even if mourned by the gods, and the gods who mourn Baudelaire cannot bring him back. Over Baudelaire's "irrevocable head," Apollo "sheds light from the under skies" (153–54). As opposed to the association of heads with sunlight in "Lycidas," the heads of "Ave atque Vale" are always associated with shadow or with extinguished light, or a light that is enigmatically repositioned and altered, as is Apollo's underworld light in the lines above. Swinburne rejects the Orpheus story as one of redemption and transformation, even while assembling its now reinterpreted motifs.

To what, then, do such sweeping revisions conduce? Swinburne writes, in a critical essay on *Hero and Leander*: "The passion of the lovers is a thin veil for that of the poet. . . . And from the very excess of pleasurable emotion, which burns and trembles through the verse as a flower trembles into the air, the whole poem is thrown back into some remote visionary land, which cannot affect or alter any human relation."[36]

Apropos of such pronouncements, Jerome McGann remarks that in this "state of trance, below or beyond ordinary consciousness . . . the light of sense goes out whereby the world is held as an aggregate of fixed things and relations. The world comes not as something to be possessed, mastered, or used, but as a vitality one is to be possessed by. . . . To be mastered by that life, rapt into it, is to discover oneself to the world as a present incarnation of such life."[37] The trance state thwarts the temporality of verse, its narrative linearity and linguistic seriality. For a form such as the elegy, which has traditionally enacted a linear and cumulative drama of apotheosis, the effect of such a disruption is radical. Since trances are temporary, however, the poem must in some measure fail, self-consciously and programmatically.

Such successful (programmatic) failure is crucial to "Ave atque Vale." Swinburne celebrates in Baudelaire's poetry a refusal, similar to his own, to conform to traditional poetic imperatives, as well as Baudelaire's solitary, perhaps Orphean, affinity for forbidden desires and realms: those of the morbid imagination, of unsocialized sexuality, and of ghosts of the dead rather than the living. Alive, the "Orphean" Baudelaire gained access, however "unprofitable," to an underworld no one else could enter, let alone survive or write poetry in: a place Swinburne generalizes as "unbreathed in," playing ambiguously on poetic inspiration as breath and wind. (Piling pun on pun, Swinburne makes the flowers "blow" as well.)

> Thou sawest, in thine old singing season, brother,
>   Secrets and sorrows unbeheld of us:
>   Fierce loves, and lovely leaf-buds poisonous,
> Bare to thy subtler eye, but for none other
>   Blowing by night in some unbreathed-in clime;
>   The hidden harvest of luxurious time,
> Sin without shape, and pleasure without speech;
>   And where strange dreams in a tumultuous sleep
>   Make the shut eyes of stricken spirits weep;
> And with each face thou sawest the shadow on each,
>   Seeing as men sow men reap.
>
>   (23–33)

This stanza envisions Baudelaire operating, as Swinburne might wish to do, within a newly conceived structure of meaning. Baudelaire's conventions are, defiantly, nonce conventions, while the poem's "work" is mainly that of undoing elegy, perhaps above all in its gendered economy of profit and loss.

Parallel to this undoing, and consistent with it, relations between the living and the dead in Swinburne's poetry are reconstituted in their irreducibly graphic aspect, exemplified by the relationship between epigraph and poem in "Ave atque Vale." The epigraph comprises five lines from Baudelaire's own "La servante au grand coeur":

> Nous devrions pourtant lui porter quelques fleurs;
> Les morts, les pauvres morts, ont de grandes douleurs,
> Et quand Octobre souffle, émondeur des vieux arbres,
> Son vent mélancolique à l'entour de leurs marbres,
> Certe, ils doivent trouver les vivants bien ingrats.
>
> [Let us bring her some flowers.
> The dead, the wretched dead, must know enormous grief,
> And when that stripper of old trees, October, vents
> His melancholy blast among their monuments,
> They surely must believe the living to be thankless.][38]

Swinburne's choice of an epigraph from Baudelaire indicates, on the one hand, the power of the dead to speak definitively, to enter and inform the language of the living, to engage, as the Baudelaire passage ironically does, the elegiac conventions. On the other hand, the powerlessness of the dead over their work or the way they are represented, and the condescension of the living toward the dead, are equally apparent. The image of Baudelaire as a discontented, petulant corpse who finds the living "bien ingrats" goes far to domesticate him; he is humanly trapped within his own words, his own irony.

Another textual domestication of the dead is hidden in the poem's removal from its original context. "La servante au grand coeur" is a poem about the death of the speaker's nurse, whose grave he has been neglecting, apparently, in favor of the lover to whom the poem is addressed:

> My old great-hearted nurse who stirred your jealousy,
> Who now beneath a humble sward sleeps quietly,
> We should in human kindness carry her a wreath.

The last eight lines of Baudelaire's poem make clear, however, that the relation of the living to the dead in this poem is that of a guilty near-son to a loving, wronged, mother-surrogate:

> If one evening, while the log fires hiss and flare
> Serenely, I should see her seated in her chair,
> If, on a frozen night of blue December gloom,
> I found her nested in a corner of my room
> Sedately, coming from the depths of her long night
> To watch her grown-up child with a maternal eye,
> To this devoted soul what reason could I plead,
> Watching the tears that swim beneath her sunken lid?

This scene further textures the already richly interwoven relations between epigraph and poem, dead writer and live writer, even between competing poetic genealogies or origins figured respectively by Orpheus and Sappho.

Yet insofar as Baudelaire, not Sappho, is the old maternal ghost, communion with "her" remains blocked as well as intimate:

> Not thee, O never thee, in all time's changes,
>   Not thee, but this the sound of thy sad soul,
>   The shadow of thy swift spirit, this shut scroll
> I lay my hand on, and not death estranges
>   My spirit from communion of thy song.
>   (100–104)

Unlike Orpheus, Swinburne's communion with the dead leaves him with only a literary relic, a "shut scroll," an ultimately unrecoverable set of meanings, no less profoundly unrecoverable in the much published poems of Baudelaire than in the incompletely surviving oeuvre of Sappho. Not coincidentally, perhaps, the following two stanzas describe a wasting Apollo:

> sparing of his sacred strength, not often
> Among us darkling here the lord of light
> Makes manifest his music and his might.
>   (133–35)

> he too now at thy soul's sunsetting,
> God of all suns and songs, he too bends down
> To mix his laurel with thy cypress crown,
> And save thy dust from blame and from forgetting.
>
> (144–47)

Significantly, Apollo appears not as he does in "Lycidas," to comfort the mourner, but instead to add to the lamentation. He comes with no gift of poetic power or promise of fame, but must conserve what little "of his sacred strength" he still possesses. Apollo, like Venus in the next stanza, is a "bitter and dying god."[39] His gesture of homage to Baudelaire is consequently an ambiguous one: when he mixes "his laurel with [Baudelaire's] cypress crown," does he bestow fame or partake of mortality?

In his final stanza, Swinburne again connects the images of an unexpressive text and an infertile mother:

> Take at my hands this garland and farewell.
> Thin is the leaf, and chill the wintry smell,
> And chill the solemn earth, a fatal mother,
> With sadder than the Niobean womb,
> And the hollow of her breasts a tomb.
>
> (189–92)

The thin leaf, like the place of the white dreams, recalls the poem's page. It is a poem of feminized loss, still partaking of that loss. In the poem, Swinburne never moves beyond the site of Sappho's death, the Ionian Sea whose waves "work her wrong"; any gods who might have redeemed her are doubly helpless, "blind gods that cannot spare" (22). This immobility represents a significant departure from elegiac linearity, no less than it does from the cyclical schema proposed by Northrop Frye, who locates the movement of elegy in the cyclical recurrences of nature: death is associated with sunset, winter, sea; rebirth with sunrise, spring, and land. Logically, hope or the possibility of hope returns with spring, as signified by the flower catalogue of pastoral elegy.[40] For Swinburne, however, "Ave atque Vale" comes to a finish with Frye's death images: the "chill" earth, Baudelaire whose "days are done," the stillness or sunset over the sea:

> all winds are quiet as the sun,
> All waters as the shore.
>   (197–98)

The final section of the poem confirms not only the irredeemability of loss and the association of that loss with poetry, but also the association of poetry and loss with women, and what is left is *only* the feminized, textual world of death. Yet this negative outcome, together with the reconfiguration of elegiac motifs entailed in it, supplies a canonical template for much of the elegiac writing with which the rest of this book will be concerned. In that sense as well as a more historical one, Swinburne's poem represents the "new" elegy.

2

"Woman Much Missed": Writing Eurydice in Hardy's *Poems of 1912–13*

Thomas Hardy's *Poems of 1912–13* constitutes a major elegiac sequence in which his dead wife, Emma, is recalled, often literally as a ghost. Both the recall and the impassioned poetic sequence are somewhat paradoxical in light of Hardy's notorious estrangement from Emma and his fatalistic "plotting" of his own marriage. In neither the mainstream elegiac tradition nor in Hardy's experience and representations of marriage does a powerful motive for mourning a dead wife suggest itself.[1] Guilt alone does not sufficiently account for Hardy's mourning of Emma; the discovery of a powerful poetic motive, necessitating a significant reworking of elegiac conventions, was required for *Poems of 1912–13*. Such a motive was at least partly elicited, as I will shortly argue, from the moment of Orpheus's backward glance and Eurydice's loss in the return from the underworld, a moment Hardy tended to conflate with the underworld moment of encounter between Dido and Aeneas in Book 6 of Virgil's *Aeneid*.[2] Before considering this seemingly generative moment in Hardy's elegies, however, I shall briefly review Hardy's assimilation of Swinburne as well as of other major elegiac predecessors.[3]

Following the precedent of Victorian elegists, Hardy refuses religious consolation. Between Shelley's *Adonais*, the last important elegy with a definitively transcendent consolation, and Hardy's sequence for Emma come Arnold's "Thyrsis" and "Scholar Gypsy" and Swinburne's "Ave atque Vale." Most twentieth-century elegies, including Hardy's, have acknowledged their relation to the extended tradition by alluding obliquely to some of its conventions, but with emphasis on those that are associated with mourning rather than consolation. Conventions of consolation or celebration they have tended to mute, diminish, turn toward sorrow, or reveal as emptied of meaning. So while Hardy presents (highly modified and contextualized) versions of the flower catalogue, of laments at the coming of winter, of the memory of scenes of poetic companionship, of a search for the dead, and of mournful invocations of water deities, he eliminates the turn in feeling which would redeem these images of loss. He allows some moments of muted consolation, as in "After a Journey," but he never suggests that they are anything more than momentary, ghostly.

To write an elegy for a woman is to alter even further the received genre. Generally, following well-known precedents that hark back at least to Moschus's "Lament for Bion," mainstream elegies have treated an admired but not intimately known male acquaintance or peer. Most often, too, these are fellow poets: in the poems they are mourned by, but seldom are, female figures. Insofar as elegy has been passed on from man to man, it has been so, as Celeste Schenck puts it, "in order both to lay the ancestor to rest and to seize the pipes of poetry from his barely cold hands."[4] Inherent in the project of seizing poetry's pipes is an insistence on the elegist's continued vitality: *his* hands are still warm, *he* can still play—and sing or speak. For at the heart of elegy are painful issues of identification and separation: the live male poet wishes to be like the man who has died, but must separate from him sufficiently to retain a commitment to life. In such negotiations, between men, of literary power and authority, women have had an important symbolic role. If elegy is a way of reaffirming patriarchal inheritance in literature, the poet will often make use of female figures in order finally to exclude them. Hardy's *Poems of 1912–13*, his most extensive and ambitious elegiac venture, is therefore particularly anomalous. Only a few elegies for women are undertaken previously to Hardy's sequence—by Spenser, Donne, Milton, Henry King, Pope—and many of these are so clearly occasional as to preclude engagement with this ambitious genre.[5] In Hardy's series of poems the conventions are subtly recomposed by their placement around a female figure in ways that allow us to see how much traditional elegy assumes an equality between elegized and elegist, despite conventional declarations of unworthiness, and how impossible that assumption is when the elegist is male and the elegized is female. No question can arise, for instance, of the elegist and elegized having shared a vocation, or even a tutor—no driving together "afield" under the benign eye of Camus with a female companion.[6] The scenes of past companionship Hardy recalls are actually those of the courtship which, when solidified into marriage, were to lead to profound estrangement. The burst of righteous anger that often precedes the turn toward consolation in traditional elegy—Milton's toward the bad priests, Shelley's toward Keats's reviewer—is transmuted into the woman's complaint, the imagined reproaches of a neglected wife. Most complicated of all by the gender change of the elegiac subject is the invocation to the muse. A muse is typically personified as a female force external to and radically different from the poet, capable of drawing poetry out of the poet and into the world. The muse is therefore distinct from, although often associated with, a beloved woman who is imagined as having an actual presence for the poet. In Hardy's ghostly elegy, the supernaturally empowering figure of the woman is also a personal muse, specially and intimately bound to the poet, as he is to her, through a conjugal tie seemingly indissoluble even by death and subsequent remarriage.[7] This dramatic extension, with its Orphean subtext, of the normative marriage plot or the Victorian companionate marriage paradigm, constitutes a major innovation on Hardy's part, to which subsequent poets would be indebted.

For all the enablement and poetic vitalization conferred by the ghostly encounter in Hardy's writing, however, the scene also remains one of ghostly contagion (i.e., of being exposed to the danger of catching death from the dead), a threat exacerbated by the ghost as female, and all the more so because women in Hardy's poetry are sources of power, pleasure, and consolation as well as of anxiety.[8] For this reason among others, many of the anxieties of the traditional elegiac genre recur in Hardy's poetry. The poetry of Orpheus, that ur-elegist, is able to overcome the power of death in order to win back Eurydice, but it is her very presence, drawing his gaze, that defeats him. The attractiveness of the dead woman requires the male elegist's wariness, lest he push beyond "negative capability" and become what he is writing about: the dead, female object. The female ghost can beckon like a siren, luring the unwary man to his death; as a spirit, she is likely to be conceived as hostile. At the same time, the body which had housed the spirit decays, so in this way too she becomes an object of repulsion and fear.[9]

Ghosts upset boundary lines—of life and death, of time and space—

and once one boundary line has been transgressed, all the others show as frangible. For Hardy's *Poems of 1912–13*, this destabilized field becomes a highly energized one for poetic production, and also one in which the "weird" estrangement of language, idiom, and diction that characterizes Hardy's lyrics can be pursued. Isobel Grundy catalogues some of Hardy's special effects: his use of riddles, crossword-puzzle clues, kennings (for instance, library as "tomb of tome"), words like "subtrude," "retrocede," picked as "nonce-words, adapted to no other occasion," and other "tongue-twister effects." She notes that his manuscript revisions often add or augment strangeness.[10] Cliché contributes to this project as a means of resurrecting dead language by giving it a new context; as a way, too, of negating, while using, convention. To defamiliarize language is, however, to ally oneself with the uncanny, with the irrational, with the feared and unknown. Even Hardy's forms of verisimilitude or prosaic realism are undermined by moments of deliberate awkwardness or employ a self-consciously unpoetic diction: "woman riding high above with bright hair flapping free" ("Beeny Cliff").

In "Lycidas," that superlative model for later elegies, the female figures, from potentially withholding Muses to shears-brandishing Furies to maenads, without exception cause or threaten destruction, while their "overcoming" confers poetic power. Hardy's sequence takes on both the threat and the empowerment; and some aspects of the "feminine," which are read only as threat in mainstream elegy, are rewritten by Hardy as power sources. The "coy" or "thankless" unreliability of the Muses in "Lycidas," a subset of the misogynist poetic tradition of women's fickleness, becomes the thrilling unpredictability of Emma's appearances in *Poems of 1912–13*:

> Where you will next be there's no knowing,
> Facing round about me everywhere,
> With your nut-coloured hair,
> And gray eyes, and rose-flush coming and going.
> ("After a Journey," 349)

Questions of identification and separation so crucial to elegy become more vexed across gender lines. Donald Davie writes of "the wildness and undifferentiation of sexual energy" with reference to Hardy's gender-destabilizing revisions of Virgil; not only is gender destabilized, but "femaleness" threatens to become contagious. (Indeed, the genre of elegy itself may seem to "feminize" the poet, mourning having been seen as dominantly woman's work at least since classical times.)[11] Finally, insofar as women are imagined as extrarational—as being at once incapable of "male" reason and possessed of powers to see into the world of the supernatural—they become an exploitable resource but a perilous one, uncanny in their otherness.

Swinburne appears to have supplied Hardy with some precedents for negotiating this difficult new terrain of male poetic ambition. Hardy's elegy for Swinburne, for example, celebrates the union between Swinburne and Sappho, his "singing-mistress":

> she the Lesbian, she the music-mother
> Of all the tribe that feel in melodies;
> Who leapt, love-anguished, from the Leucadian steep
> Into the rambling world-encircling deep
>   Which hides her where none sees.
>
> And one can hold in thought that nightly here
> His phantom may draw down to the water's brim,
> And hers come up to meet it, as a dim
> Lone shine up in the heaving hydrosphere,
> And mariners wonder as they traverse near,
>   Unknowing of her and him.[12]

This arrangement may well represent Hardy's ideal marriage; it includes a powerful communion between man and woman (they merge into a single "shine" on the water); it has all the trappings of passion—nightly meeting, talk of love—and it confirms the man's literary achievement, but it requires no actual contact, no dependencies. It is a mystical and forever liminal exchange which will feed the poet's powers.[13]

The poem nevertheless—or additionally—celebrates Swinburne as a hero of sexual emancipation, at least in poetry, in its second stanza. Swinburne's poems had come upon the literary scene:

> as though a garland of red roses
> Had fallen about the hood of some smug nun
> When irresponsibly dropped as from the sun,

In fulth of numbers freaked with musical closes,
Upon Victoria's formal middle time
His leaves of rhythm and rhyme.

(323)

These lines condense a number of Swinburnian themes and poems: a dislike of Christianity, as in "Hymn to Proserpine"; a belief in the disruptive power of the poet, as in "Ave atque Vale"; and an unconventional rendering of passion, as in Swinburne's tributes to Sappho, for which his poems were often reviled. Hardy's poem also aligns the male poets with Sappho, crossover participant in the male prerogatives of poetry and sexuality, against the sexually repressed or repressive female guardians of conventional virtue—Victoria, the nun, the poem's "real" women.[14] The description of Swinburne's conversation with Sappho develops the imagery of this stanza in its punning on "incarnadine," lifted from Shakespeare but in the spirit of Swinburne:

One dreams him sighing to her spectral form:
"O teacher, where lies hid thy burning line;
Where are those songs, O poetess divine
Whose very orts are love incarnadine?"
And her smile back: "Disciple true and warm,
Sufficient now are thine."

(324)

Her "orts" are her poems, love-embodied, but also her broken body, evoked by the "love-anguished" leap described earlier, love reddened by blood—as Swinburne depicted her in "Anactoria."[15] Sappho's fragmentation and hiddenness give way, satisfactorily, to the poetry of Swinburne. In his depictions of Sappho, Swinburne has made her unnecessary: his poetry is now "sufficient."

The sacrificial and incorporative economy of this exchange is part of its erotic preciousness for the male poet; Sappho, internalized, belongs to Swinburne and Hardy in a way that releases their poetic potentiality. The imaginary or conditional quality of the scene, its distancing from actuality—"one can hold in thought"—creates part of its pleasure; the "specters" provide an entrée to the world of imagination, a private world which appears only as an incomprehensible glow to "won-der[ing]" outsiders.[16]

It is from this ideal standpoint that something comparable yet less than ideal appears in Hardy's *Poems of 1912-13*. As "marriage poems," these elegies are curiously anticipated and glossed by "The Conver-gence of the Twain," Hardy's poem on the sinking of the *Titanic*. In "The Convergence of the Twain," the ship is decidedly "female," with her mirrors, jewels, and fiery interior; the iceberg, her "sinister mate," is "male," a silent figure of penetrative, destructive power; their coming together is an "intimate welding":

> In a solitude of the sea
> Deep from human vanity,
> And the Pride of Life that planned her, stilly couches she.
>
> (306)

Partly because this poem was published in the same volume as *Poems of 1912-13*, and written while Emma was ailing, it seems to share a continuity with the elegies. Some of the *Poems of 1912-13* recall "Con-vergence," in their evocation, first, of the couple's "fated" relationship:

> coastward bound on a night long ago,
> There lonely I found her,
> The sea-birds around her,
> And other than nigh things uncaring to know.
>
> So sweet her life there (in my thought has it seemed)
> That quickly she drew me,
> To take her unto me,
> And lodge her long years with me. Such have I dreamed.
>
> ("A Dream or No," 348)

and, second, in their insistence on the cosmic importance of the events described: what the "primaeval rocks" of Cornwall "record in colour and cast / Is—that we two passed" ("At Castle Boterel," 351). The *Titanic* poem makes explicit a strain that is muted in the sequence, namely Hardy's sense of male power and his grandiose self-image as a gigantic and vanity-reproving natural force:[17]

Well: while was fashioning
This creature of cleaving wing,
The Immanent Will that stirs and urges everything

Prepared a sinister mate
For her—so gaily great—
A Shape of Ice, for the time far and dissociate.

And as the smart ship grew
In stature, grace, and hue,
In shadowy silent distance grew the Iceberg too.

Alien they seemed to be;
No mortal eye could see
The intimate welding of their later history,

Or sign that they were bent
By paths coincident
On being anon twin halves of one august event,

Till the Spinner of the Years
Said "Now!" And each one hears,
And consummation comes, and jars two hemispheres.
(307)

Despite the catastrophe of "union" between ship and iceberg, the poem
acknowledges a poetic gain from the wreckage:

Steel chambers, late the pyres
Of her salamandrine fires,
Cold currents thrid, and turn to rhythmic tidal lyres.
(306)

However inauspicious as a marriage poem, "The Convergence of the
Twain" features a concluding exchange of the dead female body for
poetic empowerment.[18]

An explicitly Eurydicean, female, return enables the imagery of "The
Shadow on the Stone" (1917), a poem also related to the 1912–13 group.
This poem evokes what Hardy finds most poetically generative; not
pure loss or destruction as such, but the *turn* of Orpheus, that moment
of losing which comprehends both contact and irreversible separation:

I went by the Druid stone
That broods in the garden white and lone,
And I stopped and looked at the shifting shadows
That at some moments fall thereon
From the tree hard by with a rhythmic swing,
And they shaped in my imagining
To the shade that a well-known head and shoulders
Threw there when she was gardening.

I thought her behind my back
Yea, her I long had learned to lack,
And I said: "I am sure you are standing behind me,
Though how do you get into this old track?"
And there was no sound but the fall of a leaf
As a sad response; and to keep down grief
I would not turn my head to discover
That there was nothing in my belief.

Yet I wanted to look and see
That nobody stood at the back of me;
But I thought once more: "Nay, I'll not unvision
A shape which, somehow, there may be."
So I went on softly from the glade,
And left her behind me throwing her shade,
As she were indeed an apparition—
My head unturned lest my dream should fade.

(530)

"My head unturned lest my dream should fade": the last line sounds like a definitive summary. But the poem remains irreconcilably divided between not wanting to look and wanting to, between believing in the ghost and not believing in her: "And left her behind me throwing her shade, / As she were indeed an apparition." In this retelling, Orpheus will lose not only the woman but also poetry itself if he turns his head: his dream will fade, his poem's "shape" will "unvision" itself. Both she and his poetry exist in the atemporal space which cannot be looked at straight on, but which "somehow, there may be."[19]

The power of this legendary moment is further suggested by Hardy's transformation of Aeneas from a state founder into an Orphean lover and Hades quester. The epigraph for *Poems of 1912–13* is drawn from the *Aeneid*: "Veteris vestigiae flammae" (the traces or signs of an old flame).[20] This epigraph recalls the single episode of erotic beauty and excitement in the *Aeneid* as well as its tragic consequence: Aeneas's abandonment of Dido and Dido's suicide. Aeneas's defection also, eventually, reunites the original couple, Dido and Sychaeus, as ghosts: the epigraph quotes the words of Dido to her sister upon meeting Aeneas, musing that the embers of her love for her dead *first* husband, Sychaeus, stir in her again. (The fire-ring in "Where the Picnic Was" ironically recalls this moment: "the spot still shows / As a burnt circle—aye, / And stick-ends, charred, / Still strew the sward"; in that poem, however, the embers are a year old and not likely to stir again.) In several ways, then, the epigraph imports the scenario of a ghostly encounter into the poems, as well as recalling the most "Orphean" moment in the *Aeneid*.[21]

In small, the epigraph gives us the leading themes of Hardy's elegiac sequence: betrayal, remorse, the inaccessibility of the dead, the longing for them. Hardy may, more than many other poets, have needed to attach poetic invention to loss, and to have figured woman centrally in both loss and recuperation. Yet as Peter Sacks makes clear in his discussion of the Daphne and Apollo story, myths of achieving song in spite of varieties of loss and dispersal are at the heart of many myths of poetic origin and triumph.[22] They are, moreover, specifically associated with women.

Hardy's peculiarity, which is especially manifested in the power of his elegiac writing, is to have fixated on the Orphean moment of turning to look back at Eurydice and to have made this his peculiar *scene* of writing, around which an entire geography of poetic representation is organized. These scenes of almost meeting, of a fatally charged *turn*, of unforgettable looks exchanged in the absence of speech, will be replayed obsessively throughout *Poems of 1912–13*, and they represent in part the remorse of the abandoning husband. But they call up also the continuing Orphean subtext that empowers the poems' (male) elegiac imperatives.

Emma fulfills this Eurydicean part for Hardy: the dead, unloved wife is better material for his poems than the living, loved woman he was about to marry. Her posthumous role in his poetry—the immense productivity of her death for him as topic—shows that his question in "Your Last Drive" deserves more contemplation than its rhetorical presentation would suggest:

> Dear ghost, in the past did you ever find
> The thought, "What profit," move me much?
>
> (339)

Her death is a source of serious profit for him in poetic terms, yet that is too simple a way of putting it. The relations between life, literary genre, and poetic vocation overlap eerily in Hardy's biography. The ironies of this overlap were not lost on his fiancée, Florence, who, after reading these poems, wrote a letter in which she bitterly referred to her dead predecessor as "the late espoused saint" (quoting Milton's sonnet to his dead wife).[23] If any suspicion of further "profit" to come entered her mind, it may have done so on account of Hardy's curious marriage-proposal to her: he had brought her to Stinsford churchyard and shown her a corner among the Hardy graves reserved for her.[24] In "He Prefers Her Earthly," the speaker claims that the idea of a heavenly afterlife for his dead beloved is too alienating; he would rather have her simply dead:

> I would not have you thus and there,
> But still would grieve on, missing you, still feature
> You as the one you were.
>
> (496)

Paradoxically, the death rather than the apotheosis of the beloved allows her to be "the one you were."

At one time, *Poems of 1912–13* insists, the married couple had talked lovingly and fulfillingly:

> What we did as we climbed, and what we talked of
>   Matters not much, nor to what it led,—
> Something that life will not be balked of
>   Without rude reason till hope is dead,
>   And feeling fled.
>
> ("At Castle Boterel," 351)

Yet Emma and Thomas Hardy became about as estranged as a couple can while still living in the same house: as Hardy notes throughout the

series, they had their separate social lives and travels, and spoke less
and less. During the last years of Emma's life, in fact, the marriage had
become almost entirely silent, a fact referred to obliquely but obsessively from the first poem of the sequence, which juxtaposes the moment of Emma's death and the period of their courtship so many years
earlier:

> Why, then, latterly did we not speak,
> Did we not think of those days long dead,
> And ere your vanishing strive to seek
> That time's renewal? We might have said,
>   "In this bright spring weather
>   We'll visit together
> Those places that once we visited."
>   ("The Going," 339)

While one might wonder why, given the disastrous marriage, Hardy
should even imagine such a wish, the sequence constantly reiterates
Hardy's assertion that his mourning is complicated but not diminished
by the marriage's failure: the earlier loss of relatedness is superimposed
on the later, final loss. The silence of their estrangement is overlaid with
the silence of death.

In a letter to Florence Henniker after Emma's death, Hardy wrote
that "the saddest moments of all are when I go into the garden and to
that long straight walk at the top that you know, where she used to
walk every evening just before dusk, the cat trotting faithfully behind
her; & at times when I almost expect to see her as usual coming in from
the flower-beds with a little trowel in her hand."[25] Michael Millgate
comments that in this letter "the note, and even some of the vocabulary
of Hardy's rhetoric of remorse is already audible in the letter, and at
the end of 1912 and the beginning of 1913, as he later recalled, he wrote
more poems than he had ever done in a comparable amount of time."[26]
The poem it most closely resembles is the first of the sequence, "The
Going:"

> Why do you make me leave the house
> And think for a breath it is you I see
> At the end of the alley of bending boughs

> Where so often at dusk you used to be;
>   Till in darkening dankness
>   The yawning blankness
> Of the perspective sickens me!
>
>   (338)

It is a Eurydicean disappearance, and it calls forth this poem, as the poem calls forth the apparition: the "breath" he sees her for is a brief moment, but it is also the inspiration for or the actual utterance of the song or poem, and it becomes *her* breath, her vital principle. Yet another breath—the "yawn" of darkness—swallows her up again. Throughout the series, Hardy will try to befriend this ghost, will seek it, entreat it, imagine that it is speaking to him, as in "The Voice":

> Woman much missed, how you call to me, call to me,
> Saying that now you are not as you were,
> When you had changed from the one who was all to me,
> But as at first, when our day was fair.
>
>   (346)

"The Voice" ruminates upon, and leaves unresolved, questions of the possibility of any communication between the dead and the living. (Jean Brooks points out that the final "uncertainties of thought and rhythm" which take place in "The Voice" are unavailable to more conventional elegy.)[27]

The poem's very title, of course, raises questions about voice. During the series, the poet never addresses the woman by name, unlike most elegists, who constantly repeat the real or classicized name of the deceased. In "The Voice," this reticence seems fearful, recalling circumlocutory ways of alluding to spirits or the devil in order to avoid unintentionally calling them. The elliptical syntax of the two middle lines avoids any certainty of address. And in fact the speaker's belief in her existence dies away: he decides by the end of the poem that what he hears must be "only the breeze."

In "The Haunter," ostensibly the wife's answer to "The Voice," the dead woman speaks of her devotion to the man she haunts:

He does not think that I haunt here nightly:
    How shall I let him know
That whither his fancy sets him wandering
    I, too, alertly, go?—
    . . . .
Yes, I companion him to places
    Only dreamers know,
Where the shy hares print long paces,
    Where the night rooks go;
Into old aisles where the past is all to him,
    Close as his shade can do,
Always lacking the power to call to him,
    Near as I reach thereto!

                        (345–46)

The ghost's world is the world of memory and dream, of the "fancy" roaming through the past, and it is the world of poetry, where natural phenomena "print" their traces. As in "A Phantom Horsewoman," the ghost becomes an internalized spirit of poetry, causing the poet to see

            as an instant thing
        More clear than to-day,
        A sweet soft scene
        . . . .
        What his back years bring—
    A phantom of his own figuring.
        ("A Phantom Horsewoman," 354)

In "A Phantom Horsewoman," however, the poet controls the spirit of poetry: she is "of his own figuring." The relation of poet to poem and ghost in "The Haunter" and "The Voice" is more uncertain, and the tone of the passage in which she describes trying to communicate is faintly sinister, an impression heightened by the ghostly echo of the rhyme ("call to me" and "all to me," "all to him" and "call to him") between the poems. The echo is uncanny—has she implanted the rhyme in his consciousness without his actually hearing her? Or is he as much a ghost as she, each echoing the other endlessly? "The Voice" can never decide; even as it ends in the gloom of disillusion, the poet invokes "the woman calling."

Hardy's poems often capitalize upon the subtextual effects of rhyme and its ability to comment on pairings. In "The Opportunity," for example, he produces a miniature pastoral elegy by rhyming "Maytime" first with "daytime" and later with "claytime" (621). The rhyme forms a synopsis, sometimes even a subtextual counternarrative that controverts the stanza's apparent direction.[28]

Although Hardy has insisted upon the impossibility of any conversation, he has created and recorded one, ghostly though it may be, in "The Voice." This move will be repeated variously, as in "Your Last Drive," a poem about self-enclosure of the most painful kind, the awareness of missed connections. The speaker blames himself for having missed the signs of approaching death on his wife's face. Here, unlike Orpheus, he is at fault for *not* having looked at his wife's face, which might, with its "last-time look in the flickering sheen," have resembled Eurydice's at that liminal moment at the edge of the upper world, when the warmth and light of the sun had just reached her face. But he has failed her as thoroughly; like Orpheus, he has forfeited a meeting through a willful self-absorption which he now passionately regrets, an inability to imagine, and therefore connect with, a mind other than his own. He has lost his chance to "read the writing" of another's consciousness and this past failure puts in question his current project of commemorating the dead:

> I drove not with you. . . . Yet had I sat
> At your side that eve I should not have seen
> That the countenance I was glancing at
> Had a last-time look in the flickering sheen,
> Nor have read the writing upon your face,
> "I go hence soon to my resting-place;
>
> "You may miss me then. But I shall not know
> How many times you visit me there,
> Or what your thoughts are, or if you go
> There never at all. And I shall not care.
> Should you censure me I shall take no heed,
> And even your praises no more shall need."
>   (339–40)

The two kinds of "not knowing"—Hardy's now unchangeable withdrawal from his wife's concerns in the past and her current inability to know anything again—in other words, the failure to read and the use-

lessness of writing—resonate guiltily together, undoing the relation between world and text necessary for elegy and for poetic vocation. And
yet in the context of this poem, if there ever was "writing" to read on
the woman's face, it is the poet who put it there. He writes, in fact,
what he imagines not having been able to read, and ends the poem by
answering it:

> True: never you'll know. And you will not mind.
> But shall I then slight you because of such?
> Dear ghost, in the past did you ever find
> The thought "What profit," move me much?
> Yet abides the fact, indeed, the same,—
> You are past love, praise, indifference, blame.
>
> (340)

These alternations give the effect of the live poet moving between
the dead woman's consciousness and his own, as though his act of
ventriloquy allowed him to slip from one state of being into another.
The "flickering sheen" on Emma's remembered face is also an image
of absence alternating with presence, between light and dark, consciousness and death, the imagined and the actual. In this way thinking,
reading, writing, and voice, instead of replacing each other in any stable
hierarchy, move into a more reciprocal and dynamic relationship—always dependent, of course, on the imagining mind and writing hand
of the poet.

As I have suggested, however, this mobility in gender and state of
being is perilous. In "A Circular" the speaker is asked by an outsider
to respond as though he were in fact the dead woman. The poem literally presents a problem of address, since the text upon which the
poem dilates is a circular directed only contingently to him, but which
cannot be received by the dead woman to whom it has been sent:

> As "legal representative"
> I read a missive not my own,
> On new designs the senders give
>   For clothes, in tints as shown.

Here figure blouses, gowns for tea,
And presentation-trains of state,
Charming ball-dresses, millinery,
Warranted up to date.

(347)

The poem's bitter punch line comes when we are reminded that the circular is addressed to the dead woman, she "who before last year ebbed out / Was costumed in a shroud." The inappropriateness of the speaker as reader now shifts to one of gender—these are advertisements for women's fashions—and in his interest in these illustrations, the poet seems to fear falling into a psychic cross-dressing, for he carefully distinguishes himself from the true recipient of "a missive not my own." His choice of the word "figure" for the circular's pictures, with its triply layered suggestion of illustration, woman's body, and poetic trope, coalesces the poem's concerns.

The way texts circulate is itself, punningly, at issue here; in this poem the materiality of texts only deflates their value and generic status. Hardy means to insert himself in the masculine interchange of elegy, and instead finds himself stranded in a low, feminized world of textual inappropriateness. This anomalous moment is nonetheless characteristic of the speaker's predicament throughout the poems: searching for clues to the dead woman's identity in a text that cannot possibly reveal anything about her, trying to read from a perspective he has always disavowed, and longing for an identification which he repudiates even while it fascinates him.

For shifts, ambiguities, and complexities of tone, "After a Journey" displays perhaps the most virtuosity in the series. In it, Hardy superimposes the conventions of contemporary ghost story onto the Orpheus myth: here is a Eurydice who will go and come back:

Hereto I come to view a voiceless ghost;
    Whither, O whither will its whim now draw me?
Up the cliff, down, till I'm lonely, lost,
    And the unseen waters' ejaculations awe me.
Where you will next be there's no knowing,

Facing round about me everywhere,
    With your nut-coloured hair,
And gray eyes, and rose-flush coming and going.

Yes: I have re-entered your olden haunts at last;
    Through the years, through the dead scenes I have tracked you;
What have you now found to say of our past—
    Scanned across the dark space wherein I have lacked you?
Summer gave us sweets, but autumn wrought division?
    Things were not lastly as firstly well
        With us twain, you tell?
But all's closed now, despite Time's derision.

I see what you are doing: you are leading me on
    To the spots we knew when we haunted here together,
The waterfall, above which the mist-bow shone
    At the then fair hour in the then fair weather,
And the cave just under, with a voice still so hollow
    That it seems to call out to me from forty years ago,
        When you were all aglow,
And not the thin ghost that I now frailly follow!

Ignorant of what there is flitting here to see,
    The waked birds preen and the seals flop lazily;
Soon you will have, Dear, to vanish from me,
    For the stars close their shutters and the dawn whitens hazily.
Trust me, I mind not, though Life lours,
    The bringing me here; nay, bring me here again!
        I am just the same as when
Our days were a joy, and our paths through flowers.

(349)

The ghost in "After a Journey" puts the narrator in some danger of death, and it thus recalls the ghost in *Hamlet*:

What if it tempt you toward the flood, my lord,
Or to the dreadful summit of the cliff
That beetles o'er his base into the sea.[29]

The allusion brings with it that play's aura, its uncertainty, guilt, jealousy, tragic death; but perhaps also a hint of its final benediction.

Clearly different from "The Going," "After a Journey" takes place at dawn, not dusk—one rare concession to the traditional imagery of consolation—and by its end, the speaker is no longer alienated from the woman's apparition. On the contrary, he is joyously reconciled with it; the change is first marked in the shift in pronouns, from "it" to "you," accompanied suddenly by an overwhelming sense of Emma's remembered youthful beauty. By the poem's end, the whole world is newly energized and eroticized: "The waked birds preen, and the seals flop lazily." Yet it is also at this exact moment that Emma must disappear: as a ghost, she is confined to the nighttime and compelled to "vanish" at the break of day. Now, however, he is willing to count on her return.

Emma's ghost, moreover, is now fully identified as *his* imaginative creation. And she is his alone—the seals do not see her, just as the mariners in "A Singer Asleep" do not see Swinburne and Sappho. She is "voiceless," he speaks. His imagination transforms the landscape, takes hold of it, finds *his* ghost in it.

U. C. Knoepflmacher has argued, apropos particularly of *Poems of 1912–13*, that Hardy in his old age understood the importance of "a culturally defined feminine space" within his work, one that allowed him mobility in gender attitudes and a respect for female voices.[30] Knoepflmacher's later observation that *"even at its most querulous, her voice is allowed a full hearing"* (my emphasis) makes this claim less credible, however.[31] Admittedly, insofar as woman is constructed as a ghost, apostrophic, undefined, Hardy is interested in temporarily occupying that "space." In a sense, therefore, the woman does control and shape the poetic production of the male elegist, also "immortalizing" him:

> "A Shade but in its mindful ones
>   Has immortality;
> By living, me you keep alive,
>   By dying, you slay me."
>   ("Her Immortality," 56)

Yet Hardy can also suspend the woman in a feminine space defined as exterior to the process of cultural production: in short, the place of Eurydice. It is in elegies written by women that this placement, among other things, will be contested.

3

The Fading of Orpheus:
Women's Elegies

To date, the genre of the neoclassical elegy has generally not been centrally occupied by woman poets writing in English, nor have these poets generally been thought of as elegists. As Germaine Greer points out with respect to woman writers of the seventeenth century, one of the few then-sanctioned elegiac outlets for women was poetry written for the death of children.[1] This "minor" women's genre clearly stands in a subordinate, sharply differentiated, relation to the major elegiac tradition; very few such poems have made their way into standard anthologies, a state of affairs that postfeminist revision of such anthologies has done little to change. In the sentimental tradition of the eighteenth and nineteenth centuries, "poetesses" performed in a highly monitored and bounded elegiac space, establishing (but also confined to) a subordinate and largely ridiculed "female consolatory tradition" of their own.[2] As in Bradstreet's elegies, attempts to revise the tradition are painfully circumscribed by compulsions of social and religious decorum, leaving a body of work that is often interesting, even powerful, but fraught with anxiety and frustration. Poems in this sentimental tradition have generally not been canonized. Even in the modern period, when women have entered the literary marketplace in large numbers, the traditional elegy has apparently remained a problematic and relatively uncompelling form for them. Importantly, however, when they have written in the genre, they have done so in ways that tend to question the dynamics of the male elegiac tradition. Such questioning is often specifically focused on the Orphean narrative or subtext of so many canonical elegies. This questioning does not necessarily result in outright rejection of the Orphean myth or of all Orphean elegiac motifs, though it frequently does entail a destructuring of the standard Orphean narrative(s). I believe this narrative undoing implies rejection of the oppressive or sacrificial structures of the traditional elegy as well as of the ideological telos of the Orpheus story as recycled in traditional elegy.

From the perspective created by the women's elegies I will discuss, mainstream canonical elegies have a deep investment in keeping the politics of the Orpheus myth unconscious, or else in construing those politics (sometimes conceived as the politics of civilization itself) in a way that, on the one hand, maintains the redundancy of women in the process of cultural reproduction, and, on the other hand, maintains the constancy of female "threat" or "excess" as obstacles to such reproduction.

Celeste Schenck, in "Feminism and Deconstruction: Reconstructing the Elegy," focuses, as does this book, mainly on twentieth-century women's revisions of and challenges to the genre.[3] She argues that women's elegies tend to reject a career-driven, masculinist model in which the dead are to be overcome, displaced, and distanced, and in which the main goal of elegy is poetic inheritance. I believe Schenck has thus correctly located the most important area of refiguration in women's elegies: the crucial and constitutive place of the living person's ongoing affectionate relations with the dead. It is in this respect, I believe, that women's elegies have been importantly pioneering ones for other elegiac genres, notably AIDS and breast cancer elegies. Yet I would argue that women poets do not in turn unambivalently value continuity with the dead, do not only refuse to let the dead go. Nor do they necessarily reject careerist preoccupations: elegy will often remain, for women, a way of organizing, or reorganizing, poetic agendas, and of claiming creative entitlement. Nor, finally, do women elegists wholly repudiate continuity or "dialogue" with the mainstream elegiac tradition.

Jahan Ramazani, commenting on Schenck's work, makes the important point that a connective theory of women's elegy underplays the "dissociative impulse" that would later lead to the "poems of angry insubordination" by such poets as Plath, Sexton, and Rich.[4] This useful amendment tends, however, to counter affectionate association with aggressive dissociation in a manner that (again) belies the doubleness of women's elegies: the oscillations and conflictual dramas enacted, in even the angriest of those poems, between association and distancing. This doubleness of women's elegies foregrounds a question that elegy has always pondered, although its interest in the question has not always been overt: whether or not to accept the substitution of the poetic artifact for the living being. Women's elegy brings this question— muted in traditional elegy but central to decisions about poetic decorum and self-definition—to the fore.

For women, as opposed to men, an alliance and continuity with the dead, and hence a rejection of canonical poetic identity and succession, dangerously reinstate the old Orphean associations of women with death, silence, darkness, and, above all, loss of the body. Elegiac issues of presence, voice, and embodiment become central in the self-positioning of modern and contemporary women elegists. As a result, the human body takes on a new centrality in these works. The body, dead or living, its physical experiences and creative potentialities, its objecthood, all figure in newly—if not predictably—gendered representations.[5] These newly structured interrogations and explorations unsettle the elegy's traditional conventions and methods. This revisionary ethos is shared by modern elegies in general, as we have seen, but in women's elegies challenges to the genre are arranged around different, and differently politicized, preoccupations. Women's versions of elegy in the twentieth century emerge from the different perspective of women poets upon questions of bodily disappearance and poetic muting, questions that precipitate ambivalence about separation from the dead.

The critique in women's elegies of older perspectives on embodiment and poetic production, though it tends to disempower the Orpheus myth, may in part build on, or take as read, non-elegiac deployments of the myth by women. Modern women poets have periodically returned to the Orpheus myth in other genres, to assume and to reframe its preoccupations. On occasion, these poets use the myth as an allegorical mode for the representation of feminist poetic or personal history. To redress the myth's erasures, a number of modern women poets, among them H.D., Louise Bogan, Adrienne Rich, Muriel Rukeyser, alta, and Rachel Blau Duplessis, have responded in the voices of Eurydice and the maenads.[6] Sometimes, like Muriel Rukeyser, these poets have come back repeatedly to Orpheus and Eurydice in order to revise their own earlier versions, marking the myth as still a troubling source of identification and self-questioning.

H.D.'s non-elegiac poem *Eurydice*, arguably the most important re-writing of the Orpheus myth for modernism, and particularly for female modernism, reveals some of the difficulties as well as possibil-ities for a feminist revision of the myth. H.D. focuses on the turn, her Eurydice reproaching an absent Orpheus for depriving her of a second chance at life:

> So you have swept me back,
> I who could have walked with the live souls
> above the earth,
> I who could have slept among the live flowers
> at last;
>
> so for your arrogance
> and your ruthlessness
> I am swept back
> where dead lichens drip
> dead cinders upon moss of ash.[7]
>
> (I)

Eurydice in this poem offers what might properly be called a feminist reading of her situation, understanding Orpheus's act as a narcissistic appropriation, a repossession of the woman's being as part of his own:

> why did you turn back,
> that hell should be reinhabited
> of myself thus
> swept into nothingness?
> . . . .
> what was it that crossed my face
> with the light from yours and your glance?
> what was it you saw in my face?
> the light of your own face,
> the fire of your own presence?
>
> (II)

Eurydice's angry questions, enigmatic and hypothetical as they are, leave open the suspicion that Orpheus has wished to lose her as much as to keep her, to safeguard "the fire of [his] own presence" from any competing illumination from the all too legibly fervent face of the woman. A female poet and commentator upon gender politics, this Eurydice insists upon the value of her own creativity, still potentially enviable to the world of men although now protected from their depredations by invisibility:

> and the flowers,
> if I should tell you,
> you would turn from your own fit paths
> toward hell,
> turn again and glance back
> and I would sink into a place
> even more terrible than this.
>
> (VI)

What she must give up for even this limited protection, however, is visibility, presence, body, movement; the poem allows the woman poethood, but only within the terms of her diminished, disembodied, Hadean existence.

> At least I have the flowers of myself,
> and my thoughts, no god
> can take that;
> I have the fervour of myself for a presence
> and my own spirit for light.
>
> (VII)

Yet Eurydice can also embrace an alternative world in which she can withhold the self Orpheus has been overly eager to incorporate. This is at once revenge, a strategy of last resort, and, paradoxically, a way of producing new poetic modes. What can look at first like a bleakly solipsistic pleasure may in fact be richly as well as safely autoerotic: "the flowers of myself," explicitly unthreatened by the gods and men whose rapine and arbitrarily inflicted whims have governed and ended her life. Released from the compulsions and persuasions of a heterosexual, possessive, and often violently specularized form of sexuality, and consequently freed from the literary schemas that promote such sexuality, she is free to embrace a pleasure that is the manifestation of a new literary "spirit." If her world has to make do with constricting limitations imposed from without, such limitations can be made analogous to those creative restrictions, the "fit paths" of the upper world, chosen by male poets. H.D. sketches a counterpoetics of exclusion that includes loss, regret, rage, but does not comprise only those, cultivating as it does a self-directed, powerfully focused, sensual, and above all poetic pleasure.

This autoerotic reformulation of the loss of the larger world ensures that the negative relation to the Orphean will be enriched as well as impoverished. Similarly, when Rachel Blau Duplessis's "Eurydice" melds two versions of the heroine, the snake-goddess Hecate with Eurydice (her later, more familiar version of Eurydice), she produces the snake whose "deepest desire was to pierce herself."[8] This piercing will be risky, but it will be sexually reintegrative and poetically generative; she will become her own double-gendered lover, god of poetry and sexuality, and oracle. She will escape the sexual and literary dominion of Orpheus—"he can make me open, shut and open"[9]—for a self-controlled, parthenogenetic creativity, "pushing outward, of her own power":

> She will brood and be born
> girl of her own mother
> mother of the labyrinth
> daughter
> pushing the child herself outward[10]

These two woman poets, in treating the Orpheus myth, thus seem to posit Eurydice's underworld as a parallel if desocialized literary universe. The Eurydicean distance becomes a safe haven for reconsidering and reformulating. Sometimes the poet fills up this emptied world with herself, as when Muriel Rukeyser, in "The Poem as Mask," reclaims not only the maenads but also the gods and Orpheus, from whom she had distanced herself in an earlier poem. These other personae can allow her to imagine a way out of Eurydice's personal and cultural singleness; perhaps even more importantly, they are discovered to be already incorporated within her. Now she acknowledges them: "The fragments join in me with their own music."[11] Adrienne Rich's narrator in "I Dream I'm the Death of Orpheus" is a shadowy, multiple figure, manifestly derived from Jean Cocteau's 1949 surrealist film *L'Orphée*, comprising Orpheus as male poet, Death as his female guide or abductor, a female poet with "powers / . . . severely limited / by authorities whose faces I rarely see," and, finally, a fantastically forward-and-backward-looking mirror apparition:

> a woman sworn to lucidity
> who sees through the mayhem, the smoky fires
> of these underground streets
> her dead poet learning to walk backward against the wind
> on the wrong side of the mirror.[12]

Perhaps, too, the female poet wants to be *behind* the mirror's surface, invisible to the male gaze, and yet able to observe it carefully as, preserving her trammeled powers, she bides her time. These poems find the story of Orpheus and Eurydice useful as they effect transitory if crucial feminist revisions; the poems enter the narrative in order to move on, rather than to find a permanent new position within it. These women poets' ambivalent inhabiting of the myth, temporary though it is, registers gains as well as simple losses or relinquishments.

Edna St. Vincent Millay, in her early series "Memorial for D.C.," may come closest to renegotiating the Orphean scenario systematically. In one of the series' lyrics, "Prayer to Persephone," she imagines herself following a dead female friend to the underworld and appealing to Persephone in an implicitly female bond of sympathy. At the same time, some frustration and resentment with her friend's self-sufficiency leads the poet to project her as needy in the underworld, a projection that allows the poet to enter the "needed," consoling voice of Persephone:

> Be to her, Persephone,
> All the things I might not be;
> Take her head upon your knee.
> She that was so proud and wild

Flippant, arrogant and free,
She that had no need of me,
Is a little lonely child
Lost in Hell,—Persephone,
Take her head upon your knee;
Say to her, "My dear, my dear,
It is not so dreadful here."[13]

Although, like Orpheus, the poet speaking in these lines has the power
to address Persephone, she makes no attempt to regain the Eurydice
figure; in fact, she rejects the notion of a return. Nor does she embrace
a simple reward in the transmutation of loss, a specifically bodily loss,
into poetry. In "Dirge," the fourth section of "Memorial to D.C.," "Boys
and girls that held her dear" are enjoined to:

Do your weeping now;
All you loved of her lies here.

Brought to earth the arrogant brow,
    And the withering tongue
Chastened; do your weeping now.

Sing whatever songs are sung,
    Wind whatever wreath,
For a playmate perished young,
    For a spirit spent in death.

Boys and girls that held her dear,
All you loved of her lies here.
                    ("Dirge," 121)

The only option of the bereaved is to mourn the individual person for
whose soul, manifested as it is in specific bodily gestures and powers,
there can be no transcendence. Unequivocally for Millay, as in her later
poem "Dirge without Music," "the best is lost" beyond any economy
of poetic gain or restitution.[14] The focus on bodily absence is unrelent-
ing, and the "fragrant blossom" of elegy, the complex, worked, culti-
vated, poetic outgrowth of death, will not appease her.
    As often as Millay allows elegy so romantically valorized a metaphor
as the blossoming rose, she parodies this self-important genre with images of worthlessness or tininess: *"With hands that wrote you little*

notes, / I write you little elegies!" While this diminution contributes to her general devaluation of elegy, it also reveals her fear of the triviality by which women's writing is threatened. She refuses, moreover, to dismiss the possibility of commemorating the dead, especially the possibility that one woman may commemorate another. So what looks like an undermining of elegiac value can also be read as an acute awareness of the difficulty for women elegists of writing their way out of trivialization, and of gaining access to commemorative powers.

In the second section of "Memorial to D.C.," bodily absence and the body's earthly mementos are figured, as they often are in women's elegies, by the empty clothes of the dead. Friends must

> Give away her gowns,
> Give away her shoes;
> She has no more use
> For her fragrant gowns;
> Take them all down,
> Blue, green, blue,
> Lilac, pink, blue,
> From their padded hangers;
> She will dance no more
> In her narrow shoes;
> Sweep her narrow shoes
> From the closet floor.
> ("Chorus," 120)

Elegy and the detritus of a life become conflated here, in an image of women's physical, and perhaps also poetic and cultural, transience. In their evocation of the final worthlessness of the woman's objects they almost resemble misogynist listings in *vanitas* poems. The gowns, still fragrant from the last wearing—or perhaps only with the lavender they were laid in—remain nevertheless unhaunted, lifeless. The woman's trappings, moreover, suggest constriction and immaturity: her shoes are presumably "narrow" because her feet were small, but the image recalls foot binding at one extreme and childhood at the other. The stanza is narrow, too, and its nursery-rhyme jingle is undignified. The woman's full, adult bodily presence, once lost, seems unreproducible and irretrievable.

Of all the lost physical manifestations, Millay's speaker mourns most sadly the absent voice. Admittedly, the topic of voice is central to the history of elegy and of all written poetry; lyric repeatedly expresses its desire to capture an uncapturable primordial voice, not infrequently a woman's singing one. Indeed, Derrida's critique of phonological metaphysics identifies voice as the putative sign of a presence that is always and already absent. As a problematic issue for the lyric poet, however, both the captivity and the "capturing" of the female voice become strongly gender inflected in Millay's work because of the ever present threat of trivialization and incapacitation. Millay introduces this topic in the series' prefatory verse, already quoted in part:

> *O, loveliest throat of all sweet throats,*
> *Where now no more the music is,*
> *With hands that wrote you little notes*
> *I write you little elegies!*
>
> (118)

The ironic contrast in these lines between sweet-throated living music and effortful but finally inconsequential memorial poems strikes a note that will be heard throughout much of modern elegy, but with particular intensity in women's elegies.

The status of the poem as a memorial object remains a matter for debate rather than outright repudiation, however, in women's elegies, even when, as in the Millay poems, it is subjected to suspicious review. The concluding poem of "Memorial to D.C." is called, simply, "Elegy," which suggests that some of the series' elegiac concerns coalesce in it, and that the genre is finally again becoming legitimate. "Elegy" considers the disposition of body, voice, and poem once more:

> Let them bury your big eyes
> In the secret earth securely,
> Your thin fingers, and your fair,
> Soft, indefinite-coloured hair,—
> All of these in some way, surely,
> From the secret earth shall rise;
> Not for these I sit and stare,
> Broken and bereft completely:

Your young flesh that sat so neatly
On your little bones will sweetly
Blossom in the air.

But your voice . . . never the rushing
Of a river underground,
Not the rising of the wind
In the trees before the rain,
Not the woodcock's watery call,
Not the note the white-throat utters,
Not the feet of children pushing
Yellow leaves along the gutters
In the blue and bitter fall,
Shall content my musing mind
For the beauty of that sound
That in no way at all
Ever will be heard again.

Sweetly through the sappy stalk
Of the vigorous weed,
Holding all it held before,
Cherished by the faithful sun,
On and on eternally
Shall your altered fluid run,
Bud and bloom and go to seed:
But your singing days are done;
But the music of your talk
Never shall the chemistry
Of the secret earth restore.
All your lovely words are spoken.
Once the ivory box is broken,
Beats the golden bird no more.
                                   ("Elegy," 122)

Voice remains inaccessible, as it evolves and changes, is recalled and approximated. "All your lovely words are spoken": that is, "have been spoken," and are definitively spoken rather than written; therefore we don't hear the words themselves. An ellipsis follows this first evocation, "But your voice . . ."; and then only negative analogies can be produced: "Not the woodcock's watery call, / Not the note the white-throat utters, / Not the feet of children," not even the mechanical bird in the ivory box, defunct as that now is. (A male voice might be un-recoverable too, but not as likely to be programmed through the trivial and diminutive.) At the same time the voice that has been lost was "singing," was "music"; Millay attaches to it the most monumentaliz-ing and mystifying of traditional poetic ascriptions. In its wish to val-orize and even mythologize the woman's voice, Millay's elegy finally transfers at least the key Orphean attribute of voice from man to woman.

In foregrounding voice, then, Millay complicates her own anti-monumentalizing, or antimemorial, position. This poem, unlike the others in the sequence, seems almost to redeem the elegiac genre by acceding to the dissolution of the body. The material substance of the body, always mortal ("sweet flesh" sitting, only temporarily, on "little bones") is not lost but virtually resolved into its elements, which is also to say taken up into the "body" of the poem, either "blossoming in the air" or fluidly entering the "sappy stalk / Of the vigorous weed." It is the loss of the irreplaceable voice, connected emphatically throughout the series to its living intonation, at which the speaker still balks. It is this voice, characterized in the poem's last three lines as that of a golden bird, that is abruptly stilled, not transmuted, by the breakdown of its physical container (the voice box). Although "uncon-soled," this ending recovers a previously undisclosed high potential—and highly conventional potential—as a voice memorial for the "little elegy." To recover this potential is to accede substantially to elegiac norms.[15]

The poem's appreciation of the commemorative act as such seem-ingly brings us back to the speaker's characterization of the dead woman as Persephone in the first poem. The dead had no need of her when alive and able to speak, in autonomous liberty, for herself; now, returned to childhood, and silent, she must be spoken for by the poet, thus supplying the elegy with a *raison d'être.*[16]

Ambivalence about the dead, and about the unstable relation be-tween the living poet's willingness or unwillingness to give up the dead, on the one hand, and her recourse to poetic power and voice, on the other, plays out in increasingly explicit ways as the century pro-ceeds. In Sylvia Plath's excoriating, wildly indecorous, "elegies" for her father, the separation from the dead is far from definitive. In "Daddy," aside from the poem's record of the speaker's past attempts to get "back, back, back" to the dead man and of her premonitory joining with him ("I'm finally through"), the charged awareness of his ongoing centrality in her life contributes to the oscillating effect. Her division of response to the dead is expressed bodily: the dead father "bit [her] pretty red heart in two." Part of what makes the poem so disturbing is its range of bodily reference to the relations between the dead man and to herself.

A similar if lower-keyed alternation, and renegotiation of decorums, takes place in Sexton's elegy for her parents, "The Truth the Dead Know":

> FOR MY MOTHER, BORN MARCH 1902, DIED MARCH 1959
> AND MY FATHER, BORN FEBRUARY 1900, DIED JUNE 1959
>
> Gone, I say and walk from church,
> refusing the stiff procession to the grave,
> letting the dead ride alone in the hearse.
> It is June. I am tired of being brave.
>
> We drive to the Cape. I cultivate
> myself where the sun gutters from the sky,
> where the sea swings in like an iron gate
> and we touch. In another country people die.
>
> My darling, the wind falls in like stones
> from the whitehearted water and when we touch
> we enter touch entirely. No one's alone.
> Men kill for this, or for as much.
>
> And what of the dead? They lie without shoes
> in their stone boats. They are more like stone
> than the sea would be if it stopped. They refuse
> to be blessed, throat, eye and knucklebone.[17]

This poem revolves around one of the most deep-seated reactions to a death, the panicky desire not to be lost or separated oneself, either from one's own life or from the absent dead. Yet the speaker works both to dissimulate that desire and to deny it in an act of self-possessed withdrawal. The poem's turning away from any "brave" meditation on death or loss, and (with almost brutal indecorousness) from the dead themselves—"Gone, I say"—prevails throughout the first three stanzas.

Yet the speaker self-betrayingly immerses herself at once in the intensity of palpable bodily experience, in the reassurance of touching and connecting, trying even (perhaps echoing Marlowe's Jew of Malta!) to construct a territorial separation from "another country" where people die. (Again, the separatist impulse is an autoerotic one as well: "I cultivate myself.") Yet this wish rebounds hard against the speaker, apparently unable to "cultivate" herself in the present, while the dead recover agency and reject *her*.

As Schenck remarks, the speaker's refusal in this poem to participate in the conventions of the funeral is itself an act of protest against giving up the dead and, implicitly, against elegy.[18] Indeed the poem comes around again, apparently in spite of the speaker's avowal of distance, to the last stanza's empathetic meditation on the dead, on their poignant removal from pleasure and connection, yet also on their monumental, impassive persistence. The continuing connection—or circling back—remains both desiring and fearful. Pity itself unavoidably implies separation and distancing, which it reinforces by "othering" the objects: "more like stone / than the sea would be if it stopped." At the same time, the dead retain a hurtful agency, for they are stubbornly perverse in their refusal of the gifts of the living: "They refuse / to be blessed." They both are and are not corpselike, are and are not "dead"; the body in parts remains a body. The title of the poem, too, gives the dead a consciousness that sets them apart from the living, and vice versa, their agency consisting in their discomfiting rejection of touch. Finally, the subtitle of the poem situates the speaker in her parents' drama, not beyond it: the father's death, following the mother's by three months and so apparently caused by it,[19] painfully brings to the fore the mortal risks of affective connection.[20]

Another review of memorial poetry and literary modalities is undertaken in Elizabeth Bishop's poem for Robert Lowell, "North Haven." Encoding in its revaluation of elegy a history of the two poets' relationship and individual lives, this poem actively engages in dialogue not just with mainstream elegy but also with its leading contemporary practitioner. In the background of the poem is the vivid past of a decades-long, rich, generative friendship, crucial to the poetry of each, but not without its deep and troubling conflicts. In the foreground is a familiar landscape, almost empty of people (the schooner hints at human presence), but full of animation and memory:

NORTH HAVEN

In memoriam: Robert Lowell

I can make out the rigging of a schooner
a mile off; I can count
the new cones on the spruce. It is so still
the pale bay wears a milky skin, the sky
no clouds, except for one long, carded horse's-tail.

The islands haven't shifted since last summer,
even if I like to pretend they have
—drifting, in a dreamy sort of way,
a little north, a little south or sidewise,
and that they're free within the blue frontiers of bay.

This month, our favorite one is full of flowers:
Buttercups, Red Clover, Purple Vetch,
Hawkweed still burning, Daisies pied, Eyebright,
the Fragrant Bedstraw's incandescent stars,
and more, returned, to paint the meadows with delight.

The Goldfinches are back, or others like them,
and the White-throated Sparrow's five-note song,
pleading and pleading, brings tears to the eyes.
Nature repeats herself, or almost does:
repeat, repeat, repeat; revise, revise, revise.

Years ago, you told me it was here
(in 1932?) you first "discovered *girls*"
and learned to sail, and learned to kiss.
You had "such fun," you said, that classic summer.
("Fun"—it always seemed to leave you at a loss . . .)

You left North Haven, anchored in its rock,
afloat in mystic blue . . . And now—you've left
for good. You can't derange, or rearrange,
your poems again. (But the Sparrows can their song.)
The words won't change again. Sad friend, you cannot change.[21]

The third stanza engages the elegiac tradition head-on, with its brief recapitulation of the Renaissance-neoclassical flower catalogue: "Daisies pied . . . and more, returned, to paint the meadows with delight." Still coerced by the traditional elegiac linearity suggested by the reference to flowers, but at odds with it, the poem seems to wander in the "dreamy sort of way" the speaker likes to imagine the islands having done in the poem's second stanza. Characteristically for Bishop, the highly condensed dramas animating the poem—her shared past with Lowell, her relation to elegy—make little more impact on the poem's lucid, calm surface than does the poet's grief; all emerge only through allusions, echoes, resonances. The poem avoids elegiac explicitness about loss and death, affording only clues to, rather than statements of, grief: the words "loss," left," and "sad," and even the bird's song which "brings tears to the eyes," appear dissociated from Lowell as a specific referent. One might assume that the "tears" at the pastoral birdsong are for Lowell, but the speaker never says so. The "loss" is obliquely revealed in the context of Lowell's relationship to "fun," as though it were a momentary disorientation rather than the final departure of death: "sad" is displaced onto Lowell, modifying "friend" rather than the poet, who is presumably speaking out of her own grief. The dedication is the one explicit marker of Lowell's death, and only the fact of the poem insists upon the loss the speaker has sustained. The poem's cirumlocutions allow an evasion of direct statement and ultimately of fixity that even the last line, with its strong expression of closure, does not completely override.

The later stanzas clarify the speaker's wish to imagine that the islands, frozen in the stillness of the italicized first stanza, might move: Lowell's stillness, his inability to move or change or speak again, lies behind the wish. The last stanza's reference to Lowell's manically compulsive revisions of poems—often when they were in galleys, to the chagrin of his publishers—at once implies the insufficiency of poetry to stand in for the dead and Bishop's resistance to any fixation of the image: if Lowell himself could never accept a final version, why should she? The lines do suggest a reproach, not corrected away by the addition of "or re-arrange" to "derange," for the psychological burdens imposed by Lowell's mania on those who loved him, yet this derangement may have been all that saved Lowell from a conventionalizing attraction toward the "classic," the rigidified. Bishop's disavowal of fixity, so consistently if subtly anti-monumental in the poem, sets itself against the way elegy is usually created and read—and against one way in which Lowell wished to create and read himself.

Lowell was for his era a major elegist, conceivably *the* major elegist, and was regarded as such by his literary circle: John Berryman, Randall

Jarrell, Delmore Schwartz, and others, mostly male, who looked to him for poetic cues, no matter how agonistically they received his instruction or example.[22] Bishop, on the other hand, was both inside and outside of such encounters and the terms of poetic value they established, and often disagreed with those terms. At a distance from the American scene in her Brazilian retreat, and in her anomalous position as woman and lesbian, she had a certain freedom from both the traditional and the contemporary poetics of Lowell and his other intimates. This freedom, this perspective from afar, she asserts in "North Haven" with the composure and clear-sightedness of the poem's first italicized stanza: "I can see."

The poem offers an anti-paradigmatic version of elegy, one based on a radically different valuation of individual life and modes of commemoration. Bishop recognizes the inextricable embedding of her poem in conventional elegiac narrative, but nonetheless can imagine an alternative: what she substitutes is a counterpoetics of revision. Her elegy then becomes an *ars poetica*, replacing monumental closure with revision as the central principle of poetic value and vitality. Elegy usually repeats until it makes a turn toward consolation, whereas this poem, with its several starts and insertions of *correctio*, foregrounds revision. Bishop reads Lowell against himself in this regard: while he was always hoping for a perfect version that would require no further revisions, she knows that, for him, to have finished all of his poems is to be dead—and gone. Since the movement of traditional elegy, and even to a large degree of Lowell's elegies, is toward closure and monumentalization, this rejection powerfully critiques the genre while maintaining a connection to the dead poet.

Lowell's most celebrated elegies—"The Quaker Graveyard at Nantucket" and "For the Union Dead"—are literally monumentalizing, since they meditate upon large public monuments, absent from the almost entirely nonsocial world Bishop represents. Even if Lowell's monuments are threatened—the graveyard eroding, St. Gauden's bas-relief propped up and shaken by nearby construction—they are icons of value, more so in some ways because they are precarious images of a heroic past. With whatever reservations, Lowell identifies himself with these vulnerable icons. He does so in a way that Bishop's poetry rejects, and in the poetic persona of wounded narcissism he was able to make so attractive. Bishop's poem, too, rejects the self-memorializing and self-aggrandizing impulse encoded in Lowell's way of reading himself and of being read by others.

Lowell's control of the terms of elegy is a mark of power, but a limiting one, a blindness, as well. In "North Haven" blindness is subtly marked as gendered; hence, perhaps, the way she feminizes nature, with irony but also with identification. This is a convention she makes use of in only one other poem.[23] (It is nature which speaks the poem's shifting directive, "*Repeat, repeat, repeat; revise, revise, revise.*") Bishop represents Lowell as caught up in forms of vision that are not her own; and, always wary or critical of his relations with women, she is wry about what "discover[ing] girls" means for a boy, for this particular boy. In Lowell's case it seems to be no discovery at all, since the girls fit into a "classic" pattern; or else it is "discovery" in the imperialist sense, the finding but nonrecognition of a people (an island people in this poem) with their own preexisting culture, a culture imperiled by the advent of the discoverer. The poem does in fact sketch a cultural encounter: a tricky, moving, complicated one between two poets, two traditions, two poetries, two ways of reading. In refusing to reject what elegy glosses over—the deranged, provisional aspect of the man— Bishop maintains a connection to Lowell and rejects the sacrificial politics of self and other that have so largely determined the history of elegy.

The elegies of a contemporary female poet, Ruth Stone, for her husband (dead by suicide) continue the exploration of gender in forms of grief and elegy. They also confront directly the related issues of presence and embodiment, and of the relation of all of these to memorializing art objects. These poems, as obsessive in their way as Berryman's about his father's death by suicide, repeatedly reformulate the problems of writing poetry while remaining riskily connected to the dead, and do so with compelling reference to the bodily and the sexual. Unnervingly, they imagine the dead man's body, years after burial, with as vivid an attention as any love poetry has given the living. "Habit" joins the topics of erotic feeling toward the dead, the decay of the flesh in the dead and the living, and the problematic relation of both to poetic artifact:

> Every day I dig you up
> And wipe off the rime

And look at you.
You are my joke,
My poem.
Your eyelids pull back from their sockets.
Your mouth mildews in scallops.
Worm filaments sprout from the pockets
Of your good suit.
I hold your sleeves in my arms;
Your waist drops a little putrid flesh.
I show you my old shy breasts.[24]

To get to the reality of the dead man's body, the poet-speaker must wipe off a frostlike layer of mold, punningly "rime." In his physical decay the husband is at once "joke" and "poem": poetry here becomes not the antidote to decay but its ally, its "perverse" embodiment. Stone's toying with the necrophilic, in this and many of the poems, literalizes loss, the poems registering the erotic intensity of the past while eliciting a present shock of repulsion and macabre comedy. As in Sexton's poem, the dead, in a surreal sex-death nexus, remain undead objects of desire and continuing agency. Stone's focus on the dead body differs, however, in its horrific insistence on the fate of that body, and on the difficulty of conceiving continuing relations as it is transformed in decay. The quoted lines condense the vagaries of this relation: punitive and caressing, dissociative and connective, relinquishing and memorializing, indecorously exposing the dead and indecorously exposing the self. To inhabit this relational space is to be subject to the indeterminacy of presence and absence, self and other, as in "Message from Your Toes":

Down there the nerves thick as cables
in an ocean bed, collect barnacles;
clasped by octopods, send distant messages
years late, after the loved is gone,
the lips dead, after the slugs have eaten
the remembered face.

(25)

The refrain "down there," referring to the toes, but also to the subterranean, creates a surreal confusion between dead man and living woman. Whose "nerves send distant messages / years late, after the loved is gone"? Stone's minute, scientific interest in the workings of the body often produces this paradoxical indeterminacy, "science" offering no objectifying separation from the dead, but rather a new set of metaphors for bizarre connections and disconnections. In "Turn Your Eyes Away," which alludes to the death by suicide of Stone's husband, the dead man is ruefully reminded that "[i]nside your skull / there was no room for us, / your circuits forgot me."[25] Here the failure is technical, as if crucial pronouns designating human connection and recognition had been erased from a linguistic memory-bank.

Stone's poems come out of an intense engagement with the normative transactions of memorial poetry, aware of that poetry, or even of memory itself, as appropriative, reductive, and ruthlessly or "inhumanly" consuming, often at the moments when it is claiming the deepest attachment. In "Becoming You," Stone "thinks about territory / And how you invaded my skin." Now, however, it is she who invades him through poetry and memory:

> I am everywhere growing larger
> And my dimensions now include
> Your perfectly clear pattern;
> Every crystal molecule and deviant particle
> Available to my pseudopods
> As, taking my time,
> I come on digesting you.[26]

To acknowledge this process of consumption is to resist and disable it at least to a degree, even while recognizing its virtual inevitability. To acknowledge it is also to defamiliarize in macabre fashion the elegiac norm, "pseudopod" here being conflated with the writing hand or instrument, while "digesting" wittily puns on the reductive literary or scholarly summarizing of a life. A markedly different nature—or "human nature"—from that of elegy-as-usual is brought into view. Elegiac incorporation of the other as a clear "pattern"—or according to a clear pattern—to give poetic form to the self is also foregrounded and thus resisted. The self is acknowledged in all its amorphous, appetitive monstrosity. Indeed, Stone's poems for her dead husband repeatedly disrupt any perfect clarity of pattern in the poem's self-serving representation of the dead, forestalling the digestion of the other within the poetic work.

As is true of Bishop's poem for Lowell, Stone's poems raise issues that cannot be resolved into simple oppositions between embodied life and memorial poetry, or between women, love, and continuity on the one hand, and men, authorship, and agonistic overcoming on the other. Nor does elegiac reconstruction offer to Stone, or to women poets generally, a program for a fully "alternative," separatist poetics, however important the initial moment of separation may be. Nor do women's elegies, in critiquing a monumental tradition, produce a monumental countertradition. Cumulatively, instead, they make a difference to the way the tropes of the mainstream elegiac tradition are amplified, redeployed, and read, a process in which some of the familiar Orphean motifs of elegy are redistributed. As in the urging of Bishop's elegy—"repeat, repeat, repeat; revise, revise, revise"—these elegies insist on tirelessly revisionary practices of reading and writing rather than on the need to institute any homogeneous paradigm. In this way, as I have already suggested, women's elegies become important pioneering ones in contemporary elegiac writing.

4
Avatars of Eurydice:
John Berryman's *Dream Songs*

In his introduction to a volume of John Berryman's works, Saul Bellow admiringly recalls the kind of conversation Berryman provided when they were both teaching at Princeton in the early 1950s, and which illustrates, he feels, the intensity of Berryman's devotion to literature. In so doing he gives a vivid picture of one kind of life lived by male writers of the period, and of the literary imaginary inhabited by them:

> We never discussed money, or wives, and we seldom talked politics. Once as we were discussing Rilke I interrupted to ask him whether he had, the other night, somewhere in the Village, pushed a lady down a flight of stairs.
> "Whom?"
> "Beautiful Catherine, the big girl I introduced you to."
> "Did I do that? I wonder why?"
> "Because she wouldn't let you into the apartment."
> He took a polite interest in this information. He said, "That I was in the City at all is news to me."
> We went back to Rilke. There was only one important topic. We had no small-talk.[1]

Here is the Orphean "turn" with a vengeance, Catherine redescending without even the dubious satisfaction of being remembered by her poet. For Bellow and Berryman, the world of literature is virtually by definition a world of men, its borders guarded against the incursion of nonliterary women; literary women are another story. Like Berryman, Bellow apparently wishes to relegate these "big" women to the arena of small talk.[2]

In this chapter I examine Berryman's reconstruction of the Orphean-elegiac poetic persona in *The Dream Songs*. I contend that Berryman pursues this late-modernist reconstruction overtly in terms of his imagined relations with male poetic predecessors and contemporaries; I also suggest, however, that this reconstruction is strongly overdetermined by new relations in a field of poetic production imagined by Berryman as increasingly "invaded" or inhabited by talented women, live speakers rather than ventriloquized ghosts, and by the profound impact of at least one of those potentially displacing contemporaries, Sylvia Plath.

I pursue this argument, concluding with the "unmanageable" Plath, despite the critical consensus that in *Homage to Mistress Bradstreet* Berryman evinces profound sympathy both for a woman poet and for an American woman as poetic precursor. The fact that Berryman writes in the persona of Bradstreet during his extended, fantastic colloquy with her has been taken as proof of his profound empathetic identification with the woman poet and female subject.[3] This view has, however, been challenged by some recent feminist critics.[4] Even on the face of it, the poem performs no heroic reclamation of a neglected precursor. In Berryman's characterization, Anne Bradstreet remains a culturally isolated figure, a bad poet, and a nonthreatening ghostly interlocutor.[5]

In some of the earlier works before *Bradstreet*, Berryman engages with female figures, finding in them a source of comradeship, encouragement, and valuable "material," yet ultimately disposing of them. In *Sonnets to Chris*, Berryman uses the love sonnet sequence as it has nearly always been used: to pursue the poetic laurel while articulating concerns about male bonding, status, and literary production. The sequence ends, characteristically for the genre, with the poet-subject relinquishing the affair for the sake of writing poetry:

> Presently the sun
> yellowed the pines & my lady came not
> in blue jeans & a sweater. I sat down & wrote.[6]

This sacrificial equation—the woman or the poetry—also governs *Homage to Mistress Bradstreet*, which Berryman wrote directly after *Sonnets to Chris*. What then of *The Dream Songs*, Berryman's magnum opus?

In Berryman's most ambitious, powerful, and influential work, his multivoiced *Dream Songs*, women generally occupy the same liminal position as the woman does in the Bellow anecdote: wished away, generalized, or diminished from full social (certainly literary) existence. As in that exchange, the male interlocutor is a crucial ally against the invasive woman. Henry, the main speaker and Berryman alter ego in *The Dream Songs*, tellingly wishes to make *his* Orphean return from the land of the dead without his wife's knowledge. The return seems predicated, in fact, upon her not knowing, as though contact with her would nullify his cult status, his poetic vocation, his very life:

> Henry may be returning to our life
> adult & difficult.
> There exist rumours that remote & sad
> and quite beyond the knowledge of his wife
> to the foothills of the cult
>
> will come in silence this distinguished one
> essaying once again the lower slopes
> in triumph, keeping up our hopes,
> and heading not for the highest we have done
> but enigmatic faces, unsurveyed,
> calm as a forest glade
>
> for him.[7]

Here is one incarnation of the Orpheus of classical tradition, heroic—a cultural savior and inspiritor—yet wounded and melancholic. He is "distinguished" in both senses, both special and marked out for an exemplary cultural role. In this moment of poetic self-identification, Berryman appears most concerned with clearing a space for himself and for a select audience. In effect, *this* Orpheus—Berryman's Orpheus, Berryman as Orpheus—wishes to return "quite beyond the knowledge of his wife" to a new, almost exclusively masculine, Orphean scenario. Yet this wish is not granted, and it is both the persistence and the unattainability of the wish that structure much of Berryman's writing in *The Dream Songs* while opening the poem up to "invasive" female presences.

First, no matter how much Berryman's Henry might wish to slip gently back into the upper world, his lives and deaths seem fatefully to gravitate, Orpheus-like, toward the explosive, even the apocalyptic, and consistently within the turbulent dynamics of the elegiac genre:

> Whence flew the litter whereon he was laid?
> Of what heroic stuff was warlock Henry made?
> and questions of that sort
> perplexed the bulging cosmos, O in short
> was sandalwood in good supply when he
> flared out of history
>
> & the obituary in *The New York Times*
> into the world of generosity
> creating the air where are
> & can be, only, heroes? Statues & rhymes
> signal his fiery Passage, a mountainous sea,
> the occlusion of a star:
>
> anything afterward, of high lament,
> let too his giant faults appear, as sent
> together with his virtues down
> and let this day be his, throughout the town,
> region & cosmos, lest he freeze our blood
> with terrible returns.
>
>   (DS 79)

Magic and violence combine wittily in the persona's new title as "warlock Henry," and the terrible returns, celestial disturbances, stormy waters recall the threatening upheavals of "Lycidas" as well as the reappearance of Orpheus as the Christ-Lycidas amalgam of Milton's poem. (Drowned and surfacing, that hero has been ruined by "the occlusion of a star," betrayed by what in Milton's poem is the "perfidious bark / built in th'eclipse" [100–101].) The fractured, wounded, shamanic speaker is Orpheus in one classical guise, the sacrificial vegetation god or demigod of ancient ritual; his death is reenacted constantly in the sequence, and he imagines himself as the maker of a poetry charged with self-destructiveness, magical power, prophetic passion, and violence.

These traits are those of Orpheus, but they are also those of the contemporary poets whom Berryman most admires, and with whom he carries on a lifelong dialogue. *The Dream Songs*, frequently elegiac itself, includes a set of elegies for individual contemporaries and is concerned, like *The Waste Land*, with cultural loss, with the doomed modern poet, and finally, more overtly than Eliot's poem, with personal loss. Among the sequence's elegies and groups of elegies are those for, among others, Hemingway, Frost, Williams, Stevens, Jarrell, Blackmur, Roethke, Plath, Schwartz, and Yeats. The "Op. posth." poems, in which the speaking persona is dead, act as a kind of self-elegy. That *The Dream Songs* may also be read as an elegy for Berryman's father, whose suicide is mentioned more frequently than any other fact, strongly connects with Berryman's overt focus on literary forefathers and rivals.

In the previously quoted Song, the Yeats of "Under Ben Bulben" is (besides Milton) the poet most vividly recalled. Also recalled, however, is the Yeats of Auden's elegy, which itself echoes "Under Ben Bulben." The central cultural role projected for the poet, the sudden tonal shifts and "lapses" in poetic diction, the evocation of coldness (and bad weather), the statuary, the "rhymes" marking the poet's fiery passage through the world and the poem—all these admired traits of earlier poems accrue to Henry as the persona of Berryman's most ambitious poetic sequence. Concurrently, Berryman moves toward self-ordination as elegiac poet, a layered identification formed in relation to the poets who most embody and affirm for him a poetic, and especially an elegiac, vocation. He aspires to belong to death's "world of heroes," the poets of the past; he is himself the scattered hero, wrecked body and soul. At the same time, however, Berryman modernizes, by distancing, this flattering dramatization of the self, subjecting it to continual, self-conscious, deflation:

> the knowledge that they will take off your hands,
> both hands; as well as your both feet, & likewise
> both eyes,
> might be discouraging to a bloody hero.
>
> (DS 81)

Berryman thematizes this scattering modernist formal disruption. The poem's set of voices enacts a bafflement and linguistic disorientation that emerges as a bleak parody of the Orphean plot:

> —I cannot remember. I am going away.
> There was something in my dream about a Cat,

which fought and sang.
Something about a lyre, an island. Unstrung.
Linked to the land at low tide. Cables fray.
Thank you for everything.

                                                  (DS 25)

Here and throughout *The Dream Songs*, Berryman represents the poem's fragmentation as a sign of modernist pathos and connects it explicitly to the Orpheus story. Fragmentation imports the murder of the poet by an unreceptive mob, but Berryman adds his own self-undoing as well. Even the previously invulnerable lyre of Orpheus is "unstrung," as is the poetic persona in a psychological sense, and as are his connections to the mainland of American life and thought. Poetic gifts and arcane knowledge cannot protect their bearer from an Orphean, but also a specifically modernist, impotence and vulnerability: poetic "ancestors," the long dead, are "relaxed & hard, / whilst Henry's parts were fleeing" (DS 78).

The warlock figure of Orpheus-Henry manifests the violent and uncanny side of the Orpheus story rather than the erotic one represented by Orpheus the bridegroom; in fact, it does so to the virtual exclusion of the conjugal. This reconstruction of Orpheus, at once primitivist and masculinist, may indeed belong to the now widely repudiated cultural politics of the post–World War II era, with its suburban blandness and "normative" conjugal script, and may partake of the "artistic" or bohemian reaction against it. Yet Berryman's reconstruction is strongly overdetermined, as I have already suggested, by the changes in the field of poetic production brought about by the entry of women.

We can begin to take the measure of these changes by considering "Wash Far Away," a story that Berryman wrote while working on *The Dream Songs*.[8] This story, which addresses the problem for moderns of approaching the ancient tradition of elegy, at once alludes to and avoids the topic of gender relations. A world-weary professor of English is mourning the failure of his marriage, the subsequent death (perhaps suicide) of his wife, and the death some years earlier of his best friend. He is brought back to pleasure in life by a class he is teaching on "Lycidas." During this class, his students teach *him* to read the poem in a radically different, and far more personal and consoling, fashion. The tropes of the story repeat those of "Lycidas," while its narrative—of the wife, with her "fierce voice echoing," of the professor's promotion through "stepping up on her body" (367), and of the lost male idyll of early friendship, regained in the setting of an all-male class—repeats its gender politics.

This story prefigures gender relations in *The Dream Songs*, yet in its continuing proximity to the "Lycidas" tradition, it remains safely removed. It anticipates neither the drastic derealization of women in *The Dream Songs* nor the paradoxical vulnerability of the poem to "invasion." Admittedly, Berryman's Henry has marriages and love affairs; women, and the speaker's tormenting, life- and marriage-destroying lust, recur obsessively as a topic. Yet despite or because of this obsessiveness, specific or highly realized female figures hardly ever appear. The exceptions are a small group of literary women, beginning with Sappho and including Emily Dickinson, the Brontës, Plath, Adrienne Rich, and Elizabeth Bishop. The presence of some of these on the contemporary scene calls up multidirectional defenses. In an extraordinary state of passion and ambivalence, Berryman evocatively sketches these women and their achievements with one hand while he erases them with the other. Generally, women in the Songs tend to be the merest ciphers standing in for sexual possibility and yearning: "somewhere, everywhere / a girl is taking her clothes off" (DS 351). Almost none of the women are ever permanent or seem to come close to the core; "wife," "mistress," "girl," are all generic terms for replaceable units who rarely even have recognizable features, only gestures and outfits. Even when women in *The Dream Songs* assume something like traditional poetic status as muses or death figures, they are parodically flattened, caricatured, rendered voiceless. In effect, women are subjected to a stereotypical flattening along with "others" in *The Dream Songs*: African Americans and, to a certain degree, Jews.[9] (To a degree as well, all these "others" can stand in for one another in Berryman's beleaguered construction of a native, white, male poetic subjectivity.) The misogynist component in this enterprise is no paranoid projection: Berryman's hysterically tinged fraternity humor regarding the dreaded *vagina dentata* leaves little to be imagined:

> Couvade was always Henry's favourite custom,
> better than the bride biting off the penises, pal,
> remember? All the brothers

marrying her in turn & dying mutilated
until the youngest put in instead a crowbar, pal,
and pulled out not only her teeth but also his brothers' dongs & no
    doubt others'.

(DS 124)

Recalling *Homage to Mistress Bradstreet* momentarily in this perspective, we may more easily see the limitations of Berryman's "sympathy" in his address to his colonial forebear in her lonely state of death. Nevertheless, the perspective created by *The Dream Songs* also produces a more complicated sense of the poet's relations with Bradstreet than Berryman's repeated distancings of the earlier poet might suggest. The anxiety of Bradstreet's poems, the form they often take of a barely repressed quarrel with God, their focus on deaths and on bodily ills and dangers, and, most of all, their explicit and driving discomfort with traditional religious and generic forms of consolation: all of these find lingering echoes in Berryman's *Dream Songs*.

Even more striking than these echoes is that although allegedly uninterested in Bradstreet's poetry, Berryman is apparently drawn to the idea of the woman poet and the native poetic ancestor. With preoccupation growing into passion, in *Homage* Berryman, like Faust with Helen of Troy, urges the ghostly Bradstreet to become his lover, to "mistress [him] from air" (*CP*, 141). Such an affair would destroy her, Bradstreet protests in the poetic narrative, and though powerfully tempted she manages to tear away at the last minute—by thinking of her children (her resistance is thus a form of self-domestication). Yet her longing and admiration prove the poet's double mastery over her, both sexual and literary. The speaker exults in his power over her, having made her a character in his poetry. She is now *his* dead woman, firmly fixed in place:

O all your ages at the mercy of my loves
together lie at once, forever or
so long as I happen.
In the rain of pain & departure, still
Love has no body and presides the sun,
and elfs from silence melody. I run.

> Hover, utter, still,
> a sourcing   whom my lost candle like the firefly loves.
>
> (CP, 147)

Dead, she lies forever at his mercy, in a strange, bodiless captivity: because she has been magically transformed by death, her bodilessness allows her to "elf" melody for him, though she could not for herself; she may "utter" words that Berryman will use, but she must also be "still." She has made death safe for him:

> This our land has ghosted with
> our dead: I am at home.
>
> (CP, 143)

By dying, she has made America his.

Berryman's examination of Bradstreet's (woman's) work makes *Homage* his *ars poetica*. In the final analysis, Bradstreet's children, not her poems, were live births: she is his negative example. Unlike her children—and his vital poems, Berryman implies—Bradstreet's poems are stillborn:

> How [the children] loft, how their sizes delight and grate.
> The proportioned, spiritless poems accumulate.
>
> (CP, 143)

The woman poet's self-sacrificial counterpart to the male poet's choice between a woman and his poetry is, then, between her children and her poetry. But the outcome is of course antithetical: men should decide in favor of poetry; women, children.[10]

Even Bradstreet fits awkwardly into Berryman's distinction between bad female and good male poets; some female poetic contemporaries who aspired to canonical status are harder for Berryman to dismiss. Those he admires he must classify as sports of nature, in a poem addressed to the "pal" as ideal reader, to whom he often addresses asides in the Songs. This friendly auditor is definitively male: Henry (Berryman?) tends, in fact, to use the endearment to license his most overtly misogynist remarks, as in "Hey: an empty girl. / Fill 'er up, pal" (DS

250) or "biting off the penises, pal" (DS 124). Here he is warning the "pal" away from a class of women:

> Them lady poets must not marry, pal.
> Miss Dickinson—fancy in Amherst bedding hér.
> Fancy a lark with Sappho,
> a tumble in the bushes with Miss Moore,
> a spoon with Emily, while Charlotte glare.
> Miss Bishop's too noble-O.
>
> That was the lot. And two of them are here
> as yet—and: Sylvia Plath is not.
> She—she her credentials
> has handed in, leaving alone two tots
> and widower to what he makes of it—
> surviving guy, &
>
> Tolstoy's pathetic widow doing her whung
> (after them decades of marriage) & kids, she decided he was *queer*
> & loving his agent.
> Wherefore he rush off, leaving two journals, & die.
> It is a true error to marry with poets
> or to be by them.
>
> (DS 187)

"That was the lot": of women poets worthy the name, or women poets who were lesbians or unmarried and therefore not a danger to others? Or so sexually repellent, as the first stanza suggests with unpleasant triteness, that they will not cause others to be dangers to themselves? Or, most threatening of all, too "literary"? In an ambiguous placement, Plath does not make it into the original list; her suicide brings her in as an afterthought. In other poems, Berryman will attend almost obsessively to her poetry; here she is only a failed mother and, implicitly, although this suggestion comes only obliquely, a failed poet: she has handed in her credentials. The poem ends with a male example: Tolstoy, who left *his* widow miserable. But in this case, in spite of the stated moral, it is *her* fault that she is unhappy: the idea that Tolstoy is homosexual is meant to be ridiculous—only women poets are, the poem's associational structure suggests.

Without unduly emphasizing this poem, it seems fair to say that the takeover by anxiety in it—a takeover marked by a loss of wit and poise in the writing—makes it doubly important for Berryman that this poem (and perhaps others like it) do their work of erasure and exclusion. Berryman's impulses toward the erasure of women have a point. In the "Op. posth." poems, spoken from hell, in the elegies for Schwartz, and in an adoring although ostensibly combative elegiac meditation on Yeats and his occult legacy, Berryman creates an all-male land of the dead to which he will have access. He works hard to clear a space for male literary authority, both in and beyond a milieu (America, the twentieth century) which he believes devalues poetry—and in which women poets seem to be gaining the ground men are losing. Bishop, Moore, and Plath—"two of them are here"—loom large in the psychic map of the period. Yet although Berryman seems eager to set up his relationship with other male poets in the familiar terms of rivalrous agon, these bonds often seem, on one hand, more like a "feminine" plea for affection, collective security, and attention than an animated, combative form of contact, and, on the other hand, like connections to a strange male death-world of threatening intensity, spectral identity, and repressed desire.

Conventionally enough, the "Op. posth." section of *The Dream Songs* stages "the epic visit to the Underworld in preparation for future action" of Orpheus and others.[11] In his poetic persona, Berryman is preparing, at the price of giving up his body, to inherit the place of "Walt" and "the younger Hart Crane": "the know-how of the American bard / embarrassed Henry heard himself a-being" (DS 78). In the underworld are the friends and acquaintances of his lifetime, all male writers:

> where Bhain is stagnant, dear of Henry's friends,
> yellow with cancer, paper-thin, & bent
> even in the hospital bed
> racked with high hope, on whom death lay hands
> in weeks, or Yeats in the London spring half-spent,
> only the grand gift in his head
>
> going for him, a seated ruin of a man
> courteous to a junior, like one of the boarders,
> or Dylan, with more to say
> now there's no hurry, and we're all a clan.
>   (DS 88)

Instead of rebirth in spring and the raising of triumphant voices, we get a peculiarly enervated, quiet, tea party or hospital visit. Death becomes a communal, elegiac, poetic utopia, a masculine yet nonrivalrous space without competitive strife. Those whose ambition ("high hope") or fame might have called up anxiously rivalrous feeling are conveniently diminished: "ruin[ed]," "courteous," slowed. When Henry is "dug . . . up" against his will, he will try to get back, partly to get escape the maenad-like women who suddenly reappear:

> Wives came forward, claiming a new Axis,
> fearful for their insurance, though, now, glued
> to disencumbered Henry's many ills.
>
> (DS 91)

When he digs his way back to the underworld in this Song, Henry is "a single man": solitary but also unmarried, a man's man. Ironically, then, and despite his appropriation of Bradstreet, Berryman seems more uncertain of his ability to domesticate the women of his world than the men. Similarly, he seems less certain of his power to deploy or transform the traditional resources of elegy in his own defense when sexual difference is involved.

At the same time, for Berryman, traditional elegiac paradigms cannot wholly distance the threat of death or silence the importunities of the dead: "The senior population   waits. Come down! Come down!" (DS 21). Berryman's relationship to elegiac authority and to mourning has been overdetermined by his father's symbolically catastrophic death:

> My air is flung with souls which will not stop
> and among them hangs a soul that has not died
> and refuses to come home.
>
> (DS 127)

The unnamed soul is the unhallowed spirit of Berryman's father. Again, eeriness is tempered by domestic feeling: the speaker wants his father to come home, and he fears for the wandering soul. Yet as always, Berryman is haunted by that early death, feels it to beckon him, is irresistibly impelled to try to understand it:

I cannot read that wretched mind, so strong
& so undone. I've always tried. I—I'm
trying to forgive
whose frantic passage, when he could not live
an instant longer, in the summer dawn
left Henry to live on.

(DS 145)

Repeatedly, he represents his dead father's state of mind as an indeci-
pherable manuscript, as, in a sense, it must be under a regime of heroic
paternity. The poet cannot "read" his mind; he even stutters, "I—I'm,"
in approaching the unspeakable subject. Precisely such anxieties about
authorship, reading, and paternal authority pervade the complex male-
male transactions of the elegiac writings; at the same time, the disappearance of Eurydice, her functional replacement by male poetic
figures, and the corresponding loss of the *gendered* apparatus of traditional elegiac mastery make the elegiac project of *The Dream Songs* a
singularly vexed and tormenting one. Ironically, the poet's ability to
separate the dead from the living, this world from the underworld, self
from other, life from death, is compromised in the *absence* of the woman
as a heavily marked "other."

Revealingly, the important elegiac sequence for Delmore Schwartz in
The Dream Songs begins with a poem which presents the speaker's unstable place in relation to the realm of the dead:

These lovely motions of the air, the breeze,
tell me I'm not in hell, though round me the dead
lie in their limp postures
dramatizing the dreadful word *instead*
for lively Henry, fit for debaucheries
and bird-of-paradise vestures

only his heart is elsewhere, down with them
& down with Delmore specially, the new ghost
haunting Henry most:
though fierce the claims of others, coimedela crime
came the Hebrew spectre, on a note of woe
and Join me O.

"Down with them all!" Henry suddenly cried.
Their deaths were theirs. I wait on for my own,
I dare say it won't be long.
I have tried to be them, god knows I have tried,
but they are past it all, I have not done,
which brings me to the end of this song.

(DS 146)

As much as this persona tries to resist the dead who would drag him
to the underworld, the movement of this poem is steadily downward:
down from the upward images—air and breeze and "bird-of-paradise"
clothes—down to the "elsewhere," the "down . . . & down" of stanza
two, and the panicky cry "Down!" of the last stanza. At the same time,
the cry records a countermovement, the rising of the dead who would
seek him. His resistance, moreover, is only half-hearted:

he feels his death tugging within him, wild
to slide loose & to fall.

(DS 144)

His heart is "down with them." Only his body remains vertical, and
that mainly in the sexual sense so troubling to Henry: he is "fit for
debaucheries," as opposed to the dead "in their limp postures." His
energy diminishes—after the climactic moment of fear and anger—in
the flat breathlessness of the poem's last run-on sentence. The staged
lack of breath itself suggests a weakening of life force, as well as of the
poem's creative energy. That the poem may provide some kind of stay
against the draw of death is ambiguously suggested by the play on
different kinds of closure in the last two lines: "I have not done," he
protests, but the Song has.

As Sacks points out, Berryman's elegies for Delmore Schwartz "describe the dead poet in terms that surely recall the figure of the vegetation deity; we might add that they recall Orpheus in his guise as an
object of stringently tabooed homoerotic passion as well: 'Flagrant his
young male beauty . . . the whole young man / alive with surplus
love.' "[12] Schwartz, then, is the torn Orpheus, defined by song and by
pain. Though dead, he will be remembered for his "more beautiful &
fresh poems / of early manhood" (DS 150): "the young will read his

young verse / for as long as such things go" (DS 156). Delmore's
"young verse" is preserved in time, will always be young. Claiming
this time-defying poetic power for himself, Berryman identifies himself
deeply with the dead. Yet this is an identification that elicits a painful
difference: by identifying himself with this conventionally exemplary,
triumphant Orpheus, it is Henry who becomes the ghost, haunting Delmore:

> I give in. I must not leave   the scene of this same death
> as most of me strains to.
> . . . .
> fighting for air, tearing his sorry clothes
> with his visions dying O and O I mourn
> again this complex death.
>
> (DS 156)

The speaker's identification pulls him irresistibly into the scene of the
poet's dying, from which he cannot remove himself and thus separate
himself from the dead. The syntactic ambiguity created by the poem's
dangling modifiers points to a deeper one: the speaker cannot leave the
scene because he is part of it; he is the one gasping and writhing, while
"O and O" signifies the death groans as well as the apostrophic lamentation. Mourner and mourned merge in Delmore's "tearing his sorry
clothes," not only part of the physical struggle with death but also the
rending of the garments enjoined upon the bereaved Jew.

    The "Op. posth." and Delmore sections of *The Dream Songs* have
allowed Henry a disconcerting entry into "the world of the dead," yet
his curiosity remains unsatisfied:

> In his complex investigations of death
> he called for a locksmith, to burst the topic open
> where so many friends have gone
> It's crowded there, or lonely, I can't say which,
> no messages return, they preserve silence.
>
> (DS 335)

Perhaps the dead "preserve silence" not only by keeping quiet but by
preemptively disallowing the speech of the living. Nevertheless, an

elegist conceives predecessors as not only inhibiting but enabling; one examines the careers of earlier poets to see what they accomplished and how.

In this quest for knowledge, Henry is further empowered by the special gift of the medium; he can "see," in the old sense of seeing ghosts:

> O journeyer, deaf in the mould, insane
> with violent travel & death
> ....
>   ... I see you before me plain
> (I am skilled: I hear, I see)—
>
>   (DS 42)

Properly coaxed, this "skill" allows him entry to the shadowy world of spirits and literature: he sees and hears what is no longer or what is not yet. In Song 79, already quoted, Berryman makes explicit a wish elegy has persistently hinted at: that the dead person move "out of history" into another kind of being, into a highly charged, creative, unimaginable, magical "air":

>   when he
> flared out of history
>
> & the obituary in *The New York Times*
> into the world of generosity
> creating the air where are
> & can be, only, heroes?
>   (DS 79)

This magical space escapes from time and undoes all temporality; thus it becomes the space where the modernist can escape from the coercive linearity of tradition, the pressure to be original. The "world of generosity" and heroes, it releases him from rivalrous agon. But it also includes and conquers all of time: a prophetic poet, he can remember the future and surpass his predecessors. Magic summons the spirits of all the dead ancestors, so this magical space allows the modernist a way, however ironic, of incorporating tradition, of including, and safely integrating himself into, the past. Engaging modernist culture's ambivalent relation to the past, Berryman constructs the "afterlife" as a time-less dead poets' society: Berryman's "other" world is a literary one in which he can see Frost "hav[ing] it out with Horace" (DS 38).

If there is a single powerfully exemplary, authoritative figure for Berryman in the elegiac *Dream Songs*, it is Yeats, whom Berryman read, studied, and wrote about in letters, poems, and essays from his under-graduate days onward. He wrote to Yeats and later met him; this one meeting appears over and over in the poetry.[13] In *The Dream Songs* he particularly invokes the Yeats of those "last strange poems made under the shadow of death" (312). This is the Yeats who believed, or pre-tended to believe, that one could fluidly cross the borderline between life and death in both directions, through reincarnation and magical powers; it is this Yeats, a ghost who has promised to be accessible—"a brief parting from those near / Is the worst man has to fear"—whom Berryman summons.[14] Needing a definite yet permeable boundary be-tween the living and the dead, not an indeterminable space of living death, Berryman turns to Yeats, that earlier journeyer into "truths whereat the living mock,"[15] and to Yeats's home turf and burial ground, Ireland.

Berryman resists the masterful Yeats, he says, but finally brings a volume of the precursor's poems to Ireland. Becoming now a literary interlocutor with the dead literary great, as Frost did with Horace, Berryman poses a series of rhetorical questions for the dead man:

> I have moved to Dublin to have it out with you,
> majestic Shade, You whom I read so well
> so many years ago,
> did I read your lesson right? did I see through
> your phases to the real? your heaven, your hell
> did I enquire properly into?
>
> For years then I forgot you, I put you down,
> ingratitude is the necessary curse
> of making things new:
> I brought my family to see me through,
> I brought my homage & my soft remorse,
> I brought a book or two
>
> only, including in the end your last
> strange poems made under the shadow of death

> Your high figures float
> again across my mind and all your past
> fills my walled garden with your honey breath
> wherein I move, a mote.
>
> (DS 312)

"You whom I read so well": this poem is not, in fact, a gauntlet thrown
down but a wishful celebration of communion, the quality of wistful-
ness modifying the poem's confident opening in the questions that follow. "I brought my family to see me through": a singularly intimate
scenario, it at once incorporates and excludes the woman, his wife subsumed into that normative and desexualizing phrase, "my family,"
melding a religiously inflected erotic or mystical language with heterosexual reassertion. Strongly recalling the Bradstreet poem, most vividly in the carried-over word "homage," this poem effects also a
reversal of the power and gender relations in Berryman's wooing of
Anne. But rather than wooing Yeats as lover, he projects a fantasy of
being refathered by Yeats upon himself, of being the honeyed sperm,
the homunculus, in his own walled garden.

The Irish poems reflect Berryman's vexed relations with the familial:
compulsively invested in those relations, he nonetheless feels suffocated
and drearily normalized by his role as son, husband, father. This over-
determining discontent drives him cyclically both toward the occult
and towards its domestic downgrading:

> Saints throng these shores, & ancient practices
> continue in the dolmens, ruined castles
> are standard.
> The whole place is ghostly: no wonder Yeats believed in fairies
> & personal survival. A trim suburban villa
> also is haunted, by me.
>
> Heaven made this place, also, assisted by men,
> great men & weird. I see their shades move past
> in full daylight.
>
> (DS 313)

While he haunts only this family residence, for Berryman, Ireland and
its men are "weird" in every sense: prophetic, fateful, as well as

strange, they allow him to escape his cultural bounds and move freely in both past and future. Lady Gregory, Maud Gonne, Georgiana Yeats, Madame Blavatsky—all monumental figures in the later Yeats—are forgotten, for, as we have seen, this freedom of movement depends upon the disappearance of Eurydice.

Finally, however, it is Sylvia Plath who most troubles and, paradoxically, animates Berryman's masculinist world of elegy. She suffuses *The Dream Songs* with her insistent voice, more powerful than ever when it speaks from, and is understood to represent, the world of the dead. In Song 153, one of the Schwartz elegies, Berryman focuses in from the literary predicament of the age to Plath's specific case:

> I'm cross with god who wrecked this generation.
> First he seized Ted, then Richard, Randall, and now Delmore.
> In between he gorged on Sylvia Plath.
>
> (DS 153)

Against this "savage," all-consuming God whose final prey and perhaps most violently eloquent prophet was Sylvia Plath, the traditional stays and consolations of elegy seem vain indeed.[16] Plath's suicide makes her the climactic figure in Berryman's series; as agent and victim, she is identified, perhaps sublimely, with the operations of this God. With respect to this devouring figure, God or woman, Berryman takes belatedly defensive measures. At the same time, Plath's poetic giftedness and suicide make her too strong a figure of identification for Berryman to dismiss summarily or exclude as wholly "other." His sympathy and identification, torn between her and her children—"the two tots" of the "lady poets" Song (DS 187)—set up a conflict throughout the series.

Plath's mark is all over *The Dream Songs*, in almost every evocation of suicide.[17] In the Song quoted above, Henry's description of God, who "gorged on Sylvia Plath" adopts her metaphor of consumption, recalling the vampire-father-husband-God who "bit my pretty red heart in two" in "Daddy."[18] In another Delmore elegy already quoted, Henry himself has "tried" to be dead, has attempted suicide several times:

> Their deaths were theirs. I wait on for my own,
> I dare say it won't be long.

> I have tried to be them, god knows I have tried,
> but they are past it all, I have not done,
> which brings me to the end of this song.
>
> (DS 146)

"Tried" as a code word for failed suicide recalls Sylvia Plath's in "Daddy:"

> At twenty I tried to die
> And get back, back, back to you.[19]

Henry's imagining of his own funeral as spectacle imports Plath's in "Lady Lazarus," shading the gender politics differently with a black-clad Death:

> the Dancer comes, in a short short dress
> hair black & long & loose, dark dark glasses,
> uptilted face,
> . . . .
> returns to the terrible gay
> occasion hopeless & mad, she weaves, it's hell,
> she flings to her head a leg, bobs, all is well,
> she dances Henry away.
>
> (DS 382)

Like Plath, Henry does it "so it feels like hell."[20] He explicitly summons Lazarus in the final "Op. posth." poem:

> A fortnight later, sense a single man
> upon the trampled scene at 2 a.m.
> insomnia-plagued, with a shovel
> digging like mad, Lazarus with a plan
> to get his own back, a plan, a stratagem
> no newsman will unravel.
>
> (DS 91)

As Jahan Ramazani has remarked, the penultimate Song, which describes a visit to his father's grave, takes its macabre cue from Plath's murderous rage toward the dead father:[21]

The marker slants, flowerless, day's almost done,
I stand above my father's grave with rage,
often, often before
I've made this awful pilgrimage to one
who cannot visit me, who tore his page
out: I come back for more,

I spit upon this dreadful banker's grave
who shot his heart out in a Florida dawn
O ho alas alas
When will indifference come, I moan & rave
I'd like to scrabble till I got right down
away down under the grass

and ax the casket open ha to see
just how he's taking it, which he sought so hard
we'll tear apart
the mouldering grave clothes ha & then Henry
will heft the ax once more, his final card,
and fell it on the start.

(DS 384)

Ramazani comments acutely that Berryman "follows Plath in reversing the elegiac work of restoration and reintegration" (246); "splits his language between the farcical and the belligerent (247); and, in making Henry "wield an ax that functions . . . like Plath's stake, . . . is now borrowing 'phallic' authority from a literary foremother." The poem borrows also Plath's bleak and neglected paternal grave site, in "Electra on Azalea Path": "Your speckled stone askew by an iron fence . . . no flower / breaks the soil"; his undoing of "the mouldering grave clothes" recall "Lady Lazarus," "see / them unwrap me hand and foot— / The big strip tease."[22]

What may possibly have ratified Berryman's sense of rivalrous and, indeed, siblinglike identification with Plath was their shared filial longing for Yeats. Plath had the same lifelong fascination with the Irish poet as did Berryman, and she died in Yeats's London house, a house she had tried frantically to rent when she heard it was to let. Several of her early poems are reworkings of Yeats's, especially of the poem so charged for a female inheritor, "Prayer for My Daughter."[23] One cluster of associations for Berryman may well be the Lazarus story each uses;

each is likely to have absorbed the revisionary version from a passage in Yeats's "Calvary" in which Lazarus upbraids Christ:

> I had been dead and I was lying still
> In an old comfortable mountain cavern
> When you came climbing there with a great crowd
> And dragged me to the light.[24]

Berryman might well have felt that he and Plath were battling over Yeats's poetic and modernist legacy.

As Ramazani suggests, questions of literary inheritance become even more complicated across gender lines. In his critique of Anne Bradstreet, Berryman draws on a familiar cultural topos, the invidious opposition between women as the bearers of children and men as the makers of poetry, and even perhaps between mothers, powerfully haunting yet ultimately incapacitated, and (poetic) sons, overwhelmed yet ultimately victorious. In his elegy for Plath, however, Berryman complicates (in fact undoes) these familiar tropes. In a letter to his mother dated 1 August 1963 he writes, "I have no news exc. the American poetess Sylvia Plath killed herself—*The Observer* just sent me her final poems and w. extreme reluctance I wrote a Song for her."[25] He never explains this reluctance—to honor her? To let her go?

> Your face broods from my table, Suicide.
> Your force came on like a torrent toward the end
> of agony and wrath.
> You were christened in the beginning Sylvia Plath
> and changed that name for Mrs Hughes and bred
> and went on round the bend
>
> till the oven seemed the proper place for you.
> I brood upon your face, the geography of grief,
> hooded, till I allow
> again your resignation from us now
> though the screams of orphaned children fix me anew.
> Your torment here was brief,
>
> long falls your exit all repeatingly,
> a poor exemplum, one more suicide
> to stack upon the others

till stricken Henry with his sisters & brothers
suddenly gone pauses to wonder why he
alone breasts the wronging tide.

(DS 172)

Berryman makes a leap of empathetic understanding to register the
fact that it was in part domesticity that maddened Plath. Yet it is her
failure to stay on as a good mother which makes him rescind his par-
don: "the screams of orphaned children fix me anew." These screams
recall the anguish of his own sense of abandonment after his father's
suicide when Berryman was a child, and project ahead to the anguish
to which he fears he will—and in fact finally does—subject his own
children. For the moment, the screams "fix" him: they prevent him
from moving out of life, as well as riveting his attention to the case of
Plath. And, in her predicament, to his own. He and Plath, for all his
quarantining of her in *The Dream Songs*, inhabit the same space of
"grief," "torment," and of poetry-producing "agony and wrath." Perhaps Berryman fears that his increasing personal misery will not pay
off as dramatically as did Plath's in *her* "last strange poems / made
under the shadow of death." His language twins them: her face
"broods" from the photograph, he "broods" upon it—the language
again suggesting parenthood as well as sorrowful meditation—and the
"brood"/"bred" echo further connects them. Similarly, the apposition
of "hooded" does double service, modifying his brooding—perhaps he
shields his head with his hands—and her photographed face. In their
hoods, they are poetic versions of the Grim Reaper, bad examples drawing others on to death. Furthermore, for both of them marrying and
bearing is the beginning of "going round the bend." Like Plath, Berryman is tied to the familial by irrevocable bonds, and like her he cannot imagine a way out which will leave him or those who depend upon
him intact. It seems in this poem to flash upon him as a *mother*'s quan-
dary—and in a moment of uncanny return, he stays alive for the nonce
only by accepting what so much of the poem strenuously resists. By
the poem's end he has taken on the maternal signifier par excellence:
he "breasts" the tide that threatens to overwhelm him.

To what conclusions, then, does reading *The Dream Songs* as an elegiac script conduce? It appears to me that the female "threat" registered
in the Songs results, to a significant degree, from such factors as pro-

gressive expansion in women's literacy and higher educational oppor-
tunities; extension of women's legal entitlements, professional access,
political equality, and economic power; and the availability of reliable,
socially sanctioned contraception, on which women's sexual autonomy
depends. These sweeping historical changes antedated and enabled the
feminism of the 1970s, a feminism that, in many respects, laid explicit
claim to an historical fait accompli, opposing in principle any continuing, groundless, male monopolization of cultural privilege or competence. Yet the "invasive" presence of women in *The Dream Songs* also
attests to a general restructuring of the post–World War II American
world that renders untenable many of the traditional gendered antith-
eses and defenses of elegy. In the hysteric, alienated, and techno-
logically threatened American culture of the Cold War period, the
masculine poetic voice is no longer necessarily the culturally definitive
one. Not only the woman's voice, with its formerly abjected traits, but
the woman's forms of embodiment assume a new power of cultural
definition.

5

Beyond Mourning and Melancholia: AIDS Elegies

AIDS elegies have proliferated since the mid-eighties, written by male poets mainly born or resident in the United States. These poems by Thom Gunn, Wayne Koestenbaum, Essex Hemphill, Mark Doty, Paul Monette, James Merrill, and Melvin Dixon among others represent both a new, historically situated genre and an extensive refiguring of traditional elegiac motifs, including Orphean ones discussed in previous chapters. Although these elegies, like those written by women, are intensely aware of the tropes and dynamics of traditional elegy, they deliberately revise them in an attempt to write the dead—and the circumstances of their deaths—into the cultural narrative.

Even when not explicitly political, AIDS elegies typically undertake a skeptical review of elegiac consolations. Often unobtrusively, they will allude to famous elegies, especially to "Lycidas." Gunn's "Lament," with oblique allusiveness, transforms the dying man's hospital bed into something like the "watery bier" of "Lycidas." It speaks of the poem's subject as "drowning on an inland sea" and then, in a coda, describes the narrator as rebelling against a move away from the dead into a modern "pasture new": "this garden plot / too warm, too close, and not enough like pain."[1] Even in poems that are not overtly political, elegiac closure tends to be viewed as a form of collusion with mechanisms that represent those who have died as wholly other or as waste, and thereby allow or persuade the larger culture to leave unexamined its often premature "burial" of the dead.

Such allusions notwithstanding, however, this catastrophe-born genre remains relatively unmapped; perhaps the closest general precedent for it in English poetry is the poetry of World War I. Like that poetry, AIDS elegy responds to a shock that demands a different poetics and a cultural discourse dealing with death and mourning. (At least one AIDS poet, Paul Monette, explicitly makes the connection to World War I poetry, quoting Wilfred Owen's one-line manifesto: "The poetry is in the pity.")[2] A conspicuous point of linkage and disruption between traditional elegy and AIDS elegy is provided by the revision of the elegiac "marriage plot" in AIDS elegy. It is at that point of linkage and disruption that I begin. I argue that AIDS elegies not only resist or revise the elegiac marriage plot but often substitute another organizing drama: the welcome return of the dead in dream, fantasy, and ghostly manifestation. As a climactic and celebratory nonce convention, this one must be in part self-canceling: the desired moments of communion can only be temporary, so neither climax nor celebration can occur except under erasure; often the dead are recalled in a self-consciously pedantic, ironic, or even campy manner. Yet that very doubleness allows the AIDS elegy its typical refusal of consolation, maintained along with its refusal to dismiss the dead. Even the new funerary rituals poignantly devised in AIDS elegy are not ones of monumental commemoration that actually promote forgetting, object substitution, depoliticization, and a "healthy" moving on, but of closural suspension in which the dead are at once dispersed as ashes and conserved as ghostly presences.

I also contend in this chapter that relations between the living and the dead are changed definitively by the way speakers in AIDS elegies refuse to deny death by hiding that they are themselves at risk, are already infected with the HIV virus, or are, as in the case of Melvin Dixon and others, already dying. As the line between the dead and the survivors dissolves, so too does the customary elegiac politics of subject and object. (Paul Monette, rebuffing advice to move on from his grief over his lover's death, remembers the lover saying from his hospital bed, *"But we're the same person / when did that happen?"*)[3] Similarly, distinctions fade between AIDS elegy, non-elegiac poetry about people with AIDS or HIV, and poetry about people who do not have AIDS. This breakdown of categories becomes a matter of political and poetic principle, a way of always remembering that those who are not infected have been lucky rather than different in any way from the infected. Almost any gay man's poem for the living, then, shows its awareness of the reality of AIDS, insists upon the precariousness of the life that it celebrates, and asserts the endangered quality of the speaker's own life, as in James Merrill's "Farewell Performance," where the poet wonders, "will a friend enroll us / one fine day?"[4] Or in Thom Gunn's "Courtesies of the Interregnum," where a dying man seems to worry that his healthy friend will

> feel out of it,
> Excluded from the invitation list
> To the largest gathering of the decade, missed
> From membership as if the club were full.
> It is not that I am not eligible.[5]

Indeed, AIDS is so central a fact in contemporary gay consciousness that almost any poem written now by a gay man, no matter what its topic, is likely to include elegiac moments.

To begin at the point of connection and disruption with traditional elegy, however, we may say that because AIDS elegies do not need to hold the homoerotic at bay, or work to displace it, they do not require the moment of desexualizing conversion represented in traditional elegy by marriage. Central to the Orpheus story and to the traditional elegy has been a highly charged representation of marriage—the "nuptial moment" which, as Celeste Schenck has shown, functions as a climactic moment in a ritual drama of initiation into (masculine) literary production.[6] These staged marriages, however, never function as an entryway into life and sexuality: on the contrary, they function as a sacrificial offering on the altar of death, the moment when the author not only accedes to, but agrees to celebrate, the death of the other in order to insure his own authority and inheritance. (The "inexpressive nuptial song" in "Lycidas," for instance, reads two ways, signifying both Milton's poetically productive yearning toward the ineffability of God and the afterlife, and the dead man's absolute silencing in death.) Marriage is stripped of sexuality, and yet it invokes, no matter how abstractly, the figure of the woman in order to ward off the homoerotic "threat" which so imbues the genre; the woman is invoked, however, only to be erased. The importance of the marriage plot throughout the elegy tradition, and its particular way of playing out, point both to the derealization of women and to the denial of homoerotic possibility as two interconnected means of affirming (normative heterosexual male) literary authority. Brilliantly if brutally economical, this movement in elegy fuses homophobic and misogynist imperatives in the interests of a culturally privileged but only nominal heterosexuality. The injunction in "Lycidas" against the "shade" and "tangles" offered by Amaryllis and Naerea exemplifies the way sexual pleasure (entanglement) is not only banished but made the canceling other of literary power and production.

It is this normalizing dynamic of elegy that becomes apparent (perhaps hyperbolically or even hysterically) in "v." by Tony Harrison. In this poem, an elegiac interplay of sexualities comes strongly into view when an intense engagement by the poetic speaker with another male figure is forestalled by his return to a woman—a return that neutralizes the erotic pull of the other man. What is mapped onto this recognizable elegiac division is a division of class as well as personal allegiance, while class animus and homophobia appear to become intertwined.

The poem, an elegy for the speaker's parents—composed as though at Leeds Cemetery, where they are buried—consists mainly of an imaginary colloquy between the narrator and the person he might have been without education and class mobility: a skinhead who defaces gravestones with swastikas, four-letter words, and a scrawled UNITED, the name of Leeds's football team.[7] It may seem harsh to discover a "reactionary" strain in a poem that has been violently attacked in England by the right-wing press, a poem that, more germanely, asks moving and important questions about whose language, whose poetry, and whose right to memorialize will be recognized. Nonetheless, it seems to me that the outrage surrounding the publication of "v." has obscured the way the speaker's remorse and anxiety about having moved away from his class origins is displaced onto an image of a guilty male-male sexuality, to be exorcised and expunged.

Responding angrily to a taunt from his imagined skinhead alter ego, the speaker's present self lashes out in the sexualized language that characterizes skinhead speech, both speakers playing on the words the skinhead has written, but also expressing an erotic intensity beyond the apparent occasion:

> "You piss-artist skinhead cunt, you wouldn't know
> and it doesn't fucking matter if you do,

> the skin and poet united fucking Rimbaud
> but the *autre* that *je est* is fucking you."[8]

This sounds like an angry, punning moment of seduction as well as
attempted abjection. The tendentious pun is hidden in a joke on a joke,
namely, Harrison's rewriting of Rimbaud's famous epistemological-
linguistic riddle, *je* (first person) *est* (third person) *un autre*" (an other),
and in the foreign language his interlocutor can't understand: "Ah've
told you, no more Greek!" But the "fucking" here, consistently though
Harrison uses it as an intensifier, refuses to lose its gerundal directness:
"I am fucking *you*." Given this reading, the skinhead's reply can be
understood as a slangy rejection of a specific sexual appeal, or of anal
sex and by association of homosexuality in general: "no more Greek!"
The Rimbaud joke, moreover, distills the narrator's specifically sexual
but also more inclusively social longings for those made other (by class,
age, experience) but still tantalizingly the same. The skinhead's answer
is to reject the narrator's presumption of otherness, signing his grave-
stone graffiti with the narrator's own name, insisting upon their identity.

   Although the longing for communion is displaced throughout the
poem into the "aggro" of the twin speakers' political colloquy, it
emerges in the description of some boys playing in the graveyard
where the poem's meditations are set:

> The boy footballers bawl "Here Comes the Bride"
> and drifting blossoms fall onto my head.
> One half of me's alive but one half died
> when the skin half sprayed my name among the dead.
>
>   (13)

This apparently arbitrary convergence beautifully illustrates Celeste
Schenck's argument that elegy and epithalamium are deeply allied
forms which continually interpenetrate: the ceremony is half funeral,
half wedding.[9] This quatrain is oddly, and unusually for "v.," split in
its topic, reflecting the split in the narrator himself, of which he has
become aware. A deep split, in fact, since not only is the skinhead–alter
ego's graffiti now his own "signature" on the tombstone, but as a decorous poetic elegist he is displaced by the skinhead who phallically

sprays his name "among the dead." It is also the skinhead–alter ego
who unmasks the aggressive impulse of the filial elegist to deface the
parental memorial, manifesting the child's hostility to parents imagined
as still sexually connected underground rather than sentimentally re-
united in a heavenly recelebration of their earthly marriage vows.

The scene switches from the boys' play wedding to his own severed
relationship with the skinhead: that "Here Comes the Bride" makes
him think of himself suggests that his true mate is the skinhead whom
he has now left behind for a second time. Which is the live half, the
half who is willing to marry the skinhead or the half who denies him?
The narrator makes clear that what he sees is a homoerotic parody of
nuptial:

> 2 larking boys play bawdy bride and groom.
> 3 boys in Leeds strip la-la *Lohengrin*.
> I hear them as I go through growing gloom
> still years away from being skald or skin.
>   (14)

The repressed connection emerges, too, in an otherwise strange non
sequitur, an insistently anal-erotic joke from the skinhead:

> *Ah've 'eard all that from old farts past their prime.*
> . . . .
> Vicar and cop who say, to save our souls,
> Get thee behind me, Satan! *drop their breeches*
> *and get the Devil's dick right up their 'oles!*
>   (12)

No other moment in the poem—certainly no other sexual moment—
matches the graphic force of this literally demonizing representation of
homosexuality. But the narrator covers this image in the poem's final
stanzas with a heterosexual scene of communion which insists, with a
strained sentimentality that the rest of the poem carefully avoids, on
the physical difference of the lovers:

Home, home to my woman, home to bed
where opposites seem sometimes unified.
. . . .
I hear like ghosts from all Leeds matches humming
with one concerted voice the bride, the bride
I feel united to, *my* bride is coming
into the bedroom, naked, to my side.

The ones we choose to love become our anchor
when the hawser of the blood tie's hacked or frays.
But a voice that scorns chorales is yelling: *Wanker!*
It's the aerosoling skin I met today's.

(15, 17)

Again, an obscene epithet, here *"Wanker!"* (masturbator), works doubly, as generalized insult and as denotative specificity: the skinhead self insists that the relationship between the narrator and his "bride" is not marriage, it is masturbation pretending to be marriage. The erotic pull is clearly toward the vital, younger male figures with whom the speaker feels such troubled identification.[10]

In contrast to Harrison's poem as well as many mainstream elegies, AIDS elegy rarely participates in traditional elegy's consumption and silencing of women. Not required to integrate female figures sacrificially into their cultural dynamic, AIDS poems are free to include them in roles previously foreign to elegies by men. The poems are marked by expressions of love, intersubjectivity, and identification with women absent from almost all earlier depictions. These authors, moreover, invoke femininity with an ironic awareness of the politics of its traditional representations, and so generally avoid mainstream elegy's alternately possessive and demonizing forms of abstraction—Orpheus's Eurydice on the one hand, the maenads on the other.

I am certainly not suggesting that these poems are the site of a magical healing of all differences between women and gay men, or even that women figure unproblematically in AIDS elegies.[11] The much-debated issues of drag and of the relation of gay men to female movie stars reveal the difficulties and ambiguities of these issues in AIDS elegies as well. It could be argued, too, that the domain of the poems is so wholly male that they have no need to expel women. My point, however, is that is the pattern of female threat and expulsion is largely absent from AIDS elegies, a fact that allows certain politically emancipatory refigurations to be pursued.

For example, as though in answer to the versions of marriage proffered by traditional elegy, Essex Hemphill's militant "American Wedding" connects the marriage ritual with a sweeping politics of corruption and persecution, rejecting it for a redemptive—because politicizing and restorative—gay sexuality:

> In america
> I place my ring
> on your cock
> where it belongs.
> No horsemen
> bearing terror,
> no soldiers of doom
> will swoop in
> and sweep us apart.
> They're too busy
> looting the land
> to watch us.
> They don't know
> we need each other
> critically.
> They expect us to call in sick,
> watch television all night, die by our own hands.
> They don't know we are becoming powerful.
> Every time we kiss
> we confirm the new world coming.[12]

Hemphill rejects, along with the trappings of compulsory heterosexuality, the accompanying clichés about the doomed, suicidal, solitary, or passive character of the outsider. Indeed, solidarity among the doubly excluded is both affirmed and pursued in these lines: the "we" refers not to gay men in general but rather to African-American gay men who wish, like Hemphill, to admonish and reclaim both communities. At the end of "In the Life," which describes a search for sexual happiness, Hemphill's speaker urges his *mother* to understand his life and relinquish shame: if she can, he promises, she—not he—"will never notice / the absence of rice / and bridesmaids." This undoing of marriage posits a larger "we," one that can imagine a wholly unalienated yet still pleasurably fetishized sexuality.[13]

Yet marriage is not only repudiated as hopelessly normative in poetry by gay men. If epithalamium and elegy are problematically tied together, their linkage also attests to an impulse toward indissoluble union, of which a reimagined marriage may remain a signifier. Gay men's poetry sometimes reflects this recognizable and heavily invested form of desire. Paul Monette, for instance, in the last elegy of his *Love Alone: Eighteen Elegies for Rog*, imagines a retrospective wedding for himself and his now-dead lover. Searching the attic after Rog's death for mementos he might have missed, he comes across an old roll of film, and when he has the pictures developed, he finds a few from their visit to a Sienese abbey where the two had seemed to find traces of a still-extant, subterranean gay history. The old monk, Brother John, who acted as their guide, was "rapturous" in their company, joking with and touching them, and insisting on leading them down to a hidden set of frescoes. There he photographed them together in front, astonishingly, of a painting by the homosexual Renaissance painter "so-called Sodoma."[14] Later, after Rog's death, when overwhelmed with rage at the anti-gay policies of the Catholic church, Monette writes:

> I try to think of John
> and the picture he saved three years for me
> till the lost roll of Tuscany came to light
> and turned out to hold our wedding portrait
> the innocent are so brief and the rigid world
> doesn't marry its pagans any more but John
> didn't care what nothing we professed he joined
> us to join him a ritual not in the book
> . . . .
> where is the walled place where we
> can walk untouched or must I be content
> with a wedding I almost didn't witness
> the evidence all but lost no oath no ring
>
> (64)

Among the layered ironies of this passage, foremost is the speaker's experience of a wedding only after the marriage has been dissolved by

death. Perhaps, however, the only kind of male marriage available in
Monette's world, unreconstructed as he knows it to be, is such a retroactive, virtual marriage. This marriage must take place outside of
time and outside of papally enforced social norms, which have to be
angrily refused even as the speaker longs for them: "no oath no ring."
What replaces the formalized exchange of an oath and a ring is this
poignant near-miss, this self-canceling occasion, partaking both of the
kitschiness of wedding photographs and, with its image materializing
only after death, of ghostliness.

How, then, do women appear when released from their roles as cau-
tionary markers of sexual difference or threat? Mark Doty especially is
interested in representing women in a range of roles: a sister dying of
AIDS herself, in "Bill's Story";[15] Maggie, a friend tending a dying man
in "Brilliance";[16] or Carlotta, a street person with whom the narrator
makes significant contact in "Broadway."[17] "Coastal," which in the context of Doty's recent work reads as implicitly a poem about AIDS,
voices his affection for the neighbor girl's "stubbornness" in caring for
a sick loon she's found at the harbor:

> Foolish kid,
>
> does she think she can keep
> this emissary of air?
> Is it trust or illness
>
> that allows the head
> —sleek tulip—to bow
> on its bent stem
>
> across her arm?[18]

Throughout AIDS poetry, women are shown not only as camp ar-
chetypes or stereotypes—movie idols or operatic divas, for instance—
but as partners in activism: storming the White House, making panels
for the Names Project Quilt, theorizing AIDS discourse. Women also
care for the sick, and in the context of AIDS this is not a degraded
women's job but work embraced by men in a way that recasts the
gendered division of nursing labor. Maggie in Doty's "Brilliance" is no
pallid angel in the house, but a crucial interlocutor in the dying man's
approach to his own death.

Thom Gunn's "Her Pet" investigates a more complex form of relationship and identification with a female figure:

> I walk the floor, read, watch a cop-show, drink,
> Hear buses heave uphill through drizzling fog,
> Then turn back to the pictured book to think
> Of Valentine Balbiani and her dog:
> She is reclining, reading, on her tomb;
> But pounced, it tries to intercept her look,
> Its front paws on her lap, as in this room
> The cat attempts to nose beneath my book.
>
> Her curls tight, breasts held by her bodice high,
> Ruff crisp, mouth calm, hands long and delicate,
> All in the pause of marble signify
> A strength so lavish she can limit it.
> She will not let her pet dog catch her eye
> For dignity, and for a touch of wit.
>
> Below, from the same tomb, is reproduced
> A side-relief, in which she reappears
> Without her dog, and everything is loosed—
> Her hair down from the secret of her ears,
> Her big ears, and her creased face genderless
> Craning from the sinewy throat. Death is so plain!
> Her breasts are low knobs through the unbound dress.
> In the worked features I can read the pain
> She went through to get here, to shake it all,
> Thinking at first that her full nimble strength
> Hid like a little dog within recall,
> Till to think so, she knew, was to pretend
> And, hope dismissed, she sought out pain at length
> And laboured with it to bring on its end.[19]

The speaker's identifications with his subject are both obvious and sub-
tle. Like Balbiani, the speaker reads and has a pet; both (the speaker
more obliquely) are shown to confront death as the poem unfolds. The
representation of Balbiani, moreover, makes her virtually a feminine
model and alter ego in the elaboration of a crisis-defying *ars poetica*:
like Gunn in his poetry, Balbiani exhibits a calm delicacy, "plain" looks,
the "touch of wit" and reserve, that make the "strength so lavish she

can limit it." In "Her Pet," the tomb and the poetry cross, as do the conventionally gendered poet and his subject: he is shown watching a presumably macho "cop-show," but in a domestic space, and with a pet, that do not produce the image of cultural masculinity. Correspondingly, her aged, "creased," big-eared, face is finally genderless (and not unlike Gunn's, for all his handsomeness, on the book's back cover), although her body, with its aging, low-slung breasts, is definitively marked as female. *Ars poetica* overlaps with *ars moriendi*: Balbiani, but Gunn too, must work hard—or "labour," in the poem's punningly gender-ambivalent word for it—to deliver the death with which the poem ends.[20] (In "Lament," for Allan Noseworthy, Gunn describes death as "this difficult, tedious, painful enterprise.")[21]

In the poem, Balbiani's features are "worked," in a triple pun: they have moved in pain, leaving traces in lines and expression; they have been modeled by the artist; and her facial expressiveness will be part of the work she must do in order to die. That "work" is both a release and a summoning of energies, for, as the artificer of her life, at first she has toyed with fictions, "pretend[ing]" that her strength, like a charming accessory to aristocratic womanhood, "hid like a little dog within recall." ("Recall" as the power to summon at will, but also, finally, as the power of memory that links both selves, the self of the tomb's sculpted lid and that of its "side-relief.") The process of recall, generating the poem's back-and-forth motion, works against the poem's still-powerful closure, with its charged, "labour"-completing, mortal, poetic "end." Similarly, our consciousness of the speaker with Balbiani's picture in his hands, still trapped in the anxious waiting of the poem's opening, forestalls closure.

In Wayne Koestenbaum's "The Garbo Index," the tasks involved in facing death are also cast productively in a complicated identification with and through a commemorated woman he has never met. A memory of the film theorist Vito Russo leads the speaker to a meditation upon the role of Greta Garbo in Vito's and in his own imaginative self-creation:

> My dead friend Vito praised Garbo's last scene in *Queen Christina*—
> the closeup uncomprehended gays stared into, seeking dissolution.
> I remember Vito eating pizza at my table in the Village, 1986.
> He removed the sausage nuggets, placed them at plate-side.

"I don't eat pork," he said: HIV-positive precautions.
He was watching his system, as we were watching our own systems,
and are, to this day, watching. The last time I saw Vito entirely well
he was wearing pearls on his bare chest, high tea, the Pines—

never my scene. Who co-stars in *Romance*? Can't ask Vito.
When he was alive, I never helped him very much,
and now he's beyond telephone—waiting with Garbo
by the schoolyard's huddled ailanthus; waiting for the fire drill to end.

Four new Passover questions. Am I a child or an adult?
Am I a creature of memory or of action?
If I knew I were to die tomorrow, would I phrase this question
    differently?
Is it valedictory to write about Vito, or is it vanity?

My life is small, formal, and walled, and around every vista
I contain, imagine black shutters, the limits that Garbo
decreed must flank the lens filming her face in closeup,
so she could see only the camera's eye, without distracting leading man
    and crew.

Her life, if indexed, would yield surprises,
as would any life, if indexed, if reprieved.
Sea-glass, Garbo's collection of. Camellias, Garbo's paradisiacal.
Grotto, Garbo's imaginary. Ghost, Garbo's.

Once, Garbo was whispering secrets of performance
in a bandaged voice, and I was listening, and no toxins in the field
of vision arose to violate the soliloquy, unfolding
with the tranquillity of all final compositions.[22]

In this multilayered poem, Garbo becomes a figure through whom gay
men may meditate upon their identity, on their own prospective deaths
and those of their friends, and on an analogous annihilation, while they
are alive, through social misplacement, or displacement. The predicament of gay men is constituted partly by the heterosexual gaze of classic
narrative cinema, in which they are "uncomprehended" in both senses;
misunderstood and unincorporated. In the close-up, however, they may
seek "dissolution," meaning their own scopophilic pleasure, perhaps,
but also an undoing of the normative structure of cinematic narrative.
They are, "to this day, watching," choosing "scenes." Garbo's imperi-

ous self-framing—the blinders that excise the leading man, the movie's social world, everything but the yearning and nongendered viewer beyond the camera lens—contributes to such an undoing while heightening the fetishistic power of the female movie star, already threatening, in Laura Mulvey's view, to mainstream cinematic narrative.[23] (Threatening to this narrative as well is the lesbian cult aura of Garbo's screen work in *Queen Christina*.) Garbo's self-framing is presumably one of the "secrets of performance" passed on from "Garbo's ghost" to Vito, who, wounded himself, ventriloquizes her "bandaged voice" from the brink of, or beyond, the grave: "soliloquy, unfolding / with the tranquillity of all final compositions."

Like Vito, who has had to "watch his system" by eliminating potential toxins, Garbo and the speaker (whose "small, formal and walled" life apparently belongs to the circumscribed arena of classic garden poems) have found ways to watch *their* systems: to expand by reducing the field of vision. The speaker is thus able to "forget" a misplaced self and be dissolved into a glamorous star image in what seems like an act of creative misperception. This "passing over" evidently leaves the speaker wondering, however, in his new version of the Passover questions (Jewish homosexual and outsider's outsider that he is) how to "reprieve" his own and Vito's "real" lives: pedantically "indexing" or indicating these lives rather than narrating them offers itself as an ironic alternative to monumentalizing them. The speaker's fictional but passionate cross-gender identification does not necessarily chime with Vito's version of campy dressing up, but the versions are not at odds or discordant: the three voices, Garbo's, Vito's, and the speaker's, whisper together in an ending as formally closural as Gunn's in "Her Pet."[24]

Insofar as the AIDS elegy responds to earlier elegy, one way in which it does so, then, is by bringing to the fore impulses which, repressed in "v.," result in that poem's murderous agon between poet and "skin"—or between the poet and his inhabiting of his own skin. The modes of male bonding and rivalry characteristic of traditional elegy are reconstructed in AIDS elegies in a celebratory sexual context, and a relational identity is recovered, as, for example, in Thom Gunn's poem "The Missing":

> Contact of friend led to another friend,
> Supple entwinement through the living mass

Which for all that I knew might have no end,
Image of an unlimited embrace.[25]

The social and sexual are interconnected rather than compartmental-
ized and placed at odds. Gunn's classically informed, deliberate crafting
of a life requires an intense involvement with others, with a community,
but communal contact is not necessarily sentimentalized or devoid of
aggression.[26] Indeed, Gunn's poems consistently foster an unsentimen-
tal recognition of power relations, competition, and the continuing potential for victimization:

I did not just feel ease, though comfortable:
Aggressive as in some ideal of sport,
With ceaseless movement thrilling through the whole,
Their push kept me as firm as their support.

(80)

So too, in "The Man with Night Sweats," "each challenge to the skin"
creates the vitality which is in turn ruined by illness:

I grew as I explored
The body I could trust
Even while I adored
The risk that made robust,

A world of wonders in
Each challenge to the skin.

I cannot but be sorry
The given shield was cracked,
My mind reduced to hurry,
My flesh reduced and wrecked.

(57)

The gaps between stanzas, controlled yet interruptive, suggest both the
lost "world of wonders," the pleasures of offering the body up to dangers, and the calamitous disruption of those pleasures in the body's
recent wreckage. While heterosexual masculinity is often predicated
upon not being penetrated, emotionally or physically, Gunn consistently represents penetration, by needle or penis, as simultaneously

ego-enhancing and threatening. A different notion of the ego from the unitary, unviolated one of masculinist imagining is thus required in poems like "The Missing," in which pressure upon the boundaries of the self, of the body, engenders vitality, while the physical ruin of the speaker is accepted as the result of an ironically fatal coincidence rather than as the just punishment for sexual risk-taking.

This embrace of a communal and undefended version of sexuality and embodiment recalls, by contrast, the frequent struggles of mainstream elegy to distance itself from the classical love poetry that, in celebrating a male beloved, threatens to contaminate elegy with the homosexual. Mark Doty's "Turtle, Swan" has no objection to being a love poem, in spite of the loss and grief predicted:

> I read
> every week of some man's lover showing
> the first symptoms, the night sweat
>
> or casual flu, and then the wasting begins
> and the disappearance a day at a time.
> . . . .
> . . . I don't know
> where these things we meet and know briefly,
>
> as well as we can or they will let us,
> go. I only know that I do not want you
> —you with your white and muscular wings
> that rise and ripple beneath or above me . . .
> . . . .
> . . . I do not want you ever to die.[27]

And in "Homo Will Not Inherit," Doty opposes to the religious and dynastic consolations of elegy his joy in the body and in the poetry of the body:

> I'll tell you
>
> What I'll inherit, not your pallid temple
> but a real palace, the anticipated
> and actual memory, the moment flooded

by skin and the knowledge of it
the gesture and its description
—do I need to say it?—

the flesh and the word.[28]

The sexuality celebrated in AIDS poetry is not simply that of "committed relationships," however; these poems are often hymns to "casual sex." Wayne Koestenbaum muses, in "Erotic Collectibles":

> What is casual? I did not feel
> casual. My heart beat
> fast, as if this were an audition.[29]

At the funeral of Peter, in Doty's "Tiara,"

> someone said he asked for it.
> Asked for it—
> when all he did was go down
>
> into the salt tide
> of wanting as much as he wanted,
> giving himself over so drunk
>
> or stoned it almost didn't matter who,
> though they were beautiful,
> stampeding into him in the simple,
>
> ravishing music of their hurry.
> I think heaven is perfect stasis
> poised over the realms of desire.[30]

That "all he did was go down" offers a sexy, serious joke, combining a slangy evocation of oral sex with the "heaven" of three stanzas later. In Michael Lynch's *These Waves of Dying Friends*, casual sex and the pleasure of not knowing the lover's name are connected to the later evocation of particular names in a protest march, creating a perfect balance between two kinds of political resistance, sexual and activist:

> If not so long ago I fretted
> at the absence of a man, now I go for

the absence in a man, or men in whom absence
throbs. I choose that man
whose door is an eraser I walk through
to his bed so yesteryears
stay in the hall.[31]

The speaker's love of anonymous sex is offset against and yet paradoxically linked to his love for individual dead and his insistence, in
the poems and their apparatus, on naming them, on repeating ("indexing," as Kostenbaum has it) the names of the dead. (Perhaps it is
through this simultaneously political and poetic commitment to *naming* that the commemorative impulse of AIDS elegies most visibly in-
tersects with the impulse that produced the Names Quilt.)[32] In the last
poem of Lynch's sequence, protesters courting arrest at the Capitol
wear rubber gloves in parodic defiance of the police, who had worn
rubber gloves at a previous AIDS rally. They have written the names
of their dead on their gloves—the narrator's pair has "for Bill"—and
the volume is dedicated to "Bill Lewis, 18 March 1950–17 September
1987."[33]

To make connections between sensual celebration and mourning is a
way to reconstruct the epithalamium-elegy nexus of poetic tradition in
a nonsacrificial mode, and this becomes one of the most consistent en-
deavors of AIDS elegies.

It must be emphasized, however, that this double vision of sexuality
and death partakes of, and stands for, a far broader reworking of elegiac motifs in AIDS elegies. These elegies typically refuse any elegiac
narrative of reconciliation with the social, political, and ultimately "natural" order, grounded in heterosexual masculinity, that would be disrupted by further mourning. To reaffirm the naturalized sociopolitical
order described above, elegy has always had to move away from a
feminized world of the dead and of female figures.

Both grieving and reclaiming the dead become central political as
well as poetic moves in AIDS elegies. Over and over, the poems attest
to their loss and longing in the ritual of spreading the dead man's ashes
in a beloved spot—a rejection of church ritual and an embrace of the
domestic and the improvisatory, as in Koestenbaum's "Answer Is in
the Garden":

His lingering cold which no one took seriously
  Wrapped him in a coma. Now he is ashes
  Sprinkled in his backyard garden, planted just last spring.[34]

This insistence on the physicality of the ashes—"gruel of selfhood" in
Merrill,[35] "a bag of ash" in Gunn—indirectly reflects the new elegiac
sense of continuing responsibility to the dead. Grief insists, like Lynch's
naming, on the particularity of each lost person. Melvin Dixon, for instance, in "One by One," speaks of

> *Thousands. Many thousands.*
>
> Chile, I knew he was funny, one of the children,
> a member of the church, a friend of Dorothy's.
> He knew the Websters pretty well, too.
> Girlfriend, he was real.
> Remember we used to sit up in my house
> pouring tea, dropping beads,
> dishing this one and that one?
> You got any T-cells left?
>
> The singularity of death. The mounting thousands.
> It begins with one and grows by one
> and one and one and one
> until there's no one left to count.[36]

Yet the role and place of mourning in the AIDS epidemic has remained both politically and poetically problematic. In his essay " 'All
the Sad Young Men': AIDS and the Work of Mourning," for example,
Jeff Nunokawa analyzes the ambivalent place of mourning in the world
constructed for gays:

Homophobia has seldom been more obtrusive than in its current disincli-
nation to allow the gay community to grieve its own publicly; seldom
more annoying than in its refusal to honor an exigency of expression as
compelling as hunger, anger, or fear; seldom plainer than in the harass-
ment and repression, variously violent and squeamish, institutional and
intimate, by which it has worked to make the casualties of the present
crisis disappear. . . . If a homophobic reticence helped to prompt the

Names Project in the first place, a different homophobia has contributed
to its canonization in the popular media; if the majority culture is not
inclined to recognize the death of the male homosexual, it is also not inclined to recognize anything else about him; if the majority culture grants
no notice to his death, it also inters him from the start.[37]

Grieving, as this passage suggests, is connected to the desire for ritual,
but the forms of ritual expression allowed in a homophobic culture are
both limited and deeply compromised, as Nunokawa asserts later in
the essay. Referring to a poem by James Merrill, he writes: "Of course,
the submission to mortal fate—what Freud calls 'deference for reality'—
that Merrill's poem performs is a constitutive aspect of any work of
mourning. But just as Wilde and Shilts cultivate the confusion of gay
identity with a death-driven narrative, Merrill's poem characterizes the
doom as the specific fate of gay men" (317).

Here Nunokawa is discussing "Investiture at Cecconi's," the first of
Merrill's "Two Poems for David Kalstone." It describes an encounter
in a dream:

> Robe? She nods me onward. The mirror triptych
> summons three bent crones she diffracted into
> back from no known space. They converge by magic,
> arms full of moonlight.
>
> Up on my own arms glistening sleeves are drawn. Cool
> silk in grave, white folds—Oriental mourning—
> sheathes me, throat to ankles. I turn to face her,
> uncomprehending.
>
> *Thank your friend,* she cackles, *the Professore!*
> Wonderstruck I sway, like a tree of tears. You—
> miles away, sick, fearful—have yet arranged this
> heartstopping present.[38]

In these lines Nunokawa sees Merrill as colluding in the cultural understanding of homosexuality as itself fatal, and of gay men—the "sad
young men" of his title—as inherently moribund: "If at the beginning,
the speaker is like a doctor, distanced from the patients he loses after
the diagnosis, the cool silk in grave, white folds that sheathes him from

throat to ankles—the robe—as well as the dream and the poem that move him to the heartstopping end, cause the speaker to converge finally with the lost patient" (317).

While I agree with Nunokawa's contextualization of this poem within the cultural problematics of mourning, I would argue, nonetheless, that just as the speaker's identification with the dying man in Merrill's poem gives an already fated quality to his own prospective death, so too it imparts life to the man addressed. Distant, "sick, fearful," this friend, Kalstone, is not only an agent in the poem but a magician, directing his three witches in a benign, and dressy, feat of communication with his friend, coming "back," like Merrill's Ouija board acquaintances in other works, "from no known space."[39] The poem does not only collude with existing repressive structures; it finds a way to resist them as well. As a context for a communal understanding of death, AIDS requires awareness of a new relation between subject and object constituted by the realities of shared endangerment.

Relations between deference for, and defiance of, "reality" are further complicated by the second of the two poems in Merrill's pair, "Farewell Performance," which yearningly imagines a future of eternal earthly encores for his dead friend at least as vividly as it does the awareness of his transformation into ash. It starts with an assertion that the rest of the poem will prove false:

> Art. It cures affliction. As lights go down and
> Maestro lifts his wand, the unfailing sea change
> starts within us. Limber alembics once more
> make of the common
>
> lot a pure, brief gold. At the end our bravos
> call them back, sweat-soldered and leotarded,
> back, again back—anything not to face the
> fact that it's over.
>
> You are gone. You'd caught like a cold their airy
> lust for essence. Now, in the furnace parched to
> ten or twelve light handfuls, a mortal gravel
> sifted through fingers,
>
> coarse yet grayly glimmering sublimate of
> palace days, Strauss, Sidney, the lover's plaintive

Can't we just be friends? which your breakfast phone call
clothed in amusement,

this is what we paddled a neighbor's dinghy
out to scatter—Peter who grasped the buoy,
I who held the box underwater, freeing
all it contained. Past

sunny, fluent soundings that gruel of selfhood
taking manlike shape for one last jeté on
ghostly—wait, ah!—point into darkness vanished.
High up, a gull's wings

clapped. The house lights (always supposing, caro,
Earth remains your house) at their brightest set the
scene for good: true colors, the sun-warm hand to
cover my wet one. . . .

Back they come. How you would have loved it. We in
turn have risen. Pity and terror done with,
programs furled, lips parted, we jostle forward
eager to hail them,

more, to join the troupe—will a friend enroll us
one fine day? Strange, though. For up close their magic
self-destructs. Pale, dripping, with downcast eyes they've
seen where it led you.[40]

This poem's emphasis on shared ritual, the dance and the scattering of ash, sketches a cherished network of affection and affinity, of intimate relationships based on shared and ritualized pleasures that continue without the dead man but are also irrevocably changed by his absence. The speaker's hand is cold and wet after freeing the ashes, though Peter's is sun-warmed over it; the dance is overlaid with images of death and disappearance; Strauss and Sidney, not merely the dead man's memory of them or his ash, are scattered in the ambiguous syntax of the lines: "sublimate of / palace days, Strauss, Sidney, . . . this is what we paddled a neighbor's dinghy / out to scatter." After this latest loss, the speaker's perception of his own vitality is inextricably threaded through with his awareness of mortality.

At the same time, however, life impinges upon death as well: the friend is not wholly relinquished. The poem, to begin with, is addressed to him: unelegiacally, intimately, to "you." The first stanza's evocation of Prospero, moreover, and of Ariel's song, although its immediate frame of reference is the rhapsodic pleasure produced by ballet, suggests also that the image of immersion with which the poem ends may, magically, not be a final drowning, just as the ship Miranda sees going under is not, after all, irrevocably sunk. Moving between the images of death, as airy translation—into a desirably Ariel-like other way of being, akin to the "limber alembics" of dance—and life, as an absolutely final and heartbreaking performance (the "one last jeté" clapped by the gull), this poem does not want to let the dead go. The speaker's awareness that he may "one fine day" be enrolled in the troupe of the dying and dead excites him and his companions—they surge forward—but, like the dancers themselves, he is also dismayed. The dancers are, indeterminably, emanations of life, sweaty and resurgent, and of death, looking, as they do, like victims of the drowning that the first line's image had led us to hope might not have occurred.

In effect, then, Merrill's poem assists, if ambivalently, in the very critique Nunokawa levels against it. Aware of impulses within himself to embrace or accede to death, or to naturalize or romanticize a specifically gay death, Merrill works against, as well as within, a poetics of internalized doom. In doing so, he participates in the more general critique of mainstream narratives of commemoration performed by a number of AIDS elegists. Like many of those other poets, Merrill focuses suspicion, not primarily on the "fatedness" of the beloved's death, but on the consolations that have previously been offered by elegy, ones that would collude in the premature interment of the dead.

Essex Hemphill articulates a specifically African-American response to the task of mourning in a straight- and white-dominated culture that, as in Nunokawa's argument, "inters [the gay man] from the start." In his "American Wedding," the outer world "expect[s] us to call in sick, watch television all night, die by our own hands," and, in "When My Brother Fell," "wants us dead." In "Heavy Breathing," the "schizoid" nature of the world he must encounter threatens him, and those he loves, with annihilation:

> Urged to honor paranoia,
> trained to trust a dream,

a reverend, hocus-pocus handshake;
I risk becoming schizoid
shuffling between Black English
and assimilation.
My landscape is littered
with effigies of my heroes.[41]

Hemphill's response to this risk of devastating self-division—between African-American and white worlds, between the gay life and black family, is an edgily inclusive voice, joining, but without any facile harmoniousness, the languages of inside and outside. "When My Brother Fell," Hemphill's poem for the writer and activist Joseph Beam, urges a political self-awareness that he knows can be undermined by the easy gestures of memorialization, even of the Names Project Quilt, if it is allowed to take the place of other forms of joint effort:

When I stand
on the front lines now
cussing the lack of truth,
the absence of wilful change
and strategic coalitions,
I realize sewing quilts
will not bring you back
nor save us.

It's too soon
to make monuments
for all we are losing,
for the lack of truth
as to why we are dying,
who wants us dead,
what purpose does it serve?

When my brother fell
I picked up his weapons.
I didn't question
whether I could aim
or be as precise as he.
A needle and thread
were not among

his things
I found.[42]

This disruption of elegiac language—this "cussing," this invocation of "strategic coalitions," this disruption of elegiac pacing ("it's too soon") and, finally, this refusal of memorialization—amounts to a rejection of elegiac consolation in favor of a politicized urgency.

Even when not advocating political engagement, AIDS elegists tend to eschew traditional or even "respectable" consolations, not infrequently cultivating an ironic spiritualism that attests to the strategic import of James Merrill's gay-inflected Ouija board afterlife.[43] Such poems inscribe a double vision: they summon ghosts while insisting upon the finality of death. The living poets do not want the dead to be buried *in* AIDS elegies, nor, endangered as they are themselves, can they see the dead as wholly other. The poems are filled with ghosts and other revenants, while the relations of the living with these revenants are intimate, unforeclosed. In Mark Doty's "Tiara," the sad slide from the moment everyone must realize that Peter's case is terminal to the funeral—from "he *woke* in the hospice" (my emphasis) to "the wake" is reversed:

> At the wake, the tension broke
> when someone guessed
>
> the casket closed because
> he was *in there in a big wig
> and heels*, and someone said,
>
> *You know he's always late,
> he probably isn't here yet—
> he's still fixing his makeup.*[44]

The relation of the community to these ghosts is affectionate and eroticized, resisting any conception of death as bodilessness. In another poem by Doty, a dead boy contacted through the Ouija board asks the speaker and his lover to kiss in front of the TV: he can watch them through the screen.[45] And the poet recognizes the continuities of the body of the dead with his own. The narrator of Wayne Koestenbaum's "The Answer Is in the Garden," meeting the ghost of a friend whose clothing he has inherited, recognizes both his difference from and his likeness to the dead person:

> I am too corporeal
> To hold the attention of one so weightless, to say,
>   In a tone of sad confusion, that the good
> Suit he wore in life fits me well, too well, like a charm.[46]

Like Merrill, Koestenbaum can be wittily rueful about gay men's internalized sense of doom, or sense of being always and already dead. In fact, the speaker takes the apparition as a sign that he should write *his* first elegy, anticipating his own death as well as that of others:

>   I've never written
> An elegy: none of our small circle had yet died.
>   This is not musical enough to sing his
> Soul down the river mine and yours must, too, go down, but
>   Metro needs a mourning song
>   . . . .
>   When I am dead
> I may be wise enough to say it well.[47]

Similarly, Thom Gunn writes of his dream of a dead friend's return in "The Reassurance,"

>   How like you to be kind,
>   Seeking to reassure,
>   And yes, how like my mind,
>   To make itself secure.[48]

Michael Lynch, in an essay written shortly before his own death, reread his pre-AIDS poem "The Terrors of Resurrection" from a post-AIDS vantage point.[49] In the poem, as he says, "the resurrectee has every right to be jarred when his friends receive him not with rejoicing but with fretting" at *their* disrupted mourning.[50] The discomfiture of the comfortably grieving, the poem points out, is nothing compared to the discomfort—or "catastrophe"—of the dead:

facing the mourner's security
of well-done affection
and the disrupter himself jarred to find himself
this kind of disrupter.[51]

The ghosts of AIDS poetry, and the politics they enact, refuse to let the living safely die away. Conversely, the poets overwhelmingly read their own summoning of ghosts as a refusal to resign their attachment to life, the body, pleasure, political engagement.

Although elegy studies in general have tended to conflate a return to pleasure in life with resignation or acceptance of bereavement, as in so-called "normal mourning," AIDS elegies contrarily make pleasure an act of defiance against death, seen not simply as a natural fact but as the condition into which gay men are "willed" by a pathologizing or demonizing social order. The poems pursue the critique, initiated in women's elegies, of voiceless, bodiless representations of the dead, and reassert the claims of physical pleasure as well as pain.

Not least of the pleasures asserted, finally, is that of the poetic text. AIDS elegy's insistence on the particularity of individual loss makes the poem a pleasurable physical "index," not a consoling artifact-substitute. Texts have their own ghostly, erotic shimmer: in Doty's "Lament-Heaven," we read that

                    if death's like that,

          if we are continuous,
             rippling from nothing into being,
                then why can't we let ourselves go

          into the world's shimmering story?
             Who can become lost in a narrative
             If all he can think of is the end?[52]

As Cindy Patton writes in her book *Inventing AIDS*, "The insight that 'silence equals death' has spawned an international agitprop activism that circulates around the meanings elided in the legitimated discourses of science, media, public politics."[53] While Patton affirms the value of this activist "agitprop" (to which at least some AIDS elegies may be seen as contributing), it is not only agitprop that has had to circulate around the meanings elided in cultural discourses or, for that matter, in many mainstream literary texts. It is at least partly in circulating around such elided meanings that AIDS elegies have come into being as an important contemporary genre.

6

Against Elegies:
Women's Breast Cancer Poems

In 1980, after her first bout with the breast cancer that was eventually to kill her, Audre Lorde published *The Cancer Journals*, her book of prose reflections on her own experience of the disease.[1] The book urges introspection leading to political action, physical and emotional self-awareness for women with cancer, solidarity among women against the mystification of what she calls "Cancer, Inc."[2] (the National Cancer Institute, the American Medical Association, Reach to Recovery, etc.), and above all, a refusal to hide or euphemize cancer, by circumlocution, prosthesis, or any other means: "Since the supposed threat of self-actualized women is one that our society seeks constantly to protect itself against, it is not coincidental that the sharing of this knowledge among women is diverted."[3]

Repeatedly in her poetry and prose after diagnosis, Lorde insists that the trauma of cancer, if met with a spirit of conscious receptivity, can be the catalyst for a profound and definitively political reintegration of self. Lorde's poetry returns to the topic and to the delineation of this process as insistently as her prose, even if it does so in more complicated and ruminative ways. Yet the reception of Lorde's cancer writings has, ironically, forestalled the "sharing of knowledge" she advocates practically at its source. Admittedly, Lorde is mentioned in almost every book addressed to women undergoing treatment for breast cancer: in books by doctors, by survivors, by cancer activists. In a sense, however, these authors are preaching to the involuntarily converted. Beyond this specialized (if large and growing) audience, and especially in the public realm of literary response, Lorde's urgent attempt to articulate a politics—and a *discourse*—of breast cancer has been thwarted, as if by design, even if unconsciously for the most part.

Reading the jacket of Lorde's last book of poems, for instance, *The Marvelous Arithmetics of Distance*, no one would know how Lorde had died. The back cover quotes some of Lorde's most famous allies and admirers. Adrienne Rich speaks of "a great talent too soon forced to give up her pen, but assured in her place by all the books she lived to write." Alice Walker remarks that these poems show "the same vibrant, brave, and generous soul we knew before." Robin Morgan: "Now the poet is gone—but the work lives, and sings." And Michelle Cliff speaks of "an individual coming to terms, in which Lorde describes a self at the end of her life span." Possibly each of these women wrote more, and the editors have chosen what they felt to be the most market-worthy selections. Yet it is remarkable that the editors could put together, from the words of four famously radical women, a tribute so perfectly aligned in its naturalizing banality with the most unreflective and conventional forms of elegiac expression. If some satisfaction is to be gained from the Orphean positioning of Lorde, a woman, as the "singer," the immortal poet, in these tributes, that satisfaction must surely be qualified by her assimilation to the very values which that status represents, and that I have described in depth throughout this book. Moreover, the tributes show no trace of the rage and anguish that I assume some of these writers must feel; they are also devoid of any sense of the political as well as cosmic injustice of Lorde's long physical struggle and early and painful death; of any reference to *The Cancer Journals*, to the topic of many of the poems, or to the cause of Lorde's death. In short, the tributes are exclusively anodyne, performing an act of silencing so complete as to pull the reader up short.

Such, one could argue, is the world of bookselling, yet that would hardly be a reassuring explanation. The world of bookselling is putatively that of the political culture in and for which books are written. Disconcertingly, this silencing in the marketplace recurs in the academy. A survey of recent articles on Lorde's poetry, all written since she published *The Cancer Journals*, many written since her death, turns up not one which mentions her struggle with cancer or her extensive writings on the topic.[4] Among these are articles by politically engaged, sophisticated women—feminists, many of them strongly and explicitly identified with an African-American or lesbian identity—and therefore not inclined to discount outsider perspectives. These writers, in fact, record and argue for deliberate, conscientious attention to experiences of marginalization, particularly as they are experienced in terms of poverty, of physical dislocation, of lesbian exclusion, of racial injury. Yet even authors in this group who quote from *The Cancer Journals* do not mention the reason Lorde wrote it, or relate its topic to the poems; instead they cite Lorde out of context so as to generalize her specific insights, ones that she drew in anguish, but with determined clarity of vision, from the experience of having breast cancer in a racist and misogynist culture. In effect, such generalizing makes her insights disappear. This erasure is so far from being the apparent, or in any way a plausible, intention of the writers involved that a mechanism of repression must surely be at work. Perhaps that repression attests to the widespread cancer phobia of a culture in which, all too often, the equation cancer death prevents people from seeking timely diagnosis. Perhaps, too, breast cancer is especially dreaded by women insofar as it afflicts the organ that serves as the prime cultural signifier of womanhood in its sexual and maternal aspects. The rhetoric of the prosthetic and reconstructive industries makes it all too clear that an immediate restoration of the pre-surgery silhouette is the best remedy, a reclamation of womanhood and an erasure of mastectomy. (It is not presented, in other words, as a mere stopgap, or as a comfort for some, not all, women.) Yet if these academic women in particular, who have trained themselves to hear Lorde's specific, detailed, localized language, are unable to hear what she says, how can the culture at large? How can these writers seemingly assent to the view that death from breast cancer is simply a natural fact of the "life span" about which it is useless to complain, and from which only transcendent consolations and sentimental memories are to be gleaned? How, finally, can they continue to inhabit the very ideological assumptions in elegy that have been so punishing to women?

These troubling questions will be at issue throughout this chapter. So will the related question of silence(s) between and among women, as well as between men and women, regarding breast cancer. To declare my personal stake both in the topic of this chapter and in some of the larger topics addressed in this book, these questions trouble me as an academic woman and a breast cancer survivor. The questions become all the more pointed given certain affinities between the politics of AIDS and breast cancer, as well as between AIDS and breast cancer poems.

The analogies between the discourses of AIDS and breast cancer are important—both are increasingly powerful, effective, and politically sophisticated sources of activism, and both are the necessary response by groups who consider their lives particularly vulnerable to public indifference or hostility. The outcomes, however, have been very different. The relative attention to the bodily and psychic realities of each disease, in everyday life as well as in the poetry which emerges from it, has been markedly asymmetrical. Among other strange asymmetries has been the relative inarticulateness of women poets in response to breast cancer. The AIDS-activist slogan "Silence = Death," which is given peculiar force by the elegiac tradition I have been considering, seems curiously suspended in relation to breast cancer.

The tabooing of breast cancer as a cultural topic as distinct from a medical one has evidently inhibited its poetic representation. In general, and for reasons already suggested, women poets have had a more ambivalent relation to elegy than men; nevertheless, they have written powerful (if relatively few) breast cancer elegies. Yet whereas AIDS elegies have become a major genre in contemporary poetry, the poetry of breast cancer is still a mostly unrecognized subgenre. This disparity is a matter of both production and reception. Aside from the work of Audre Lorde and Marilyn Hacker, which has given the topic some visibility, and to which I shall shortly return, the poems tend to be rare and scattered. Not in every case, but far more often than not, the poetry of breast cancer bears all the marks of having been wrung out with difficulty in the face of a world of resistance. Often the poems are so muted, so indirect, so encoded, that one needs specific biographical information in order to see the references the poems make to this particular form of illness and death, which affects so very many women in the latter part of the twentieth century. (For example, as I shall show, in Anne Sexton's elegies for her mother, who died of breast cancer, one needs to read clues in crossword-puzzle fashion to find specific references to the disease.) To go from full-voiced, expressively varied AIDS elegies, with their uninhibited embrace of grief, rage, and pleasure, to comparatively reticent breast cancer elegies is to retrace an uncannily familiar path: though women elegists have largely rejected the story of Eurydice as a pattern for their poetry, they still can be absorbed very quietly into their own deaths. In this respect, the Orphean patterning of so much previous elegiac writing not only sets an ominous precedent for women with breast cancer, it also gives the "Silence = Death" slogan a peculiarly threatening inflection in the context of women's poetry.

The topic of breast cancer raises urgently, then, the question of how women's discourse can be voiced, and especially in culturally sanctioned forms like poetry. Elegy, situated at or close to the top of the generic hierarchy of poetry, is even less readily accessible to women poets. What seemingly intervenes between the experience or awareness of breast cancer and public discourse is a profound censorship, in some ways as much among women as between women and men. This censorship cannot be regarded simply as form of gender oppression or of deliberate silencing, as in so much traditional elegy, although those modes persist: the censorship will always be manifestly and inescapably overdetermined by codes of patriarchal inscription. The peculiarity of breast cancer elegies is that of an elegiac discourse that disappears even as it forms—a discourse that becomes almost impossible to speak or hear.

The "inaudibility" of breast cancer poetry is partly a matter of tone, in contradistinction, say, to Paul Monette's unabashed utterance of grief and rage in AIDS elegy, or to Michael Lynch's mordant political commentary. Yet it is also a matter of quantity. Until November 1994, when Marilyn Hacker published her *Winter Numbers*, no single author's volume of poetry, as far as I am aware, has been mostly devoted to poems about breast cancer.[5] Only one, very slim, anthology of collected breast cancer poetry, *Her Soul beneath the Bone,* has been published.[6] Poems, then, have been written about breast cancer both by poets who have personally experienced the disease and by ones who have not; although I will be discussing these poems, they are hard to find and, as I will show, likely to be hidden, erased, or forgotten. In fact, in almost every case the poems carry a subtextual or overt knowledge of that likelihood—an awareness of the difficulty of being heard so profound as to constrict the voice at the outset. In spite of this difficulty, or because of it, these poems make a specific and important contribution: they consider the limits and dangers of speech and writing and explore the possible value of certain forms of silence and reticence. In other words, the "inaudibility" of breast cancer poems is not necessarily to be construed wholly negatively, or as merely symptomatic of women's predicament. Even if silencing represents a threat, breast cancer writing is capable to some degree of incorporating and transforming it.

This chapter, then, will outline not only the difficulties of creating a discourse of breast cancer but women poets' double relation to those difficulties: desiring adequate speech on one hand, yet rejecting the dream of any simple, univocal utterance or true representation attained by a lifting of taboos or the undoing of ideological censorship. Crucially, these poets proceed by exploring the multiplicities of their own subject positions and discourses. When doing so within existing frameworks and conventions of elegy—the teleological movement of which has traditionally been towards resolution, female silencing, and detachment from the dead—they almost necessarily mobilize a critique of elegy and a resistance to its norms. At the same time, it is not clear that those frameworks and conventions necessarily *obstruct* the articulation of a discourse of breast cancer (even a fully political one); indeed, they powerfully enable it in many local instances and, finally, in one breast cancer survivor's landmark volume, Marilyn Hacker's *Winter Numbers*.

Adrienne Rich, in an early and influential breast cancer elegy, addresses the problematic relatedness of taboos on sexual and other kinds of communication. In "A Woman Dead in Her Forties," the issue of communication is vexed, the poet's most fervent wishes being exactly that which cannot be spoken. Although the poem passionately regrets the silences it records, it does not propose speech as a simple alternative:

> Your breasts / sliced-off   The scars
> dimmed as they would have to be
> years later
>
> All the women I grew up with are sitting
> half-naked on rocks   in sun
> we look at each other and
> are not ashamed
>
> and you too have taken off your blouse
> but this was not what you wanted:
>
> to show your scarred, deleted torso

I barely glance at you
as if my look could scald you
though I'm the one who loved you

I want to touch my fingers
to where your breasts had been
but we never did such things

You hadn't thought everyone
would look so perfect
unmutilated

you pull on
your blouse again: stern statement:

There are things I will not share
with everyone[7]

Refusal to euphemize the mastectomy was already, at the moment the poem was written in the mid-seventies, a radical statement about what normally could be said. Insofar as the italicized lines can be read as a quotation of the addressed woman's imagined thoughts, they suggest that such candor might be received as a violation as well as an act of political solidarity. So too, sexual, or sexualized, touching, is at once proffered and withdrawn as a healing gesture; the connection between sexual contact and political solidarity is left unfixed. The italicized lines, technically unassigned, are therefore attributable to any or all of the women depicted, and so draw attention to the fact that "the personal" encloses and therefore censors everyone: all shelter "things [they] will not share / with everyone." Both admiring of and distressed by the dying woman's silent insistence on what has set her apart, this introductory section foregrounds problems of communication and silence, of connection and separation:

Most of our love from the age of nine
took the form of jokes and mute

loyalty: you fought a girl
who said she'd knock me down

we did each other's homework
wrote letters   kept in touch, untouching

lied about our lives: I wearing
the face of the proper marriage

you the face of the independent woman
We cleaved to each other across that space

fingering webs
of love and estrangement   till the day

the gynecologist touched your breast
and found a palpable hardness[8]

Speaking is not necessarily to be valued over silence, or "truth" over
lies; the "space" between the two women is unbridgeable by speech
alone, attesting as it does to something deeper and more pervasive
than ordinary social conventions.[9] Admittedly, social convention, nar-
rowly conceived, diminishes and constrains the lives of those excluded
from the norm—people with cancer, single women, lesbians—and so
the poem embodies a social critique. Yet the separation between
women is a constitutive fact of daily life, a patriarchally induced division, perhaps, but for all that a mode of being central to women's
lives. This separation correlates with the scarred woman's feeling of
exclusion from the world of the perfect and unmutilated: such feeling
is too deeply embedded in the cultural matrix to be cured simply by
addressing it in plain language. Not saying the wrong things, or saying foolish ones, is as important in its way as saying the right things.
Making this distinction and adhering to it in practice constitutes one of
the chosen political as well as poetic disciplines of women poets writing about breast cancer, calling forth a comparable discipline of atten-
tive reading and critical commentary, perhaps especially from
academic women.

In her ultimate, if vexed, refusal to be governed by ordinary social
conventions about breast cancer, and in her exploration of the specific
results of social regulation between women, Rich is responding to a
history of silence in poetry on the topic, yet in a sense she cannot get
beyond silence even if she can specify or relocate it. She hints sadly at
a politics half-imagined, or at least sensed as a need, but not yet
brought to fruition; to realize it, neither poetry as usual nor "plain
language" suffices:

we never spoke at your deathbed of your death

but from here on
I want more crazy mourning, more howl, more keening

We stayed mute and disloyal
because we were afraid

I would have touched my fingers
to where your breasts had been
but we never did such things[10]

Rich's call for "more crazy mourning, more howl, more keening," invokes not only a mourning freed of modern conventions of propriety (or "sanity") but also a new understanding of what makes the highly educated and deeply bonded women of the poem unable to speak of death or to touch meaningfully, in sexual or non-sexual ways. An inexpressible residue will remain as haunting guilt and even as aggression against the patient:

Time after time in dreams you rise
reproachful

once from a wheelchair pushed by your father
across a lethal expressway

Of all my dead it's you
who come to me unfinished

You left me amber beads
strung with turquoise from an Egyptian grave

I wear them wondering
How am I true to you?

I'm half-afraid to write poetry
for you   who never read it much

and I'm left laboring
with the secrets and the silence

in plain language: I never told you how I loved you
we never talked at your deathbed of your death

(254–55)

Plain language spoken only posthumously is neither a political language nor one of effective connection with the living or with the dead.

Rich may be responding not only to silencing but to "deep" encoding. Anne Sexton, for example, wrote a number of elegies for her mother, and though they at times say the word "cancer," the word often remains phobically unspecified; it might be lung or skin cancer rather than the sexually charged cancer of the breast. Nevertheless, these elegies as well as other poems written by Sexton reveal a deep, troubled consciousness of the mother's cause of death. This consciousness is made fully explicit at least once, in the poem "Dreaming the Breasts":

> In the end they cut off your breasts
> and milk poured from them
> into the surgeon's hand.[11]

More often, this consciousness is obliquely focused on the legacies— genetic, emotional, existential—passed on from mothers to daughters. A poem for *her* daughter, endangered, as Sexton herself would have been, by this genetically matrilineal disease, shows the speaker taking fright at a mole on the child's face, "inherited from my right cheek: a spot of danger / where a bewitched worm ate its way through our soul / in search of beauty":[12]

> Darling, life is not in my hands
> life with its terrible changes
> will take you, bombs or glands,
> your own child at
> your breast, your own house on your own land.
> Outside the bittersweet turns orange.
> Before she died, my mother and I picked those fat
> branches, finding orange nipples
> on the gray wire strands.
> We weeded the forest, curing trees like cripples.[13]

" 'Fat arm,' " Sexton's biographer tells us, "was a term of disgust Mary Gray [the poet's mother] connected to her mutilation by surgery," the lymphedema of the arm that is often an aftereffect of radical mastectomy.[14] Knowing that, we can connect the "fat / branches" to her fear of the treacherous "glands" and again to the parasitic—if also beautiful and imaginably nourishing—"orange nipples" of the bittersweet vine, which must be cut away in order to save the trees. Fatness and glands further intimate a relation between the hormonal "excess" of women and desexualizing or isolating forms of disease, including cancer and obesity. Within this same network of associations, the nightmare of the child destroyed at its mother's breast makes the sanctified, breast-giving relation between mother and girl-child itself the danger. The nipples, only apparently a source of sustenance, really poison, their "bittersweet" gift making the humans the afflicted as well as the healers (the word "cripples" belongs syntactically to both "we" and "trees").[15] Yet at the same time Sexton rejects any demonizing reading of mothers as responsible for all possible damage incurred in a woman's life: "Darling, life is not in my hands."

The deep coding of breast cancer in this and other poems may attest to the dread induced by the disease, but it also reveals a complex of fears, hostilities, and resentments, painfully difficult to admit let alone theorize, between women. The widely believed myth that breast cancer is primarily a disease transmitted from mothers to daughters undermines idealization of the mother-daughter bond and matrilineal transmission. While such idealization may always be questionable, even as a conscious feminist strategy, an undermining of the ideal will almost inevitably force into consciousness and language whatever the idealization has suppressed. Unacknowledged forms of suspicion, resentment, and violence between mothers and daughters, and between women in general, thus gain tortured expression in breast cancer poems. Generally speaking, insofar as violence between women remains unacknowledged, whether from motives of solidarity in the face of patriarchal oppression or because such violence may seem guiltily complicit with its masculine counterparts, the admissions wrung out in breast cancer poetry may seem like betrayals. Yet these poems insist that such acknowledgment may be the necessary preliminary to any clear-sighted return to the larger world in which the family is constructed and breast cancer is experienced.

Sometimes, the fact of having breast cancer is fantasized as the omnipotent mother's curse (although the mother's cancer can also be fantasized as an analog of the daughter's devouring greed, as in Sexton's "Dreaming the Breasts": "I ate you up" [314]). In Helen Webster's

"Child," the speaker believes that "Momma wants me / dead, drowned / like the kitten," and the coming of death from breast cancer is seen as a helpless submission to the mother's wish:

> Some days
> I oblige her—
> stop my ears
> with mud
> fill my mouth
> with stones
> plug my nose
> with clay
> block my eyes
> with leaves
> bind my body
> with rags.
> Then wait, cocooned.[16]

Perhaps, however, the accession is not as helpless as the poem initially suggests. The speaker's self-burial becomes an act of furious if perverse agency that "exceeds" the mother's wish, while the word "cocooned" jumps out of the poem as the designation of a state to be desired. Is the cocoon a way of sheltering from the mother? Of returning to the womb in a different kind of sheltering? Or of hatching, as a kind of motherless self-delivery? Or of healing, in bandages from surgery? The cocoon both is and is not a birth image and a maternal image, its indeterminacy allowing the speaker's relation to nativity to be restructured as desired. So, too, being "cocooned" is both death and a waiting game, as the speaker waits out the uncertainty of a prognosis which will end, sooner or later, with her death or with her metamorphosis. In the language of the poem, as distinct from "real life," the mother's curse is and is not fulfilled.

Similarly, in Michelle Murray's "A Haunting," the mother is a terrifying childhood figure of magical agency, disciplinary power, and inexplicable malice:

> My mother's hand is fiddling with the spoon
> but my face, grown monstrous,

stares back at me from the bowl's tipsy
reflection
before it ripples in the clear soup—
shattered!
Ah Madam my hand trembles.
Food spatters on the cloth,
food and the old terrors staining.
My mother's hand is breaking off the flowers.
Petal by petal they die
in the fierce grip of her hands.
My house is littered with dying flowers.
The stink of them fouls the gracious walls.

I dance on the lawn under the sun.
My shadow springs with me
lightly . . .
mine, mine!
My mother's feet are crushing the grass
in my dance.
All of us pregnant with our ghosts.[17]

The poem compares the helplessness, the frustrated simultaneous crav-
ings for autonomy and for safety, of the person with breast cancer to
that of the fearful child of a parent perceived as both threatening and
consoling. The remembered presence of the mother, like the threat of
death, and like the rampant tumor cells, dissolves the speaker's human
edges, making the speaker reappear, "grown monstrous" in the soup
bowl's reflection. She is further dehumanized when she sympathizes
with the grass crushed under her mother's feet. For a daughter to think
about her mother's breast cancer is to confront some of the sources of
her own misogyny, specifically her fears of female embodiment and of
likeness to other women, especially likeness to the mother. "All of us
pregnant with our ghosts": we uncannily contain our dead parents, and
also our own deaths. Similarly, the swelling and loss of control in pregnancy is made to suggest the bodily effects of cancer, thus conflating
the images of demonic possession, cancer, and maternity.

Even when less explicit or primordially charged, breast cancer poems
often mobilize a critique of the mother. In "To My Mother," Claire Henze
obliquely accuses her mother of collusion with the forces of suppression

and, making a move frequent in poems about breast cancer, skips a generation to identify with the grandmother as opposed to the mother:

> You told me the maid fainted
> when she saw my grandmother
>   in her bath.
> Naked, upright, cheerful and witty
> A terrible gash across her chest
> No breasts.
> And I picture the maid lying limp on
>   the tile floor
> of this vast French bathroom,
> my grandmother sitting in the big tub.
> You say she was amused by the
>   maid's shock,
> and the picture doesn't hearten
> or amuse or reveal her spirit,
> or do anything but form a knot in my stomach
> and make me weep.
> My grandmother died long before I was born,
> of the disease I have now.
> I never knew her
> but I know her now.
> I know how she felt at that moment
> when the maid fainted.
> I know more about her now than
>   anyone else.
> And I know she was not amused.[18]

The maid's response, of terror, disgust, withdrawal, is what the post-
mastectomy woman in Rich's poem imagines that unscarred women
must also feel. Like Rich, Henze insists on describing what everyone
else looks away from: the missing breasts, the still-raw scar. And like
Rich, she examines the damage done by speech: "You told me," "You
say," as opposed to the "I know's" of the poem's ending. The speaker
moves through the silences of the past—the grandmother's absence, the
mother's denial, the maid's withdrawal—to a definitive statement. To
insist on her grandmother's lonely anguish is to make a new beginning,
from a position of age, denudation, and threatened mortality.

As I have suggested, the poets of breast cancer often tease out the network of family relations, particularly between women, in order to return more clear-sightedly to the world in and by which family is constructed. A view of that world can reveal the way the politics of silencing between women passes through the family and the experience of breast cancer to other forms of social division and repression. Yet it can also suggest modes of poetic and political reconstruction.

Michelle Murray's "Poem to My Grandmother in Her Death" registers the larger losses sustained in her relationship with her grandmother through the representation of breast cancer. The speaker notes the diminishing connection with the dead woman across distance in time and experience, and across boundaries of class and education:

> After a dozen years of death
> even love wanders off, old faithful
> dog tired of lying on stiff marble.
>
> In any case you would not understand
> this life, the plain white walls
> & the books, a passion lost on you.
>
> I do not know what forced your life
> through iron years into a shape of giving—
> an apple, squares of chocolate, a hand.
>
> There should have been nothing left
> after the mean streets, foaming washtubs,
> the wild cries of births at home.[19]

Despite the losses inherent in the passing of time, distance can allow the speaker to perceive her grandmother anew, moving beyond imagining her only in the conventionalized maternal "shape" of selfless nurturing, a shape ambivalently associated in the poem with that other "shape of giving," the rounded breast. What the speaker recovers is a shared experience of bodily and emotional *damage* that allows her to understand how the grandmother's silences could, and still can, speak:

> Never mind. It's crumbling in my hands,
> too, what you gave. I've jumped from ledges
> & landed oddly twisted, bleeding internally.
>
> Thus I learn how to remember your injuries—
> your sudden heaviness as fine rain fell,
> or your silence over the scraped bread board.
>
> (25)

As the poem progresses, the speaker finds herself caught up in a complex new process of identification and distancing, the difficulty and provisionality of which is indicated by the heavy enjambment and syntactic tortuousness of the lines:

> Finding myself in the end is finding you
> & if you are lost in the folds of your silence
> then I find only to lose with you those years
>
> I stupidly flung off me like ragged clothes
> when I was ashamed to be the child
> of your child. I scrabble for them now
>
> In dark closets because I am afraid.
> I have forgotten so much. If I could meet you
> again perhaps I could rejoin my own flesh
>
> And not lose whatever you called love.
> I could understand your silences & speak them
> & you would be as present to me as your worn ring.
>
> (25)

This recovery of mutuality and empathy in the face of "injuries" brings her back to her own familial betrayals and silences, as she reaches to undo an earlier, shamed, rejection of her mother. That mother is also "your child," the product, presumably unlike herself, of "mean streets" and home birth. In wishing to retrieve the past, its material and psychic details, she finds a versatile articulateness that allows her to inhabit her grandmother's silences: if the grandmother is "lost in the folds of your silence," the speaker will "lose" with her "those years." To uncover old wounds allows her to value what is absent: the unspoken word, the lost "flesh." That flesh comprises the cast-off family (flesh of my

flesh) and its social reality, but also the severed breast, the grandmother's lost body, and finally, a self for which she wishes a new kind
of psychosocial integration. This reunion of self with self will not be
only inward: "I could rejoin my own flesh / And not lose whatever
you called love."

The damaged "shape" of the third stanza is that of the lost flesh, the
breast, yet it is also an emblem of the grandmother's life, distorted by
pain and deprivation. These circumstances the speaker now wants to
recall, imagining the ways in which the grandmother's life was and
was not constrained by them:

> In the shadows I reach for the bucket of fierce dahlias
> you bought without pricing, the coat you shook
> free of its snow, the blouse that you ironed.
>
> There's no love so pure it can thrive
> without its incarnations. I would like to know you
> once again over your chipped cups brimming with tea.
>
> (25)

Knowledge of her grandmother's life as definitively constituted by
lacks and silences allows its lost fullness to be conceived, just as those
full chipped teacups, formed like rounded if damaged breasts, recall
the "shape" that has haunted the poem. Yet the imagining remains
insufficient, or indeed a further sign of lack: the imagined resurrection
is incomplete without the body and the specific life that body has lived,
without its "incarnation" of love.

In making connections between the politics of silencing in breast cancer and a broader politics, lesbian poetry—starting with the Rich poem
already cited—has generally been the most politically explicit. Lesbian
critiques take as their starting point the experience of marginalization,
an experience already theorized in and across a community. The need
for a supportive community is taken as self-evident, but at the same
time, the ways of imagining that community constantly shift and refine
themselves under the pressure of ongoing political analysis. This self-
revising ideological dynamic is particularly urgent among African-
American lesbians who write about breast cancer. Audre Lorde is the
major example, her work as an activist poet mobilizing not only an
energetic and focused sense of community but a usefully fluid sense of

identity politics. None of this, however, results in a reductive simpli-
fication of the politics of breast cancer or supplies a ready-made discourse for the illness.

In *The Marvelous Arithmetics of Distance*, Lorde's last book of poems
before her death from breast cancer, the poet explicitly, intensively, and
with painstaking deliberateness describes the processes of coming to
terms with her approaching death from cancer.[20] The front flap of *The
Marvelous Arithmetics of Distance* quotes her hopes for the book: "Beyond the penchant for easy definitions, false exactitudes, we share a
hunger for enduring value, relationship beyond hierarchy and outside
reproach, a hunger for life measures, complex, direct, and flexible. . . .
I want this book to be filled with shards of light thrown off from the
shifting tensions between the dissimilar, for that is the real stuff of
creation and growth." Strikingly and characteristically, Lorde locates
valuable communication both inside and outside ordinary speech,
which tends to produce the "easy definitions" and "false exactitudes"
that inhibit creativity and change. Yet she wants her language to be
directly available as well as complex, her project being a matter of
deeply political as well as personal conviction:

> I am not afraid to say
> unembellished
> I am dying
> but I do not want to do it
> looking the other way.[21]

This insistence on seeing clearly and on speaking fearlessly charges the
whole volume. "Unembellished" does not mean plain, however, and
the disorienting experience of cancer can leave her, as in the title of one
poem, "speechless":

> At the foot of the steps a forest
> strewn with breadcrumb fingers
> sticky with loss
> stuffed with seductive chaotic songs
> like a goose bound for the oven
> giddy trees wait   shaken.

In the wild arms of a twilit birch
the void of course moon
hangs like a spotlit breast.

Death
folds the corners of my mouth
into a heart-shaped star
sits on my tongue like a stone
around which your name blossoms
distorted.[22]

In this terrifyingly condensed nightmare version of a fairy tale, dangers recede confusingly beyond the access of ordinary speech. The appositions float: what or who is "stuffed with seductive chaotic songs," the forest or the speaker? Hansel and Gretel's defenses against being lost and killed merge with the dangers, the consumers with the consumed. Their trail of bread crumbs becomes the finger tested by the witch for fatness, edible and easily lost. The witch's sticky candy house is the sign of loss, the trees are as disoriented as the children, words are bound for the oven with the goose they fill. Traumas from the adult world infiltrate: the moon, no longer celestially removed from any sources of change in its perfect pattern, has lost its course, snagged in a tree, medically spotlighted like the human breast whose hormonal flux it is popularly supposed to regulate.

The poem's ending suggests the difficulty of reaching back to any reader, political or otherwise, from this setting, full of specters too strange, numerous, and dark to convey except in nonliteral metaphors. Distanced by her immersion in horrors from the poem's "you," an amalgam of love object, reader, and political ally, the speaker finds speech an almost anatomical impossibility: "Death / folds the corners of my mouth / into a heart-shaped star." Certainly this image resists visualization. The single necessity of language in this context is that it must change. Finally only surreal images can intimate the experience, only "chaotic songs" can hope to do it justice. Lorde implies that we will have to read her despite and through her distortions of "ordinary" language; the reader is being asked to produce the clarity on the other side of the thicket, but the poem also identifies the request as an impossible one, a dream of plain speaking that would posit some nonexistent simple or shared reality to be lucidly expressed.

Lorde continues to call upon a wide range of discursive modes in her cancer poetry, from perfect explicitness to deep encoding. These modes illustrate differently her experience of the political and material world after surviving cancer and its treatments. For example, "Restoration: A Memorial—9/18/91" is set in Berlin after hurricane Hugo has devastated her Carriacou home and "after chemotherapy":

> In this alien and temporary haven
> my poisoned fingers
> slowly return to normal
> I read your letter dreaming
> the perspective of a bluefish
> or a fugitive parrot
> watch the chemicals leaving my nails
> as my skin takes back its weaknesses.
> Learning to laugh again.[23]

Here, the most alien place, Berlin, becomes contradictorily a "haven" and a place of relearned laughter: in other poems it is named as the site of increasing violence against Blacks: "Afro-German woman stomped to death / by skinheads in Alexanderplatz."[24] Like her bodily health, however, and like her hurricane-torn island, Berlin is being "reconstructed" by global forces beyond the control of individuals, including corporate ones simultaneously producing the environmental "poisons" that may induce cancer and the harsh chemotherapeutic agents that treat it. The city becomes both a social refuge from and an ironic analog for her cancer. The apparent health and order of the Caribbean world is attractive ("no other life / half so sane") but not immune: the parrots are "fugitive" like herself, because Hugo blew parrots from one island to another.

Hugo and the cancer are persistently associated in Lorde's poetry. However, she generally makes Hugo the vehicle of which cancer is the tenor, thus maintaining a certain allegorical indirectness. In the last two stanzas of "Hugo I," the hurricane acts as a reproach to human delusions of immortality, and it is the ostensible subject of a poem that touches only indirectly if unmistakably on cancer-related death or bodily alienation:

This skeleton was an almond tree.
That stalk a prickly pear cactus
green as a gourd
a peep of red fruit
promised and warned
in the same sticky breath.

All the rest is rubble.
Constructions
that fester and grow loathsome

because they cannot self-destruct.
In some fantasy of immortality
a wilted wisdom formed them
to last 10,000 years.

But the wind is our teacher.[25]

Among the lessons the wind "teaches" is that of mortality, perhaps specifically the mortality denied by Horatian poetic claims to have built edifices—shelters; monuments—more lasting than bronze. Not only are these leveled to uniform "rubble," but cancer as a form of growth has made the very process of "construction" almost indistinguishable from its opposite. Growing and festering are now comprised in the same movement, while the "immortal" art of cancer cells, apparently dreamed into being by some "wilted" divine or human wisdom, makes them the paradoxical agents of human mortality.

The following poem in the collection, "Construction," makes the connection between cancer and the hurricane more overt, at the same time apparently reclaiming a certain local knowledge of the craft of building for weatherproof efficacy:

Timber seasons better
if it is cut in the fourth quarter
of a barren sign.

In Cancer
the most fertile of skysigns
I shall build a house
that will stand forever.[26]

Despite the apparent choice of local craftsmanship over alien technology, however, Lorde is drawing consciously as well on the conventional Western metaphors of poetic construction while repositioning her Caribbean-engendered poetry in the context of the canonical Western literary tradition. It is Cancer as an archaic astrological influence but also as a "modern" disease that paradoxically empowers Lorde: her condition makes her want to master Western signification ("skysigns") as one source of power and certainty.

In "125th Street and Abomey," Lorde pursues her strategy of combining her worlds:

> Seboulisa mother goddess with one breast
> eaten away by worms of sorrow and loss
> see me now
> your severed daughter
> laughing our name into echo
> all the world shall remember.[27]

In the original Dahomeyan myth, Seboulisa had cut off her breast in the Amazon manner of female archer-warriors.[28] Lorde is Seboulisa's "severed daughter" in that sense, yet also in another, disempowering sense: she is separated from the culture in which Seboulisa is a self-determining goddess. Lorde's loss is more passively and unredeemably sustained, closer both to mastectomy and to the suffering evoked throughout her poetry as that of the disenfranchised:

> the surest way of knowing
> death is a fractured border
> through the center of my days.[29]

Death is specifically related to cancer: Lorde evokes not just the "scar" of surgery but the "fractured border" of microscopically enlarged cancer cells. The cancer is a part of larger world events, indifferent to "natural" borders, that cause misery and deepen inequities. Yet Lorde's cancer also becomes a source of her activism, partly because it is not conceived as a purely natural fact, isolated from global politics:

I still patrol that line
sword drawn
lighting red-glazed candles of petition
along the scar.[30]

In these cancer poems, as in "Restoration," a sense of purpose sustains Lorde as the "ravishment fades / into compelling tasks." Loss is constant nonetheless, and Lorde rebels against it, as in her elegies for Pat Parker, her friend and fellow black, lesbian activist-poet, who died of breast cancer in 1989, and to whom the volume is in part dedicated. These poems represent no poetic retreat from the political to the personal, however, and they reengage the poetics of elegy in such a way as to conserve the dead and reaffirm the bond between women across boundaries, including the one between the living and the dead:

It's almost a year and I still
can't deal with you
not being
at the end of the line.

I read your name in memorial poems
and think they must be insane
mistaken   malicious
in terrible error
just plain wrong.

not that there haven't been times before
months passing   madly   sadly
we not speaking
    get off my case, will you please?
    oh, just lighten up!

But I can't get you out
of my air   my spirit
my special hotline phone book
is this what it means to live
forever   when will I
not miss picking up the receiver
after a pregnancy of silence
one of us born again
with a brand-new address or poem

miffed
because the other doesn't jump
at the sound
of her beloved voice?[31]

This poem is at once an elegy and a disavowal of elegy, seeing "memorial poems" as wrong in any number of ways. Lorde focuses first on her resistance to the idea of Parker as absent through death or separation: simply "not being" as well as "not being at the end of the line." Wishfully, the poem confuses the two states of absence, imagining this period of noncommunication as merely another temporary estrangement. Here, as other poets of breast cancer do, Lorde comments on silences between women, silences and resentments certainly fostered by the larger culture but also more personal, more chosen and textured, creative as well as destructive. Each rivalrous, irritable time-out in the friendship has been "a pregnancy of silence." Silences are thematized in the poem's form, in pauses that break up sentences and allow meanings to proliferate, setting apart groups of words which read as both suspended phrases and sentence components.[32] The personal silences have alternated, also, with periods of grace and shared love—a word that does not appear until the last line of the poem—and with shared literary and political projects. In "Lunar Eclipse," another poem written for Parker, "Being sisters / wasn't always easy / but it was never dull."

Lorde's technique of loading a phrase with different possible meanings implies both division and an interdependence that overrides divisions between the two women: "I can't get you out / of my air   my spirit." The epithet "my spirit" is both possessive and vocative, Parker being inside Lorde's spirit (meaning soul) or being the soul itself. The separated addressee is also a ghost-spirit, living in the limbo of Lorde's "special hotline phone book," her awaited return yet another of the literary reunions celebrated in their friendship. That "hotline," like the line Parker had been "at the end of," is also the poetic line that Lorde works so productively in this piece—its temperature high, its urgency raised. Each woman's poetic project has touched and mutually fertilized the other's, so that now, even if she wanted to, the living woman could not get the dead one out of her "air," or poem. Finally, then, this poem that refuses to give up the dead is placed in contradistinction to the "insane" and "wrong" memorial poems of the opening. Rather than acceding to an eternal silence, it ends by invoking a "beloved voice."

Lorde's own life, too, she finds hard to relinquish, separation from the dead being, in effect, a painful rehearsal for separation from the self, from its forms of self-connection, from its personally inflected language (or languages), from its forms of erotic connection and social belonging:

> when I am gone
> another stranger will find you
> coiled on the warm sand
> beached treasure   and love you
> for the different stories
> your seas tell
> and half-finished blossoms
> growing out of my season
> trail behind
> with a comforting hum.
>
> But today
> is not the day.
> Today.[33]

The posthumous perspective on the self is almost necessarily one that seeks to defer its own arrival.

Another exemplary negotiation between the personal and the political is undertaken by Marilyn Hacker in her *Winter Numbers,* a collection of poems responding to her own breast cancer. Like the poetry of World War I, these poems detail the inadequacies of traditional elegiac tropes and narratives as a response to massive, general loss. (In a phrase brilliantly conflating the experiences of that war with those of contemporary women, she refers to her post-cancer self as "cell-shocked.")[34] "No one," Hacker reminds her readers in the first section, "Against Elegies," "was promised a shapely life / ending in a tutelary vision." At the same time, "Against Elegies" takes on, with a certain poetic and historical self-consciousness, the fate her particular generation, "the young-middle-aged," devastated by AIDS and suicide as well as well as breast cancer. The volume's title reflects Hacker's sense that the elegiac modes, implicitly including Orphean ones, are on the verge of becoming inoperative: while she evokes the "winter" of classical elegiac mourning, she foregrounds the insufficiency of poetic "numbers" to encompass the various numbers in question:

> Catherine is back in radiotherapy.
> Her schoolboy haircut, prematurely gray,
> now frames a face aging with other numbers:
> "stage two," "stage three" mean more than "fifty-one"
> and mean, precisely, nothing.
>
> ("Against Elegies," 12)

The poems insist upon the numerical fact and numerical "staging" of the deaths they are recording, too many for elegies. Figures, statistics, stages, all resist assimilation to normalizing or naturalizing erasure of the deaths occurring before the normal life span has been completed. The public, political world wishes to perform exactly this naturalizing erasure: "Tell me, senators, what you call abnormal?" ("Year's End," 76). At the same time, as in AIDS elegies, the easily forgettable individual names matter: "James has cancer. Catherine has cancer. / Melvin has AIDS."

Numbers tell an undeniable story of "unnatural" death, both collective and individual, but not the whole story:

> Twice in my quickly disappearing forties
> someone called while someone I loved and I were
> making love to tell me another woman
> had died of cancer.
>
> Seven years apart and two different lovers:
> underneath the numbers, how lives are braided,
> how those women's deaths and lives, lived and died, were
> interleaved also.
>
> ("Year's End," 75)

Beneath the serial march of numbers, lives may become textually braided or "interleaved," the poem—the poetic volume—functioning as a space of conservation and reconnection to the dead, not of elegiac disconnection. "Cancer Winter," the volume's final group of poems, is a sonnet series on her own cancer; it looks back over the preoccupations and emotional states of the other sections. Every sonnet in the sequence begins with a version of the last line of the last sonnet but one, thus producing a closed or braided sequence reminiscent of Donne's "La Corona." In the volume's ironically titled middle section, "Elysian Fields," in poems set before Hacker's diagnosis but already surveying the scene of death around her in anticipation, so to speak, Hacker writes:

> Our friends are dying
> and between us nothing at all is settled
> except our loving.
> . . . .
> Seize the days, the days, or the years will seize them,
> leaving just the blink of a burnt-out lightbulb
> with a shard of filament left inside that
> ticks when it's shaken.
>
> Fix the days in words and the years will seize them
> anyway: a bracket of dates, an out-of-
> print book, story nobody told, rooms locked and
> phone disconnected,
>
> cemetery no one will ever visit.
>
> ("Dusk: July," 58)

This anticipatory rumination on mortality, somewhat predictably post-modern in sensibility, is fully attuned to such post-elegiac tropes of mortality as the disconnected phone. It is equally well attuned to the ironical treatment of textual residues as remainders rather than re-minders: the bracketed dates of birth and death and the out-of-print book attest to the passing of a life. Yet the poem remains safely unspe-cific. In "Cancer Winter," by way of contrast, Hacker ruminates on her shifting connection to elegy as she faces her own treatment for cancer:

> It's become a form of gallows humor
> to reread the elegies I wrote
> at that pine table, with their undernote
> of cancer as death's leitmotiv, enumer-

ating my dead, the unknown dead, the rumor
of random and pandemic deaths. I thought
I was a witness, a survivor, caught
in a maelstrom and brought forth, who knew more
of pain than some, but learned it loving others.
I need to find another metaphor.
                              ("Cancer Winter," 81)

"Cancer Winter" deals with Hacker's own experience with cancer
and medical treatment, yet this subject, as in Lorde's poems, connects
her poetic discourse to a broader political world and the mass traumas
of this century:

But this was another century
in which we made death humanly obscene:
Soweto El Salvador Kurdistan
Armenia Shatila Baghdad Hanoi
Auschwitz   Each one, unique as our lives are,
taints what's left with complicity,
makes everyone living a survivor
who will, or won't, bear witness for the dead.

I can only bear witness for my own
dead and dying, whom I've often failed:
unanswered letters, unattempted phone
calls, against these fictions. A fiction winds
her watch in sunlight, cancer ticking bone
to shards. A fiction looks
at proofs of a too-hastily finished book
that may be published before he goes blind.
                              ("Against Elegies," 14)

Above all, the Holocaust shadows the entire volume, as does the imperative of recording and bearing witness—a responsibility that can
neither be relinquished nor effectively discharged, there being no language or construction of the witness in which that global imperative
can effectively be discharged. For one thing, all is "taint[ed] with complicity";[35] for another, it is enough for the speaker to "bear witness for
[her] own dead," whom she has "often failed." Even the identities for
which she seeks to bear witness are "fictions." Yet these fictive acts of

witnessing remain compelling. Hacker's ambiguous Jewishness—
"though you are not my past, you are my past / (there are no atheists
in a pogrom)" ("August Journal," 95)—is implicated in her discussion
of identity and responsibility. She neither rejects nor embraces her likeness as a sufferer to those dead in the Holocaust, but explores it in an
increasingly politicized, retroactive drama of identification and positioning:

> It's not Auschwitz. It's not the Vel d'Hiv.
> It's not gang rape in Bosnia or
> gang rape and gutting in El Salvador.
> My self-betraying body needs to grieve
> at how hatreds metastasize. Reprieved
> (if I am), what am I living for?
>   ("Cancer Winter," 85)

The stretched rhymes "Vel d'Hiv"/"grieve"/"reprieved" connect
seemingly disparate fields of personal identification and cultural experience in the poem, in keeping with Hacker's multiple, perhaps post-
modern, self-characterization as a lesbian, mother, Jew, Yankee,
feminist, Francophile, breast cancer survivor. Yet Hacker is ethically
committed to making distinctions in all these arenas, making fastidi-
ously negative rather than sensationalizing positive connections between the situation of the breast cancer patient and the victims of
historical atrocity: "not Auschwitz," "not gang rape in Bosnia."

Hacker sets this drama of self-positioning and political identification
in the scene of writing, both metaphorically and actually. In the opening sonnet of "Cancer Winter,"

> I watched a young man at his window write
> at a plank table, one pooled halogen
> light on his book, dim shelves behind him, night
> falling fraternal on the flux between
> the odd and even numbers of the street.
>   ("Cancer Winter," 77)

The "odd and even numbers" draw attention to the fact that two genders are writing, opposite and separated by space as well as time, but

"fraternal"; the fact of writing in a sonnet sequence implies dialogue with male figures, reciprocal though not without possible tension and difficulty. "[O]dd and even" refers also to the book's other, medically referential numbers (stages of treatment, statistics about the dead), and finally, in their arrangement, to the braiding of sonnets in the sequence:

> The odd and even numbers of the street
> I live on are four thousand miles away
> from an Ohio February day
> snow-blanketed, roads iced over, with sleet
> expected later, where I'm incomplete
> as my abbreviated chest. I weigh
> less—one breast less—since the Paris-gray
> December evening when a neighbor's feet
> coming up ancient stairs, the feet I counted
> on paper were the company I craved.
> My calm right breast seethed with a grasping tumor.
> The certainty of my returns amounted
> to nothing. After terror, being brave
> became another form of gallows humor.
>   ("Cancer Winter," 85)

Hacker's dependable "returns," to Paris, or to the sonnet form, or to the last lines of earlier poems, have apparently "amounted/ to nothing," however, in comparison with the medical event that has resulted in an "abbreviated" chest, and have weighed nothing in comparison with the weight lost as a result of mastectomy. Rooted in writing, and yet not saved by it in any physical or metaphysical sense, the poet still finds in poetry a way of sustaining herself as a witness to the absent presence of the dead in an "interleaved" community of mourning.

The last sonnet of the series leaves her in that scene of writing. The pine table on which she writes is, like her, "scarred":

> Friends, you died young. These numbers do not sing
> your requiems, your elegies, our war
> cry: at last, not "Why me?" but "No more
> one-in-nine, one-in-three, rogue cells killing
> women." You're my companions, traveling

from work to home to the home I left for
work, and the plague, and the poison which might cure.
The late sunlight, the morning rain, will bring
me back to where I started, whole, alone,
with fragrant coffee into which I've poured
steamed milk, book open on the scarred pine table.
I almost forget how close to the bone
my chest's right side is. Unremarkable,
I woke up, still alive. Does that mean "cured"?
                                        ("Cancer Winter," 90)

Other ironies aside, the principal irony of this ending inheres in the increasingly well-known fact that breast cancer, unlike many other forms of cancer, is never "cured," at least insofar as other cancers may be pronounced cured after five years of remission. Nor can a "cure" readily be envisaged for a condition as overdetermined as breast cancer; indeed, Hacker's poems imply that neither the ailment nor its drastic remedies can be separated from a world of contemporary violence, medical technology, and postmodern dislocation. Yet the poems, in being written "against elegies," resist both a certain self-elegizing impulse and a premature leave-taking. Resisted as well is a culturally over-determined alienation from the sensual woman's body, including the diminished one, of which the new dimensions can "almost" but never quite be forgotten. Among other things, "I woke up alive" means not dead, not voiceless, not in the preordained place of Eurydice, not buried in elegy. That in itself constitutes a cultural politics as well as a poetics of breast cancer.

Afterword:
Why Elegies?

My general premise has been that it is important to consider modern and contemporary elegies in conjunction with older ones. At one time this view might have seemed like a virtually uncontentious premise of literary study, requiring little explicit justification. Yet the current application of labels like "mainstream" or "canonical" to older poems is often pejorative, as is categorizing them as "high-cultural." This labeling often implies a desire to separate contemporary writing from traditional forms. The disruptive, subversive, democratizing, or simply *accessible* potentialities of pop culture are now increasingly opposed, even in the academy, to high-cultural forms seen as authoritarian or elitist; conversely, high culture is increasingly seen as both remote from and inimical to any politics of emancipation or identification. Tracing generic or literary-historical continuities, especially in the context of AIDS or breast cancer crises, might thus seem like an empty literary formalism or, worse, like a perverse subjection of resistant contemporary texts to long-standing norms of denial, alienation, and oppression. In the foreshortened temporality of postmodern criticism, a reexamination of premodern elegies may even seem like an exercise in sheer irrelevance.

As I have tried to show, however, contemporary poets writing about AIDS and breast cancer do in fact maintain a generic commitment, however problematical or resistant, to high-cultural elegy: they do so as a matter of life and death, no less. These poets make a knowledge of traditional elegy one condition for reading their poems. Literary nostalgia becomes a paradoxical mode of reentry into contemporary pop culture, activist politics, and the representation of crisis. The commitment of these poets to poetry as such constitutes a renewed act of faith against the odds.

What could motivate such a commitment? Among other things, recognition that high and low culture are neither stably opposed nor immutably at odds. For contemporary elegists, "high" and "low" designate different yet not mutually exclusive registers in a common cultural discourse, which remains a source of power as well as oppression, a resource as well as a threat. These poets refuse to relinquish poetry's forms of representation, intellectual frames, or deep historical roots to the deadly politics with which they are now increasingly associated, and sometimes exclusively identified. For my argument, it is crucial that AIDS and breast cancer elegists have shown the way toward a productive engagement with a poetic genre freighted with ideology, oppression, and a tragic past. Out of that difficult engagement has emerged a more complex relation to what we call politics; indeed, elegy advances political theory in the most unexpected guises.

In her essay "Queer and Now," Eve Kosofsky Sedgwick remarks, apropos of her own diagnosis and treatment for breast cancer, that despite the fear and exhaustion of the process, she still has found intellectual sustenance in "a confrontation with the theoretical models that have helped [her] make sense of the world so far." Having breast cancer has meant "hurling my energies outward to inhabit the very farthest of the loose ends where representation, identity, gender, sexuality, and the body can't be made to line up neatly together."[1] The political payoff of this dispersal of energies, she notes, is not immediate or certain; but she believes one must persevere, given the limits to any localized activism in a generally unaltered political culture.

Sedgwick specifically refers to her engagement, both affectionate and skeptical, with her own deconstructive training. Yet her argument refers more generally to an ongoing project of rereading the texts of "high culture." If this rereading enables her, as she says, to learn and teach how to read destructive codes—codes that deny value to certain lives or importance to certain losses—it is also a rereading in quest of pleasure and hitherto unclaimed forms of enablement *in* canonical writing. Similarly, it is not only against but through the complexities of mainstream elegiac writing that I see cultural notions of representation, identity, gender, sexuality, and the body being tested and rethought.

As I said in my introduction, however, I propose no simple continuity or alignment between the poems in this book. No single literary-historical narrative or generic paradigm can encompass them all. If I am reading contemporary elegies in the light of earlier, canonical poems, I am also rereading and differentiating those earlier poems in the light of contemporary elegy. None of the poems I have discussed speak entirely for themselves; they speak in and through one another. Canonical elegies reveal a heterogeneity and resistance to oppressive normalization; their embedded countertexts not only anticipate contemporary elegy but constitute a resource on which contemporary elegists draw. Then, too, contemporary elegies provide a way of locating and reading earlier elegiac counterdiscourses. In other words, contemporary poets—and readers—who immerse themselves in earlier poems derive much more than mere technical competence or normative "cultural literacy."

The question Why elegies? has nevertheless been directly posed by readers for whom the production of effective agitprop, as Cindy Patton calls it, remains the compelling task of the crisis-ridden present.[2] The obvious reason for elegies—so many women and men have died from AIDS and breast cancer, and they need to be mourned and remembered—may seem like no reason at all, or a bad one, to activist readers. I have already suggested, however, that poetry and agitprop are not sharply distinguished or mutually exclusive in the poems I have been considering; indeed, this is one of the sacrificial separations that the poets refuse. The story of Orpheus and Eurydice and its history within elegy caution against unreflecting or aggressive separation, however strongly motivated. Another reason for elegies, then, is that these poems inevitably pose the question of separation—not just the final separation between the living and the dead, but also a wide range of contingent disconnections. Elegies pose this question and respond to it productively; and this, I am convinced, justifies both the poems themselves and their critical study.

Notes

Introduction

1. Edmund White, *The Burning Library: Writing on Art, Politics, and Sexuality, 1969–1993* (London: Picador, 1995), 138–39.

2. Sigmund Freud, "Mourning and Melancholia," in *The Standard Edition of the Complete Psychological Works of Sigmund Freud*, ed. James Strachey, 24 vols. (London: Hogarth Press, 1953–74): 14:243–58.

3. Louise Fradenburg, " 'Voice Memorial': Loss and Reparation in Chaucer's Poetry," *Exemplaria* 2 (March 1990): 184. My reading of Sacks and my thinking about the gender politics of elegy are greatly indebted to Fradenburg's important essay.

4. Peter Sacks, *The English Elegy: Studies in the Genre from Spenser to Yeats* (Baltimore: Johns Hopkins University Press, 1985), 4–5.

5. Sacks, *Elegy*, 6.

6. Walter Benjamin's *Theses on the Philosophy of History, Illuminations*, trans. Harry Zohn (New York: Schocken, 1968), includes a caveat often ignored by literary historians: "Whoever has emerged victorious participates to this day in the triumphal procession in which present rulers step over those who are prostrate. According to traditional practice, the spoils are carried along in the procession. They are called cultural treasures, and a historical materialist views them with cautious detachment. . . . there is no document of civilization that is not also a document of barbarism" (265).

7. Celeste Schenck, "Feminism and Deconstruction: Re-Constructing the Elegy," *Tulsa Studies in Women's Literature* 5 (spring 1986): 13–27.

8. Fradenburg, "Voice," 196 n. 15.

9. Juliana Schiesari, *The Gendering of Melancholia: Feminism, Psychoanalysis, and the Symbolics of Loss in Renaissance Literature* (Ithaca: Cornell University Press, 1993).

10. If not expressed by the male melancholic, the sufferings of women may nevertheless be "understood" by the (male) psychotherapist or physician, who translates women's ailments into an "intelligible" language.

11. In *The Acoustic Mirror: The Female Voice in Psychoanalysis and Cinema* (Bloomington: Indiana University Press, 1988), 1–15, Kaja Silverman argues that the focus on sexual difference as the site of loss—or to put it crudely, on the castration complex—covers for a far more profound sense of loss that would be symmetrical for both genders: the loss

of the phenomenal world associated with the entry into language. That loss both constitutes and threatens subjectivity: one may say that the subject is based on loss. This general
loss must always be repressed, however, not only because it threatens subjectivity but
also because, unlike the lack assumed in sexual difference, it produces no possible consoling superiority for the masculine subject.

12. "When Dionysus invaded Thrace, Orpheus neglected to honour him, but taught other
sacred mysteries and preached the evil of sacrificial murder to the men of Thrace, who
listened reverently" (Robert Graves, *The Greek Myths* [Baltimore: Penguin, 1955], 1:112).

13. Even Eurydice, the ultimate victim, has her dangerous side in the myth's history,
for she is a version of the snake-goddess Hecate, also known as Agriope ("savage face"),
herself a killer by snakebite (Graves, *Greek Myths*, 1:115).

14. John Milton, "Lycidas," in *Complete Poems and Major Prose*, ed. Merritt Y. Hughes
(New York: Odyssey Press, 1957), 120–25, ll. 50–61. All other citations of "Lycidas" are
from this text.

15. John Berryman makes this point in his short story "Wash Far Away," in *The Freedom of the Poet* (New York: Farrar, Straus & Giroux, 1976), 381. Noted by Mary Ann
Radzinowicz, "How John Berryman Read Milton's 'Lycidas,'" unpublished manuscript.

16. Ellen Zetzel Lambert, *Placing Sorrow* (Chapel Hill: University of North Carolina
Press, 1976), 166, remarks that *"tangles* is a suggestive term linking this image to all those
other images of dark mazes and tangled woods in Milton's poetry."

17. Percy Bysshe Shelley, "Adonais," in *Shelley's "Adonais": A Critical Edition*, ed. Anthony D. Knerr (New York: Columbia University Press, 1984), 39, ll. 316–24. Earlier, Orpheus has been somewhat more distantly evoked by the description of the "mountain
shepherds . . . their magic mantles rent" (262–63).

18. Shelley, "Adonais," 42.

19. I was alerted to Shelley's presentation of an enervated, diminished version of Keats
by James A. W. Heffernan's "Adonais: Shelley's Consumption of Keats," *Studies in Romanticism* 23 (fall 1984): 295–315.

20. Matthew Arnold, "Thyrsis," in *The Poems*, ed. Kenneth Allott (London: Longmans,
1965), ll. 81–90.

21. Harry Berger, "Orpheus, Pan, and the Poetics of Misogyny: Spenser's Critique of
Pastoral Love and Art," *English Literary History* 50 (spring 1983): 28. This article and the
piece it uses as a starting point, Thomas Cain's "Spenser and the Renaissance Orpheus,"
University of Toronto Quarterly 41 (1971): 24–47, are essential reading for the history of the
status of marriage in the Orpheus myth. See also Jonathan Goldberg's trenchant commentary on both of these discussions in *Voice Terminal Echo* (New York: Methuen, 1986),
172 n. 17. Notable as well is Goldberg's critique of Sacks in *Sodometries: Renaissance Texts,
Modern Sexualities* (Stanford: Stanford University Press, 1992), 86–94.

22. Aurelia Ghezzi, "Quis Tantus Furor," *Southern Comparative Literature* 7 (1983):
9–10.

23. Emmett Robbins, "Famous Orpheus," in *Orpheus: The Metamorphoses of a Myth*, ed.
John Warden (Toronto: University of Toronto Press, 1982), 13.

24. See, for instance, Margaret Alexiou, *The Ritual Lament in Ancient Greece* (London:
Cambridge University Press, 1974), 10.

25. G. W. Pigman III, *Grief and English Renaissance Elegy* (Cambridge: Cambridge University Press, 1985), 2.

26. Mary K. DeShazer, *Inspiring Women: Reimagining the Muse* (New York: Pergamon
Press, 1986), 7, sees the Orpheus myth as partly responsible for "the Muses' symbolic
transformation from active singers to passive inspirers." That this conversion would seem

desirable to male poets is suggested by the stories of malevolence on the part of the older, more powerful Muses. Elisabeth Bronfen, *Over Her Dead Body: Death, Femininity, and the Aesthetic* (New York: Routledge, 1992), 363, notes that the Muses' "intolerance for rivalry" is recorded in the myth of Thamyris, whose voice and memory were confiscated after he boasted of poetic skill superior to that of the Muses.

27. This way of putting it may seem to beg the question, posed by Michel Foucault in *The History of Sexuality*, vol. 1, trans. Robert Hurley (New York: Pantheon, 1978), whether "homosexuality" existed before that category was invented in the nineteenth century. While I do not suggest that "homosexuality" designates a single, transhistorical phenomenon, it still seems like a term that can be used intelligibly and nonpejoratively in this context.

28. Ovid, *Metamorphoses*, bk. 10, trans. Frank Justus Miller (Cambridge: Harvard University Press, 1946), 71.

29. R. B. Martin, *Tennyson: The Unquiet Heart* (New York: Oxford University Press, 1980), 94–95, quoted in Richard Dellamora, *Masculine Desire: The Sexual Politics of Victorian Aestheticism* (Chapel Hill: University of North Carolina Press, 1990), 28.

30. Shelley, "Adonais," ed. Knerr, 42, l. 320.

31. Wilfred Owen, "Anthem for Doomed Youth," in *Complete Poems and Fragments*, ed. Jon Stallworthy (London: Chatto and Windus, 1983), 76; Virginia Woolf, *To the Lighthouse* (New York: Harcourt, Brace, 1927), 201; Ezra Pound, "Hugh Selwyn Mauberly," in *Selected Poems of Ezra Pound* (New York: New Directions, 1957), 64.

32. Rudyard Kipling, "Epitaphs of War," in *Rudyard Kipling's Verse: Definitive Edition* (New York: Doubleday, Doran, 1940), 388.

33. The now often vilified theses of Sandra Gilbert and Susan Gubar about this socio-literary situation in "Soldier's Heart: Literary Men, Literary Women, and the Great War," in *No Man's Land: The Place of the Woman Writer in the Twentieth Century* (New Haven: Yale University Press, 1989), 2:258–323, retain significant explanatory power. According to these authors, the First World War resulted in a radical rethinking of the social structures and ideology that had produced the war and in a distaste for existing cultural, social, and familial arrangements. The thrilled reaction to the war on the part of many women who were allowed to work for the first time gave grounds for the suspicion of men in the trenches that women were pleased to have them removed. As these critics have argued as well, male authors, including poets, were angry at the infiltration of women into the literary marketplace, particularly since, as men claimed, it was often the women who issued the most jingoistic statements in favor of the war. The experience of war as sexual wounding and the pro-war writings of women inevitably reinforced men's fear that "all the world is topsy-turvy since the War began" (to quote a triumphant poem by a woman) and thus intensified the resentment with which male writers defined this war as a major turning point in the battle of the sexes.

34. Siegfried Sassoon, "Glory of Women," in *The War Poems of Siegfried Sassoon* (London: William Heinemann, 1920), 57.

35. In the chapter "Soldier Boys," in *The Great War and Modern Memory* (New York: Oxford University Press, 1975), 270–309, Paul Fussell comments extensively on homo-erotic idyll in World War I poetry.

36. Edward Thomas, "Tears," in *Poems by Edward Thomas* (New York: Henry Holt, 1917), 10–11.

37. Ivor Gurney, "To His Love," in *Collected Poems of Ivor Gurney*, ed. P. J. Kavanagh (New York: Oxford University Press, 1982), ll. 1–5.

38. Sassoon, "The Rear-Guard," in *War Poems*, 36–37.

39. Owen, "Strange Meeting," in *Complete Poems*, 148.

40. The problematic recovery of power to love and mourn, whether in the "submerged" version represented by Eliot's *The Waste Land*, composed as a mourning poem for Jean Verdenal, or in the overt versions represented by the elegies of Yeats and Auden, has been extensively discussed by critics including Sacks and Jahan Ramazani, *The Poetry of Mourning: The Modern Elegy from Hardy to Heaney* (Chicago: University of Chicago Press, 1994). The now classic "homosexual" readings of *The Waste Land* as elegy for Verdenal are John Peter, "A New Interpretation of *The Waste Land*," *Essays in Criticism* 2 (1952): 242–66, and James Miller, *T. S. Eliot's Personal Waste Land* (University Park: Pennsylvania State University Press, 1977). For an analysis of the anxiety about gender and sexuality governing not only Eliot's composition but Pound's revision of the poem, see Wayne Koestenbaum, "*The Waste Land*: T. S. Eliot's and Ezra Pound's Collaboration on Hysteria," *Twentieth Century Literature* 32 (summer 1988): 113–39.

41. Tony Harrison, *V. and Other Poems* (New York: Farrar, Straus & Giroux, 1990).

42. Gregory Woods, "Coping with Loss," in *This Is No Book: A Gay Reader* (Nottingham: Mushroom Publications, 1994), 69.

43. A partial context for Swinburnian Decadence and the proliferation of spectral female figures is supplied by Bram Dijkstra, *Idols of Perversity: Fantasies of Feminine Evil in Fin de Siècle Culture* (New York: Oxford University Press, 1986), 153, 230, 266.

44. Gilbert and Gubar, *No Man's Land*, 2:259, 264, see these changes as, in large part, the culmination of other more generalized shifts in the relations between the sexes. "Metamorphoses of sexuality and sex roles," Gilbert and Gubar argue, "together with gender transformations, [were] connected with the decline of faith in a white male-supremacist imperialism; with the rise of the New Woman; with the development of an ideology of free love; and with the emergence of lesbian literary communities."

45. See Ivy Schweitzer, "Puritan Legacies of Masculinity: John Berryman's *Homage to Mistress Bradstreet*," in *The Calvinist Roots of the Modern Era*, ed. Aliki Barnstone, Michael Manson, and Carole Singley (Hanover, N.H.: University Press of New England, 1997).

46. Simon Watney, *Policing Desire: Pornography, AIDS, and the Media* (Minneapolis: University of Minnesota Press, 1987), 9.

47. Paula Treichler, "AIDS, Homophobia, and Biomedical Discourse: An Epidemic of Signification," in *AIDS: Cultural Analysis, Cultural Activism*, ed. Douglas Crimp (Cambridge: MIT Press, 1991), 31.

48. Cindy Patton, *Inventing AIDS* (New York: Routledge, 1990), 131.

49. Jack Collins, untitled introductory essay in *City Lights Review* no. 2 (1988): 25.

50. Some important AIDS poems by women—Olga Broumas, June Jordan, Heather McHugh, Honor Moore, Carol Muske—appear in the collection *Poets for Life*, ed. Michael Klein (New York: Persea, 1992), and elsewhere. In Chapter 6 I discuss poems by Marilyn Hacker which mourn friends dead through AIDS and breast cancer. Yet because the first literary response to AIDS has come overwhelmingly from gay men, and because the gay response so purposefully engages the gender politics of elegy, I will not be writing, except in passing, about AIDS in women, IV drug users, or heterosexuals, even though this focus may seem to reinscribe AIDS as a "gay men's disease." The gay poets I am discussing have themselves worked effectively to cancel that inscription. It must be admitted, nevertheless, that the adequacy of any current discourse to AIDS as a global epidemic encompassing all sexual orientations and driven by acute poverty, ignorance, sexual exploitation, and often-willful disinformation, is questionable.

51. Eve Kosofsky Sedgwick thoughtfully retraces and questions these unproductively naturalized divisions throughout her work, most specifically in "White Glasses," 262–64,

and in "Queer and Now," 12–15, in *Tendencies* (Durham, N.C.: Duke University Press, 1993). See also her poems about her own negotiations of breast cancer and her friends' experiences of AIDS in *Fat Art, Thin Art* (Durham, N.C.: Duke University Press, 1994).

52. Joseph Cady, "Immersive and Counterimmersive Writing about AIDS: The Achievement of Paul Monette's *Love Alone*," in *Writing AIDS: Gay Literature, Language, and Analysis*, ed. Timothy F. Murphy and Suzanne Poirier (New York: Columbia University Press, 1993), 244.

53. Elaine Scarry, *The Body in Pain: The Making and Unmaking of the World* (New York: Oxford University Press, 1985), 22.

54. David Bergman, "In the Waiting Room," *Poetry* 149 (December 1986): 138.

55. Audre Lorde, *The Cancer Journals* (San Francisco: Sisters/Aunt Lute, 1980), 16.

56. Michael Lynch, *These Waves of Dying Friends* (New York: Contact II, 1989), 26, 91.

57. Lee Edelman, "The Mirror and the Tank: 'AIDS,' Subjectivity, and the Rhetoric of Activism," in *Writing AIDS*, ed. Murphy and Poirier, 22–23.

58. Edelman, "Mirror and Tank," 23.

59. Douglas Crimp, "How to Have Promiscuity in an Epidemic," in *AIDS*, ed. Crimp, 270.

60. Marilyn Hacker, "Year's End," in *Winter Numbers* (New York: Norton, 1994), 75–76.

61. See Celeste Schenck, *Mourning and Panegyric: The Poetics of Pastoral Ceremony* (University Park: Pennsylvania State University Press, 1988), 7.

1. Unwriting Orpheus: Swinburne's "Ave atque Vale" and the "New" Elegy

1. Swinburne wrote the poem on hearing a report, which proved false, that Baudelaire had died. This embarrassingly premature elegy was, however, made good by Baudelaire's death in August 1867, and Swinburne brought out the poem in January of the next year. See Donald Thomas, *Swinburne* (New York: Oxford University Press, 1979), 36–37.

2. For the best discussion of Swinburne's intense, if intensely ambivalent, interest in sexual feeling and practice unacceptable to the Victorians, especially with regard to male-male desire, see Richard Dellamora, *Masculine Desire: The Sexual Politics of Victorian Aestheticism* (Chapel Hill: University of North Carolina Press, 1990), 69–85. Dellamora does not argue that Swinburne acted on sexual feelings for men but rather that in an early phase of life, he seems "imaginatively receptive to male-male desire" (70).

3. *The Complete Works of Algernon Charles Swinburne*, ed. Sir Edmund Gosse and Thomas James Wise, Bonchurch Edition (London: William Heinemann, 1925), 3:44, ll. 12–22. All references to "Ave atque Vale" are to this edition; line numbers are cited in the text.

4. I am indebted to Terry Holt, who first pointed out this correspondence to me.

5. Emmett Robbins, "Famous Orpheus," in *Orpheus: The Metamorphoses of a Myth*, ed. John Warden (Toronto: University of Toronto Press, 1982), 14.

6. See the discussion of Swinburne's feelings about Sappho in Dellamora, *Masculine Desire*, 75. On the Ovidian "appropriation" of Sappho as deserted lover of Phaon, see Elizabeth D. Harvey, "Ventriloquizing Sappho: Ovid, Donne, and the Erotics of the Feminine Voice," *Criticism* 31 (spring 1989): 115–38.

7. Thaïs Morgan, "Violence, Creativity, and the Feminine: Poetics and Gender Politics in Swinburne and Hopkins," in *Gender and Discourse in Victorian Literature and Art*, ed. Antony H. Harrison and Beverly Taylor (De Kalb: Northern Illinois University Press, 1992), 96.

8. Jahan Ramazani, *Yeats and the Poetry of Death: Elegy, Self-Elegy, and the Sublime* (New Haven: Yale University Press, 1990), 40. Celeste Schenck, *Mourning and Panegyric: The Poetics of Pastoral Ceremony* (University Park: Pennsylvania State University Press, 1988), 3, argues that crossings of elegy and epithalamium center on the figure of Orpheus as both bridegroom and mourner because his story reflects the inextricable twinings of loss and gain: "Either poems successfully evolve consolation by means of denial or loss or creation of ample compensation for it—symbolically represented by the singing head spilling forth its spell-binding notes even after decapitation—or else they articulate the impossibility of filling the void by means of a compensatory vision—orphically signalled by the bridegroom's failing voice decrying the loss of the absent, dead, repressed Eurydice."

9. Thomas Hardy, "Your Last Drive," in *Poems of 1912–13*, vol. 2 of *The Complete Poetical Works of Thomas Hardy*, ed. Samuel Hynes (Oxford: Clarendon, 1982), 49, ll. 27–28.

10. Generally speaking—and in Sacks's reading of elegy—elegiac scenarios of mortality are strongly connected to ones of castration. It is the paradoxically privileged masculine relation to castration that becomes the enabling condition of poetic rebirth, "chastened" song, and posthumous vitality. Women are excluded from this endless dynamic of regeneration and empowerment; they are too "lacking" from the start, and cannot participate in the empowering dynamic of oedipal succession. They are therefore excluded and threatening, yet also marginally seductive as figures of death, but then also of stasis as ecstasy, relief, arrested *telos*.

11. Thomas, *Swinburne*, 159.

12. Practically all of Swinburne's critics have observed, however, that the depiction of liberty and political struggle in his work retains a distanced abstraction that contrasts strongly with his poetry of a more "subjective" landscape. Antony Harrison has argued recently that Swinburne (despite his frequent assertions to the contrary), like Wordsworth, ultimately saw art as the only means of escape, in the social and political sphere, from historical contingency. See Antony Harrison, *Victorian Poets and Romantic Poems: Intertextuality and Ideology* (Charlottesville: University Press of Virginia, 1990), 200.

13. Algernon Charles Swinburne, *Poems and Ballads*, vol. 1 of *The Poems of Algernon Charles Swinburne* (New York: Harper and Bros., 1904), ix.

14. See, for example, Edmund Gosse, *The Life of Algernon Charles Swinburne* (London: Macmillan, 1917).

15. See Leslie Brisman, "Swinburne's Semiotics," *Georgia Review* 31 (fall 1977): 578–79.

16. He refers dubiously to Alcibiades' report of his chaste night with Socrates in that work, in a letter dated 7 February 1878 to Theodore Watts (later Watts-Dunton), in Cecil Y. Lang, ed., *The Swinburne Letters* (New Haven: Yale University Press, 1959), 4:42.

17. Plato, *The Symposium*, 179d, in Plato, *Collected Dialogues*, ed. Edith Hamilton and Huntington Cairns (Princeton: Princeton University Press, 1961).

18. Lang, *Swinburne Letters*, 1:164.

19. Swinburne, *Poems and Ballads*, 155–62.

20. See Douglas Bush, *Mythology and the Romantic Tradition in English Poetry* (New York: Norton, 1961), 329.

21. Swinburne, *Poems and Ballads*, 156.

22. Swinburne, *Poems and Ballads*, 158.

23. Swinburne, *Complete Works*, ed. Gosse and Wise, 2:271.

24. The poem's form reveals its self-consciousness about creating new narrative. In Romantic fashion, Swinburne mingles Italian and English sonnet conventions, creating a

small second turn in the last couplet: the couplet's opening ("Turn yet") makes it a pun on its own form.

25. "Eurydice" is printed with a companion piece to another sonnet, " 'Non Dolet,' " in which the republicans of Italy are represented by a Lucretia-like figure of heroic suicide for the honor of her husband (that is, the Italian people):

> It does not hurt.
> . . . .
>   not that which had been done
> Could hurt the sweet sense of the Roman wife,
> But that which was to do yet ere the strife
>   Could end for each for ever, and the sun.
>   (*Complete Works*, 2:270, ll. 1–6)

This sonnet, too, creates in small space a charged scene of female heroism, a self-sacrificing but also vengeful female figure standing for the republic, defeating its enemies, and yet to be outlived by it. In their new orbits around Hugo, both Italy, addressed as "Italia," and Eurydice alter gender proprieties and call into question the agency of the male lover-hero.

26. Lang, *Swinburne Letters*, 1:164.

27. This familial positioning of Baudelaire may partly explain his choice of title, after Catullus's elegy for *his* brother. Catullus, "Ave atque Vale," in *The Poems of Catullus*, trans. Peter Whigham (New York: Penguin Books, 1966), 213.

28. Thäis Morgan, "Male Lesbian Bodies: The Construction of Alternative Masculinities in Courbet, Baudelaire, and Swinburne," *Genders* 15 (winter 1992): 37–53, cautions usefully against reading this different kind of discourse, however, as "subversive" or feminist.

29. Jacques Derrida, *Disseminations*, trans. Barbara Johnson (Chicago: University of Chicago Press, 1981), 65; quoted in Jonathan Goldberg, *Voice Terminal Echo: Postmodernism and English Renaissance Texts* (New York: Methuen, 1986), 61.

30. By a conflating slippage, Swinburne may identify his own and Baudelaire's poetry, both violently attacked for their eroticism and sometimes actually suppressed, with the poetry of Sappho, which was censored in its Victorian editions and is available only in fragments at best. For a good discussion of the history of these censorships, see Richard Sieburth, "Poetry and Obscenity: Baudelaire and Swinburne," *Proceedings of the 10th Congress of the International Comparative Literature Association* (New York, 1982), 464–71.

31. See Peter Sacks, *The English Elegy: Studies in the Genre from Spenser to Yeats* (Baltimore: Johns Hopkins University Press, 1985), 210, for his discussion of this echo.

32. Jerome J. McGann, *Swinburne: An Experiment in Criticism* (Chicago: University of Chicago Press, 1972), 292.

33. "Ave atque Vale" is most obviously in dialogue with "Lycidas," but it takes on the entire tradition. Swinburne knew his literary forebears thoroughly—Greek and Latin as well as English and French—and he shows that the conventions of elegy (presided over, in the tenth stanza, by the "Muse funereal") are still his raw materials, to be discriminated among at will. His single most important revision is that he admits no consolation in "Ave atque Vale"; this refusal of redemption, apotheosis, or compensation is Swinburne's link to modernism in poetry and elegy.

34. Sacks, *Elegy*, 210.

35. Sacks, *Elegy*, 116, does, however, offer a persuasive reading of the formal under-

mining of "Lycidas" 's closure by its own "frame of fictionality," thus alerting us to the dangers (not always avoided by Sacks himself) of taking closure in "Lycidas" or any other elegy too literally or referentially.

36. Cecil Y. Lang, ed., *New Writings by Swinburne* (Syracuse: Syracuse University Press, 1964), 34–35.

37. McGann, *Swinburne*, 164.

38. Charles Baudelaire, "La servante au grand coeur," in *The Flowers of Evil and Paris Spleen*, trans. William H. Crosby (Brockport, N.Y.: BOA Editions, 1991), 190–91.

39. In an influential reading of "Laus Veneris," Jerome J. McGann, *Swinburne*, 292, notes the near identity of Venus and Proserpine, arguing that

> the Proserpine/Venus of "Ave Atque Vale" . . . becomes in the elegy a positive source of power and sympathy, an ideal figure to be solicited as a source not only of sleep, rest and death, but also of eternal life, power, and light. The difference between the fallen Venuses of "Laus Veneris" and "Ave atque Vale" is simply this: in the former poem she is not associated with Proserpine whereas in the latter she is. Tannhäuser cannot die, being an unnatural, that is a Christian, believer, but Baudelaire, the believer in the Proserpine/Venus, can and does. Tannhäuser is set off from the actions and continuities of natural cycle; Baudelaire is not.

While McGann is right to acknowledge Baudelaire's affinity with Proserpine, he seems to me to misinterpret cycles of nature in "Ave atque Vale." Baudelaire does represent here, like the hero of classical pastoral elegy, a dying spirit of nature. The trouble is that he will not be brought back, preferring, in a sense, to remain underground: nature in Swinburne's elegy is no longer cyclic. See also Bram Dijkstra, *Idols of Perversity: Fantasies of Feminine Evil in Fin de Siècle Culture* (New York: Oxford University Press, 1986), 230.

40. Northrop Frye, "Lycidas," in *Twentieth-Century Literary Criticism* (New York: Longman, 1977), 433.

2. *"Woman Much Missed": Writing Eurydice in Hardy's* Poems of 1912–13

1. Precedents do exist for such mourning, as, for example, in Milton's "Methought I saw my late espoused saint." Before Hardy, however, the death of a wife had not served as a major elegiac topos like that of the dead male friend, or as a motive for extensive revision of elegiac conventions.

2. William E. Buckler, *The Victorian Imagination: Essays in Aesthetic Exploration* (New York: New York University Press, 1980), speaks of the Orpheus and Eurydice story as a "mythic subtext" to Hardy's elegies. Cited in Peter Sacks, *The English Elegy: Studies in the Genre from Spenser to Yeats* (Baltimore: Johns Hopkins University Press, 1985), 356 n. 7.

3. Both Sacks and Ramazani treat this sequence at length, in Sacks, *Elegy*, 234–69; Jahan Ramazani, *The Poetry of Mourning: The Modern Elegy from Hardy to Heaney* (Chicago: University of Chicago Press, 1994), 47–61. Both concentrate on the sequence's revisions of the elegiac and psychological work of mourning; neither is primarily concerned with the workings of gender.

4. Celeste Schenck, "Feminism and Deconstruction: Re-Constructing the Elegy," *Tulsa Studies in Women's Literature* 5 (spring 1986): 13.

5. Pope's "Elegy on the Memory of an Unfortunate Lady" makes an interesting exception: the lady is never named, however, and Pope keeps the status of the poem—

fictional? occasional?—in doubt. Spenser's "November" and Donne's "Anniversaries" are exceptions, too, mostly by virtue of the transitory change in hierarchical relation created by Elizabeth I's queenship: they try to contain the cultural anomalies of the female ruler in the dominant elegiac forms, but her disruptive powers and transcendent self-fashioning manifest themselves insistently.

6. These scenarios are theoretically more possible in the second half of the twentieth century, when women have access to education. Elegies by men for women still tend to be hierarchical, as in Theodore Roethke's "Elegy for Jane: My Student, Thrown by a Horse." A moving exception is Douglas Dunn's *Elegies* (London: Faber and Faber, 1985), poems written for his artist wife.

7. In making his muse a ghost, Hardy is drawing on a contemporary resurgence of interest in the supernatural, and particularly in the ghost story. In broad terms, this resurgence has been explained by Julia Briggs, *Night Visitors: The Rise and Fall of the English Ghost Story* (London: Faber and Faber, 1977), 16–17, as an effect of historical transition between waning religious belief and nascent scientific materialism, a diminished echo, so to speak, of the great crises of faith registered by such Victorian poets as Tennyson and Swinburne: "If, as [Freud] implies, the form [of the ghost story] depends upon the existence of a relationship between an outmoded, but not entirely abandoned belief and an enlightened scepticism, such tension was notably present in the last century, when the material and spiritual conceptions of life were locked in a continuous conflict which no intellectual could entirely avoid."

Every kind of ghost appears in Hardy's poems, from the talkative and reproachful dead soldier of "A Christmas Ghost Story" to the flitting memory-vision of "After a Journey." The very proliferation and variability of these ghosts is literary. As Hardy himself notes, these ghosts trace a line of literary tradition and their appeal stretches from high to low culture: in a letter to the *Daily Chronicle* titled "A Christmas Ghost Story," Hardy reviews the nature of warrior ghosts from Homer and Virgil through Dante and Shakespeare (Harold Orel, ed., *Thomas Hardy's Personal Writings: Prefaces, Literary Opinions, Reminiscences* [London: Macmillan, 1967], 202).

8. Hardy himself wrote a number of ghost stories, mainly, he asseverated, as a way of recording and affirming folk traditions, yet often distancing himself from these traditions with titles like "A Superstitious Man's Story." About the ghosts who inhabit every volume of his poetry, he writes, "Half my time—particularly when writing verse—I 'believe' (in the modern sense of the word) . . . in spectres, mysterious voices, intuitions, omens, dreams, haunted places, etc., etc. But I do not believe in them in the old sense of the word any more for that" (Florence Emily Hardy, *The Life of Thomas Hardy: 1840–1928* [London: Macmillan, 1962], 370). These qualifications, so typical of Hardy's writings about himself, suggest an anxiety about how he will be perceived; but they also point to a genuine concern with the troubling yet tenuous persistence of the supernatural. This is the Hardy who urges his correspondents to read Darwin and Huxley in order that they may assure themselves that there is no God, and who rejects not only traditional religion but also any belief in an afterlife, yet it is also the Hardy who tells an interviewer that he would give ten years of his life in order to see an "authentic, indubitable, spectre," and who describes himself as, though not a churchgoer, "churchy." See William Archer, *Real Conversations, Recorded by William Archer* (London: Heinemann, 1904), 37; F. E. Hardy, *Life*, 376.

9. The specific literariness and metapoetic aspiration of Hardy's elegiac project presumably contributed to its exemplariness for other poets. Ghosts strongly instantiate such poetic figures as prosopopeia and apostrophe (that is, speech by or to an absent, dead,

or imaginary figure, impossible speech). Ghosts, like these rhetorical figures, are bridges to "absence" and nonbeing, and the strategic value of a bridge, as well as its danger, is that it permits crossings in both directions. Paul De Man notes that through prosopopeia "one moves, without compromise, from life or death to life and death," yet he notes that "the latent threat that inhabits *prosopopeia*, namely that by making the death [sic] speak, that the living are struck dumb, frozen in their own death" (Paul De Man, "Autobiography as De-Facement," in *The Rhetoric of Romanticism* (New York: Columbia University Press, 1984), 74, 78). The problems of voice that so mark Hardy's sequence both reveal and defend against anxiety: fading in and out of ventriloquy, Hardy manipulates rapid alternations of voice with deft evasiveness.

10. Isobel Grundy, "Hardy's Harshness," in *Thomas Hardy*, ed. Patricia Clements and Juliet Grindle (London: Vision Press, 1980), 5–8.

11. Donald Davie, "Hardy's Virgilian Purples," in *The Poet in the Imaginary Museum* (New York: Persea Books, 1977), 224; Margaret Alexiou, *The Ritual Lament in Ancient Greece* (London: Cambridge University Press, 1974), 10.

12. Thomas Hardy, "The Singer Asleep," in *The Complete Poems* (New York: Macmillan, 1976), 324. All further references are to this edition, and page numbers will the cited in the text.

13. Ray Evans claims that, like Swinburne, Hardy is "concerned with the singing qualities of his poems": in the Swinburne elegy, Hardy refers to Sappho as "the music-mother / Of all the tribes that feel in melodies" (Ray Evans, "The Setting of Hardy's Elegy on Swinburne in *Satires of Circumstance*," *Thomas Hardy Society Review* 1, no. 7 [1981]: 222).

14. Their shared antagonistic stance toward the sexual status quo was a matter of pride and friendship for the two poets: "[Swinburne] spoke with amusement of a paragraph he had seen . . . 'Swinburne planteth, Hardy watereth, and Satan giveth the increase.' . . . We laughed and condoled with each other on having been the two most abused of living writers, he for *Poems and Ballads*, I for *Jude the Obscure*." Quoted in J. O. Bailey, *The Poetry of Thomas Hardy* (Chapel Hill: University of North Carolina Press, 1970), 283.

15. That this praise contains a submerged set of power relations seems to have struck Katherine Mansfield, who wrote in a letter that she and J. Middleton Murry had read "A Singer Asleep," "which J. adored. I, being an inferior being, was a little troubled by the picture of Sappho and Algernon meeting *en plein mer* (if one can say such a thing) and he begging her to tell him where her manuscript was. It seemed such a watery *rendez-vous*." Quoted in Bailey, *Poetry of Hardy*, 282.

16. This conditional quality is also Hardy's concession to Swinburne's different belief system, which would disallow any such ghostly meeting: Hardy depicts it, but within a distancing frame of conditionality.

17. Jon Stallworthy ("Read by Moonlight," in *Thomas Hardy*, ed. Clements and Grindle) speaks of Hardy's "moon's-eye view, his wraith's perspectives, [which leave] him free to play his leading role in his own poems: here [in "Convergence of the Twain"], the Shape of Ice destined to 'mate' with the hot-hearted ship" (178); in the same poem, the "moon-eyed fishes . . . embody the narrator's detached imagination" (177). Throughout, the moon's-eye view represents Hardy's wish to "impose his own frigidity and sterility on the loves of others" (182).

18. Ramazani, *Poetry of Mourning*, 33, refers to the encounter between ship and iceberg in the poem as a "marriage" and notes that the term "wedding" is thinly masked by the poem's "welding."

19. The poem reaches, too, to a complicated mystical and personal past in its central

prop: the old stone of this poem was dug from Hardy's lawn at Max Gate and he believed it to be a Druid altar. When one visitor photographed him with the stone in 1898, he asked, "with a smile," "Do you believe in ghosts? If you do, you ought to see such manifestations here, on a moonlit night" (Clive Holland, "My Walks and Talks in Wessex with Thomas Hardy," *John O' London's Weekly*, 30 March 1951). It may be, too, that in evoking a Druid stone in his elegy he was considering "Lycidas" and the magic power of the poet-priests buried in that poem. But if a note from one of Florence Hardy's friends is true, the mention of the stone is as much an exorcism as a conjuring: "Mrs. Hardy, the second, walking round the garden with me, the first time I stayed at Max Gate (1933) on coming to the erected stone, remarked: 'Hardy found his first wife burning all his love-letters to her behind that stone, one day' " (Irene Cooper Willis, quoted in Bailey, *Poetry of Hardy*, 412–13).

20. William E. Buckley, *The Poetry of Thomas Hardy: A Study in Art and Ideas* (New York: New York University Press, 1983), 155–56, 196.

21. As Donald Davie has noted, Hardy wrote these poems, which recall his courtship of Emma, at the time he was preparing to marry his second wife, Florence, who had lived with the Hardys as secretary to the poet and companion to the wife. Aligning Hardy's real-life situation with that in the *Aeneid*, Davie writes: "If we recall that Hardy in 1913 was presumably already attached to Florence Emily Dugdale, whom he was to take as his second wife in the next year, the 'complex relation' would work out: Hardy equals Dido; Emma equals Sychaeus: Florence Emily equals Aeneas. (We have already seen the sexes thus switched when Elfride in *A Pair of Blue Eyes* was said to be 'like Aeneas at Carthage')" (Davie, "Hardy's Virgilian Purples," 224).

The issue of sexual triangulation had troubled the marriage almost from its beginnings, and Emma in 1898 wrote that she felt "crucified" over Hardy's poems to other women. Hardy spoke of the *Poems of 1912–13* as "an expiation," and despite his protestations to Florence Henniker, he had, as Robert Gittings's biography has shown, much in the way of neglect and emotional if not physical infidelity to expiate. Gittings also notes that Hardy reworked older love poems, some of them to Emma, to address them to Florence, and that these appeared as *More Love Lyrics* (Robert Gittings, *Thomas Hardy's Later Years* [London: Heinemann, 1978], 133).

22. Sacks, *Elegy*. Sacks's emphasis, however, is on the psychological "work" of substitution and displacement that the hero, or any mourner, must undertake; he does not discuss gender specifically in this passage.

23. Robert Gittings and Jo Manton, *The Second Mrs. Hardy* (London: Heinemann, 1979), 71.

24. Gittings and Manton, *Mrs. Hardy*, 71. The physical landscape of cemeteries fascinated him in a literary way. His secretary reported having said of Stinsford churchyard, "It's a Gray's Elegy sort of place, isn't it?" To which Hardy replied, "It *is* Stoke Poges" (May O'Rourke, *Thomas Hardy: His Secretary Remembers*, Monographs on the Life, Times, and Works of Thomas Hardy, no. 8 [Benjamin, Dorset, England: Toucan, 1965], 8).

25. Michael Millgate, *Thomas Hardy: A Biography* (New York: Random House, 1982), 487.

26. Millgate, *Thomas Hardy*, 487.

27. Jean R. Brooks, *Thomas Hardy: The Poetic Structure* (Ithaca: Cornell University Press, 1971), 82–83.

28. See S. C. Neuman's " 'Emotion Put into Measure': Meaning in Hardy's Poetry," in *Thomas Hardy*, ed. Clements and Grindle, 33ff.

29. *Hamlet*, in *The Riverside Shakespeare*, ed. G. Blakemore Evans (Boston: Houghton Mifflin, 1974), 1.5.69–71.

30. U. C. Knoepflmacher, "Hardy Ruins: Female Spaces and Male Designs," *PMLA* 105 (October 1990): 1055–68.

31. Knoepflmacher, "Hardy Ruins," 1067.

3. The Fading of Orpheus: Women's Elegies

1. Germaine Greer, Introduction to *Kissing the Rod: An Anthology of Seventeenth Century Verse*, ed. Germaine Geer, Susan Hastings, Jeslyn Medoff, and Melinda Sansome (New York: Farrar, Straus & Giroux, 1988), 9–12.

2. Jahan Ramazani's phrase, in *The Poetry of Mourning: The Modern Elegy from Hardy to Heaney* (Chicago: University of Chicago Press, 1994), 296. See his illuminating discussion of this history, 295–97.

3. Celeste Schenck, "Feminism and Deconstruction: Re-Constructing the Elegy," *Tulsa Studies in Women's Literature* 5 (spring 1986): 13–27.

4. Ramazani, *Poetry of Mourning*, 22.

5. Women elegists, then, write from an awareness and rejection of the Orphean politics underlying traditional elegy. Yet this awareness is not always necessarily expressed in overtly political ways, or in ways continuous with an activist politics. For that reason, the concluding chapters of this book examine shifts in elegiac writing in inescapably and unquestionably politicized AIDS and breast cancer elegies.

6. I have been directed to many of these poems by references throughout Alicia Ostriker, *Stealing the Language* (Boston: Beacon Press, 1986), and Mary K. DeShazer, *Inspiring Women: Reimagining the Muse* (New York: Pergamon, 1986). Louise Bogan imagines herself as not Eurydice but one of the raging maenads: these figures offer the female poet what DeShazer, 64–65, calls a "demonic alternate self," whose reach to poetry neither requires the silencing of women nor accepts that silencing for herself.

7. H.D., *Collected Poems, 1912–44*, ed. Louis I. Martz (New York: New Directions, 1983), 51–55. Numbers following in the text refer to sections of the poem.

8. Rachel Blau Duplessis, *Wells* (New York: Montemora Foundation, 1980), sec. 6. This insight, that Duplessis is drawing upon the archaic representation of Eurydice in the myth, is DeShazer's, *Inspiring Women*, 65.

9. Duplessis, *Wells*, sec. 4.

10. Duplessis, *Wells*, sec. 11.

11. Muriel Rukeyser, *Collected Poems* (New York: McGraw Hill, 1978), 435. See also Ostriker, *Stealing the Language*, 212, 237.

12. Adrienne Rich, *The Fact of a Doorframe: Poems, Selected and New, 1950–84* (New York: Norton, 1984), 119–20.

13. Edna St. Vincent Millay, "Memorial to D.C.," *Collected Poems* (New York: Harper and Row, 1956), 118–23. Numbers following in the text are page numbers.

14. Millay, "Dirge without Music," in *Collected Poems*, 240.

15. This appearance of accession is paradoxically heightened by Millay's recourse to the conventional elegiac claim of unworthiness. Yet the form this takes, the "littling" of elegy, continues to recall the woman poet's miniaturized relationship to the genre. The epigraph's phrase "I write you little elegies" is picked up by Elinor Wylie in "Little Elegy," in her last volume of poetry, *Angels and Earthly Creatures* (New York: Alfred A. Knopf, 1929), 63. In turn, Millay's series for Wylie after her death, "To Elinor Wylie," in *Collected Poems*, 368–75, takes up this implicit conversation with Wylie about elegiac value.

16. In her poems for Elinor Wylie, too, the eroticized body of the beloved dead both

remains as a precious and irredeemably lost memory for the poet and is placed in relation to the dead woman's poetic legacy to the living poet.

17. Anne Sexton, *The Complete Poems* (Boston: Houghton Mifflin, 1981), 49.

18. Schenck, "Feminism," 18.

19. See Diane Middlebrook, *Anne Sexton: A Biography* (Boston: Houghton Mifflin, 1991), 116–17.

20. The echo in "iron gates" of Marvell's already echoing "To His Coy Mistress" may maintain the perverse association produced in Marvell's poem between the erotic and the mortal, elegy and epithalamium, also recalling the ruthlessly voiced poetic persona who speaks "seductively" of the approach of death and the decay of the body.

21. Elizabeth Bishop, *The Complete Poems: 1927–1979* (New York: Farrar, Straus & Giroux, 1994), 188–89.

22. See Ramazani, *Poetry of Mourning*, 241–42.

23. That poem is also—and much more violently—critical of existing gender arrangements: Bishop, "Brazil, January 1, 1502," in *Complete Poems*, 91.

24. Ruth Stone, *Cheap* (New York: Harcourt Brace Jovanovich, 1972), 15. Page numbers are cited in the text.

25. Ruth Stone, "Habit," in *Second Hand Coat* (Boston: David R. Godine, 1987), 25.

26. Stone, *Cheap*, 14.

4. Avatars of Eurydice: John Berryman's Dream Songs

1. Saul Bellow, introduction to *Recovery/Delusions, etc.*, by John Berryman (New York: Delta, 1973), x.

2. Or no talk. In 1961, Berryman wrote to Bellow when he was planning to marry for the third time: "She is beautiful as well but the best thing about her is Japanese submissiveness, silence, & attention." Quoted in Marjorie Perloff, "*Poètes Maudits* of the Genteel Tradition: Lowell and Berryman," in *Robert Lowell: Essays on the Poetry*, ed. Steven Gould Axelrod and Helen Deese (Cambridge: Cambridge University Press, 1986), 109.

3. Even in the most recent volume of criticism, this view tends to hold: see Christopher Benfey, "The Woman in the Mirror: John Berryman and Randall Jarrell," and Joseph Mancini, Jr., "John Berryman's Couvade Consciousness: An Approach to His Aesthetics," in *Recovering Berryman*, ed. Richard J. Kelly and Alan K. Lathrop (Ann Arbor: University of Michigan Press, 1993): 153–68; 169–78.

4. See Ivy Schweitzer, "Puritan Legacies of Masculinity: John Berryman's *Homage to Mistress Bradstreet*," in *The Calvinist Roots of the Modern Era*, ed. Aliki Barnstone, Michael Manson, and Carole Singley (Hanover, N.H.: University Press of New England, 1997); Barbara Hardy, "Re-reading Berryman: Power and Solicitation," *Journal of the English Association* 40, no. 166 (1991): 37, succinctly notes the tendency of most of Berryman's commentators to participate uncritically in his "self-sympathy."

5. Something similar applies to Berryman's representation of Henry as subaltern male interlocutor in *The Dream Songs*. A black, or rather blackface, persona derived from nineteenth-century minstrel shows, who calls Henry "Mr. Bones," he is the feet-on-the-ground comforter to a metaphysically anguished Henry:

> The high ones die, die. They die. You look up and who's there?
> —Easy, easy, Mr. Bones. I is on your side.
> I smell your grief.
> —I sent my grief away. I cannot care

forever. With them all again & again I died
and cried, and I have to live.

—Now there *you* exaggerate, Sah. We hafta *die.*
That is our 'pointed task. Love & die.
—Yes; that makes sense.
But what makes sense between, then? What if I
roiling & babbling & braining, brood on why and
just sat on the fence?

(DS 36)

This praise of the commonsensical folk wisdom of African Americans is obviously con-
descending—no "braining" for them—while the put-downs of Henry by the blackface
voice really show forth as praise. More germane here is the poem's exclusion of the black
interlocutor from any elegiac engagement; commonsense and stoic endurance ("We hafta
die") are set up in opposition to poetic gift and melancholy glamor. In keeping with
praise of Berryman's sympathy with the feminine, it has been argued that through blackface Berryman signals his identification with oppressed peoples in general and African
Americans in particular; that Berryman's social conscience, suffered as personal anguish,
finds expression in blackface dialogue. See, for example, Mary Lynn Broe, "White Man
in the Woodpile: John Berryman's Burnt Cork Poetic," *American Poetry* 1 (winter 1984):
22–33. One bracing exception, however, is the discussion by Sally Gall and M. L. Rosen-
thal in *The Modern Poetic Sequence: The Genius of Modern Poetry* (New York: Oxford
University Press, 1983), 416–22. In "Tongue-Tied in Black and White," an elegy for Berryman, the African-American poet Michael Harper charges Berryman with the use of a
technique "dangerous" to African Americans but "needful" to him as a white man
steeped in but refusing to acknowledge his own racism (Harper, *Images of Kin: New and
Selected Poems* [Urbana: University of Illinois Press, 1977], 10).

6. John Berryman, *Collected Poems, 1937–1971,* ed. Charles Thornbury (New York:
Farrar, Straus & Giroux, 1989), 129, Sonnet 117. Hereafter cited in the text as *CP* followed
by a page number.

7. John Berryman, *The Dream Songs* (New York: Farrar, Straus & Giroux, 1969), 87.
All references to this collection are given as "DS" followed by the Song number rather
than the page.

8. John Berryman, *The Freedom of the Poet* (New York: Farrar, Straus & Giroux, 1976),
367–86.

9. Berryman sees Jews as a special case. In an autobiographical story called "The
Imaginary Jew" (*Freedom of the Poet,* 359–66), he identifies with Jews as possessing arcane,
ancient knowledge gleaned from suffering, and capable, unlike African Americans in his
work, of full consciousness and intellectual endeavor. At the same time Jews are unthrea-
tening, too neurotic and "harmed" by the past—more debilitatingly so than he claims
for himself—to usurp the place he wants. Berryman quotes Delmore Schwartz as saying
"I am the Brooklyn poet Delmore Schwartz / Harms & the child I sing" (DS 149).

10. For a nuanced reading of motherhood envy and poesis in the context of American
Puritanism, see Schweitzer, "Puritan Legacies."

11. Gary Q. Arpin, *The Poetry of John Berryman* (Port Washington, N.Y.: Kennikat,
1978), 74.

12. Peter Sacks, *The English Elegy: Studies in the Genre from Spenser to Yeats* (Baltimore:
Johns Hopkins University Press, 1985), 326.

13. For instance, in "Yes, yes, I offered him a cigarette," from "Eight Previously Unpublished Poems," special Berryman issue of *Gettysburg Review* 4 (autumn 1991), 561.

14. Yeats, "Under Ben Bulben," in *The Collected Poems of William Butler Yeats*, ed. Richard J. Finneran (New York: Macmillan, 1989), 325.

15. Yeats, "All Souls' Night," in *Collected Poems*, 227.

16. "Savage god" is also, of course, the title of the well-known book by A. Alvarez, in which Sylvia Plath features centrally (*The Savage God: A Study in Suicide* [New York: Random House, 1972]).

17. It appears also in Song 92, in which Berryman claimed to be rewriting Plath's "Tulips," also set in the hospital and describing tulips as unwelcome messengers from the world of the living (Jeffrey Meyers, *Manic Power: Robert Lowell and His Circle* [New York: Arbor House, 1987], 140).

18. Sylvia Plath, "Daddy," in *Collected Poems* (New York: Harper and Row, 1981), 222.

19. Plath, "Daddy," 224.

20. Plath, "Lady Lazarus," in *Collected Poems*, 245.

21. Jahan Ramazani, *The Poetry of Mourning: The Modern Elegy from Hardy to Heaney* (Chicago: University of Chicago Press, 1994), 293.

22. Plath, *Collected Poems*, 117.

23. Elizabeth Cullingford, "A Father's Prayer, A Daughter's Anger: W. B. Yeats and Sylvia Plath," in *Daughters and Fathers*, ed. Lynda E. Boose and Betty S. Flowers (Baltimore: Johns Hopkins University Press, 1989), 278–97.

24. Quoted in John Berryman, "The Ritual of W. B. Yeats," in *Freedom of the Poet*, 249.

25. Richard J. Kelly, ed., *We Dream of Honour* (New York: Norton, 1988), 359. This is the only prose comment by Berryman on Plath that I have been able to find. He does not mention Plath again in this or any other collected letter, but this one ends with "My mail is the maddest thing you ever Saw."

5. *Beyond Mourning and Melancholia: AIDS Elegies*

1. Thom Gunn, "Lament," *The Man with Night Sweats* (New York: Farrar, Straus & Giroux, 1992), 64.

2. Paul Monette, *Love Alone: Eighteen Elegies for Rog* (New York: St. Martin's Press, 1988), xi.

3. Monette, "The Very Same," in *Love Alone*, 20.

4. James Merrill, *The Inner Room: Poems by James Merrill* (New York: Alfred A. Knopf, 1988), 94.

5. Gunn, "Courtesies of the Interregnum," in *Night Sweats*, 73.

6. Celeste Schenck, *Mourning and Panegyric: The Poetics of Pastoral Ceremony* (University Park: Pennsylvania State University Press, 1988), 7.

7. The poem is written in the stanzas of Thomas Gray's "Elegy Written in a Country Churchyard." Its setting in a graveyard at dusk, its consideration of working class lives and possibilities, and even the heaving earth recall Gray's poem, as do, more mutedly, its ambivalently homoerotic musings on an unknown young man. (The earth is heaving in "v.," however, because mining has hollowed out the ground below, not because it is disturbed by wild tree roots.)

8. Tony Harrison, "v.," in *V. and Other Poems* (New York: Farrar, Straus & Giroux, 1990), 10. Numbers following in the text are page numbers.

9. Schenck, *Mourning and Panegyric*.

10. It simultaneously screens a passionate longing for the dead father. Although the elegy ostensibly mourns both parents, the father is the center of anguish, and the mother's death is memorialized mainly as the father's loss.

11. A sense of political solidarity is by no means universal in gay and feminist thinking. Conflict over funding between AIDS and breast cancer activitists exposes tensions within both groups, often internalized from a larger oppressive structure. For what is still one of the best overviews of tensions in the academic community, see Craig Owens, "Outlaws: Gay Men in Feminism," in *Men in Feminism*, ed. Alice Jardine and Paul Smith (New York: Methuen, 1987): 219–32. See also David Van Leer, "The Beast of the Closet: Homosexuality and the Pathology of Manhood," *Critical Inquiry* 15 (spring 1989): 587–605, attacking Eve Kosofsky Sedgwick for "misappropriating" the terms of male gayness, and her reply, "Tide and Trust" (with a rejoinder by David Van Leer), *Critical Inquiry* 15 (summer 1989): 745–63.

12. Essex Hemphill, *Ceremonies* (New York: Plume, 1992), 170–71.

13. Hemphill, *Ceremonies*, 172.

14. Monette, *Love Alone*, 62.

15. Mark Doty, *My Alexandria* (Champaign: University of Illinois Press, 1993), 68.

16. Doty, *My Alexandria*, 65.

17. Doty, *My Alexandria*, 21.

18. Doty, "Atlantis," in *Atlantis* (New York: Harper Perennial, 1995), 59–60.

19. Gunn, "Her Pet," in *Night Sweats*, 71–72.

20. James Miller, "Dante on Fire Island: Reinventing Heaven in the AIDS Elegy," in *Writing AIDS: Gay Literature, Language, and Analysis*, ed. Timothy F. Murphy and Suzanne Poirier (New York: Columbia University Press, 1993), sees a similarly cross-gendered understanding of how to work towards death in Doty's "Tiara," discussed above: "Peter could marvel at Bette Davis as Queen Elizabeth one moment and replay her death scene the next (for real) complete with wig and diadem as dictated by the *ars moriendi* tradition. The old art of dying was, for the new saint, simply an extension of his theatrical art of living" (285).

21. Gunn, "Lament," in *Night Sweats*, 64.

22. Wayne Koestenbaum, *Rhapsodies of a Repeat Offender* (New York: Persea, 1994), 45–46. The answer to the poem's first question—"Who co-stars in *Romance?*"—is answered not without animus, by Leonard Maltin, *TV Movies and Video Guide* (New York: New American Library, 1988), 895: "Garbo is miscast in this static, hokey early talkie about an Italian opera star who philosophizes about love and has a relationship with an inexperienced young priest limply played by Gordon." These terms suggest how closely that movie might fit in with Koestenbaum's preoccupations; he is also the author of *The Queen's Throat: Opera, Homosexuality, and the Mystery of Desire* (New York: Vintage, 1993). Another intertext for this poem is almost certainly Roland Barthes's cult-status essay, "The Face of Garbo," in *Mythologies*, trans. Annette Lavers (New York: Hill & Wang, 1972), 56, in which he describes the taste for Garbo (as opposed to that for Audrey Hepburn) as reflecting the ethos of an era.

23. Laura Mulvey, "Visual Pleasure and Narrative Cinema," in *Visual and Other Pleasures* (Bloomington: Indiana University Press, 1989): 14–28.

24. Peter Saccio, in an unpublished manuscript I am grateful to have received, speaks of drag in Doty's work as exhibiting "the potential of a cliché considered apolitical and frivolous to turn into a public identity, an in-your-face, luscious, oppositional discourse, [to become,] through upgrading, the ultimate sensual fulfillment, the expression of civilization, and an independent construction of the self."

25. Gunn, *Night Sweats*, 80.

26. In Gunn, sexual radicalism and defiance of norms coexist with an insistence upon a classical decorum. They do so in apparent contrast to his way of life and chosen surroundings, as represented in his poems.

27. Mark Doty, *Turtle, Swan* (Boston: David R. Godine, 1987), 23.

28. Doty, *Atlantis*, 78.

29. Koestenbaum, *Rhapsodies*, 32.

30. Mark Doty, *Bethlehem in Broad Daylight* (Boston: David R. Godine, 1991), 34–35.

31. Michael Lynch, *These Waves of Dying Friends* (New York: Contact II, 1989), 34.

32. Most AIDS elegies I have read, however, express serious reservations about the Quilt, seeing it as placatingly normalizing or anti-activist, or as simply inadequate, emotionally or aesthetically. Derek Jarman writes that "when the AIDS quilt came to Edinburgh during the film festival, I attended just out of duty. I could see it was an emotional work, it got the heartstrings. But when the panels were unveiled a truly awful ceremony took place, in which a group of what looked like refrigerated karate experts, all dressed in white, turned and chanted some mumbo jumbo—horrible, quasi-religious, false. I shall haunt anyone who ever makes a panel for me" (*Derek Jarman's Garden* [London: Thames and Hudson, 1995], 91. See also Eve Kosofsky Sedgwick, on the "big, ever-growing, and sometimes obstructive niche in the ecology of gay organizing and self-formation" ("White Glasses," in *Tendencies* [Durham, N.C.: Duke University Press, 1993], 265).

33. Lynch, *These Waves*, 88.

34. Wayne Koestenbaum, "The Answer Is in the Garden," in *Poets for Life*, ed. Michael Klein (New York: Persea, 1992), 135.

35. Merrill, "Farewell Performance," in *Inner Room*, 93.

36. Dixon, "One by One," in *Poets for Life*, ed. Klein, 63.

37. Jeff Nunokawa, " 'All the Sad Young Men': AIDS and the Work of Mourning," in *Inside/Out: Lesbian Theories, Gay Theories*, ed. Diana Fuss (New York: Routledge, 1991), 319.

38. Merrill, "Investiture at Cecconi's," in *Inner Room*, 92.

39. A few days after Kalstone's death, the author Edmund White mentioned to Merrill that he was missing their mutual friend, to which Merrill replied that he had already been in touch with Kalstone and that "everything was going swimmingly" (*Village Voice*, 21 February 1995).

40. Merrill, "Farewell Performance," in *Inner Room*, 93–94.

41. Hemphill, "Heavy Breathing," in *Ceremonies*, 17.

42. Hemphill, *Ceremonies*, 32–33.

43. James Merrill, *The Changing Light at Sandover* (New York: Atheneum, 1982).

44. Doty, "Tiara," in *Bethlehem in Broad Daylight*, 34.

45. Doty, "Fog," in *My Alexandria*, 34.

46. Koestenbaum, "The Answer Is in the Garden," in *Poets for Life*, 136.

47. Koestenbaum, "Answer Is in the Garden," 135.

48. Gunn, "The Reassurance," in *Night Sweats*, 67.

49. Michael Lynch, "Terrors of Resurrection," in *Confronting AIDS through Literature*, ed. Judith Pastore (Champaign: University of Illinois Press, 1993), 79–83.

50. So, too, Lynch is "jarred" by the general resistance to AIDS activitists' attempts to "shift the focus from death to chronic illness, from palliative care to means for coping with reduced energies, from revising wills to demanding treatments." This resistance, he asserts, occurs in those who will accept marginalized persons only "as long as they are safely dying away" ("Terrors of Resurrection," 82).

51. Lynch, "Terrors of Resurrection," 80.
52. Doty, *My Alexandria*, 83.
53. Cindy Patton, *Inventing AIDS* (New York: Routledge, 1990), 131.

6. Against Elegies: Women's Breast Cancer Poems

1. Audre Lorde, *The Cancer Journals* (San Francisco: Sisters/Aunt Lute, 1980).
2. Lorde, *Cancer Journals*, 62.
3. Lorde, *Cancer Journals*, 63. It must emphatically be remembered that breast cancer is a life-threatening disease not only of women but of men as well, even if women make up by far the majority of sufferers. It is partly because of this preponderance that breast cancer is thought of as a woman's disease (with whatever negative or alienating consequences for men who happen to be afflicted by it), but partly as well because of the degree to which the breast remains the fetish and signifier of womanhood in our culture.
4. See, for instance, Mary J. Carruthers, "The Re-Vision of the Muse: Adrienne Rich, Audre Lorde, Judy Grahn, Olga Broumas," *Hudson Review* 36 (summer 1983): 293–322; AnneLouise Keating, "Making 'our shattered faces whole': The Black Goddess and Audre Lorde's Revision of Patriarchal Myth," *Frontiers* 8, no. 1 (1992): 20–33; Sagri Dhairyam, " 'Artifacts for Survival': Remapping the Contours of Poetry with Audre Lorde," *Feminist Studies* 18 (summer 1992): 229–56; Pamela Annas, "A Poetry of Survival: Unnaming and Renaming in the Poetry of Audre Lorde, Pat Parker, Sylvia Plath, and Adrienne Rich," *Colby Library Quarterly* 18 (March 1982): 9–25. Exceptions are almost all from two special issues of *Auto/Biography Studies* on the writing of illness, and all discuss *The Cancer Journals* to the exclusion of the *poetry* about breast cancer: Jeanne Perreault, " 'That the pain be not wasted': Audre Lorde and the Written Self," *Auto/Biography Studies* 4, no. 1 (1988): 1–16; G. Thomas Couser, "Autopathography: Women, Illness, and Lifewriting," *Auto/Biography Studies* 6, no. 1 (1991): 65–75; and Kay C. Cook, "Filling the Dark Spaces: Breast Cancer and Autobiography," *Auto/Biography Studies* 6, no. 1 (1991): 85–94.
5. Marilyn Hacker, *Winter Numbers* (New York: Norton, 1994). The middle section of *Winter Numbers* focuses not on breast cancer but on other losses, and the first, "Against Elegies," is about the way AIDS and suicide as well as cancer are devastating Hacker's generation. But the final section, "Cancer Winter," reflects on both the others and looks at them through the perspective of the experience of cancer.
6. Leatrice H. Lifshitz, ed., *Her Soul beneath the Bone: Women's Poetry on Breast Cancer* (Urbana: University of Illinois Press, 1988).
7. Adrienne Rich, *The Fact of a Doorframe* (New York: Norton, 1984), 250–55, sec. 1. Numbers following in the text are page numbers.
8. Rich, "A Woman Dead in Her Forties," in *Doorframe*, 253.
9. See Willard Spiegelman, *The Didactic Muse: Scenes of Instruction in Contemporary Poetry* (Princeton: Princeton University Press, 1989), 156, for a discussion of the ambivalent nature of language in this poem, and as a central problematic in Rich's poetry.
10. Rich, "Woman Dead," 255.
11. Anne Sexton, *The Complete Poems* (Boston: Houghton Mifflin, 1981), 315.
12. Breast cancer is not, of course, necessarily matrilineal, although it is quite widely thought to be so; a concentration in the mother's family puts a woman at somewhat higher risk, but most women who get the disease have no known risk factors.
13. Anne Sexton, "The Fortress," in *Complete Poems*, 67.
14. Diane Middlebrook, *Anne Sexton: A Biography* (Boston: Houghton Mifflin, 1991), 159.

15. This complex of anxieties is an ancient one, featuring in a Latin maxim applied by Erasmus to rhetorical copiousness: *ubi mel, ibi fel; ubi uber, ibi tuber*, "where there is honey, there is poison, where the (nourishing) breast is, there is cancer." Cited in Jonathan Goldberg, *Voice Terminal Echo* (New York: Methuen, 1986), 3.

16. Helen Webster, *Bulletins from a War* (Washington, D.C.: Word Works, 1980), 11.

17. Michelle Murray, *The Great Mother and Other Poems* (New York: Sheed and Ward, 1975), 11.

18. Claire Henze, "To My Mother," in *Cancer Stories: Creativity and Self-Repair*, ed. Esther Dreifuss-Kattan (Hillsdale, N.J.: Analytic Press, 1990), 163–64. In this moving and fascinating book, Dreifuss-Kattan also comments tellingly on the preferring of the grandmother to the mother as a psychoanalytic splitting off of the bad breast from the good body, 165–67.

19. Michele Murray, "Poem to My Grandmother in Her Death," in *Great Mother*, 67. Numbers following in the text are page numbers.

20. Audre Lorde, *The Marvelous Arithmetics of Distance* (New York: Norton, 1993).

21. Lorde, "Today Is Not the Day," in *Arithmetics*, 57.

22. Lorde, "Speechless," in *Arithmetics*, 48.

23. Lorde, "Restoration: A Memorial—9/18/91," in *Arithmetics*, 40–41.

24. Lorde, "East Berlin," in *Arithmetics*, 50. See also the collection she inspired, *Showing Our Colors: Afro-German Women Speak Out*, ed. May Opitz, Katharina Oguntoye, and Dagmar Schultz, trans. Anne V. Adams (Amherst: University of Massachusetts Press, 1992).

25. Lorde, "Hugo I," in *Arithmetics*, 45–46.

26. Lorde, "Construction," in *Arithmetics*, 47.

27. Lorde, "125th Street and Abomey," in *The Black Unicorn* (New York: Norton, 1978), 12.

28. Carruthers, "Re-Vision," 319.

29. Lorde, "The Night-Blooming Jasmine," in *Arithmetics*, 52.

30. Lorde, "Jasmine," 52.

31. Lorde, "Girlfriend," in *Arithmetics*, 54.

32. For a helpful and politically contextualized discussion of this rhetorical figure in Lorde's work, see Amitai F. Avi-ram, "*Apo Koinou* in Audre Lorde and the Moderns: Defining the Differences," *Callaloo* 9 (winter 1986): 193–208.

33. Lorde, *Arithmetics*, 59.

34. Hacker, "Cancer Winter," in *Winter Numbers*, 81. I will cite by section title and page number.

35. See Shoshana Felman and Dori Laub, eds., *Testimony: Crises of Witnessing in Literature, Psychoanalysis, and History* (New York: Routledge, 1992).

Afterword: Why Elegies?

1. Eve Kosofsky Sedgwick, "Queer and Now," in *Tendencies* (Durham, N.C.: Duke University Press, 1993), 12–13. In a footnote, Sedgwick explains: "That deconstruction can offer crucial resources of thought for survival under duress will sound astonishing, I know, to anyone who knows it mostly from the journalism on the subject. . . . I came to my encounter with breast cancer not as a member of a credal sect . . . but as someone who needed all the cognitive skills she could get. I found, as often before, that I had some good and relevant ones from my deconstructive training" (12).

2. Cindy Patton, *Inventing AIDS* (New York: Routledge, 1990), 131.

Index

Reading Women Writing

A SERIES EDITED BY

Shari Benstock and Celeste Schenck

*Melissa F. Zeiger
is Associate Professor of English
at Dartmouth College.*

www.ingramcontent.com/pod-product-compliance
Lightning Source LLC
Chambersburg PA
CBHW022313280326
41932CB00010B/1086